DIARY
OF A
HIP-HOP
PUBLICIST

BY
LYNN K. HOBSON
www.lynnhobson.com

Thank You

First, I'd like to thank my Lord and Savior Jesus Christ. I'd like to thank my mother, Patricia Robinson Hobson-Wilson; my dad, Julius W. Hobson, Jr.; my stepmom, Diane "Dinie" Lewis; my stepdads, Eugene Phillips and Richard Wilson; my sister, Faye Hobson Rencher and brother-in-law, T. Rencher; my nieces, Siena and Savannah; my grandmother, Carol "Mama Carol" Joy Smith (I love you sooo much!); my aunts (Jean, Arnona, and Larna); my uncle Bashan; Eulalia Robinson and family; all of my cousins; my brothers, Javon Floyd and Rob Young; my godsons, Jaeden Smith & Cash Stackhouse; the Dowe Family; the Stackhouse Family; the Cropp Family; Sam and Linda Botts; and Curtis and Myrna White.

To my TRUE friends, I'd like to thank the Gucci Girls (Kimberly Mossy Smith; Retha Nicholson Fernandez; Joy Harris; Tanya Dooley Adijah; Joell Barnett; and Kenyatta Ferguson; RIP Jill Ferguson); my ROCK Trina Stackhouse; Daina "Baby D" Hannibal; Yasmin Amira Davis; Joy King; and Leslie Duomoh.

The Cummins Family (Robert "Don Pooh Cummins, Nikki Hunter Cummins, and Greg Cummins); DipSet and the James Family; Kariem Cyrus; and Reginald Dunn.

The Powerhouse Girls (Kita Williams; Monique Jackson; Arian Reed; and Jocelyn Coleman) and Kellie Dutton.

Kaylin Garcia; Cisco Rosado; Priscilla Rainey; and Bebe (Kouture Konnections).

Special thanks to World Changers Church New York (Dr. Creflo A. Dollar; Pastor Taffi L. Dollar; Kirk Tomlinson; and Alnisa Reed). Thanks for teaching me the word with simplicity and understanding.

Thanks to all of my Haters. You have been the wind beneath my wings.

And yes... my Thank You's are long, but I'm grateful and this is MY book! LOL!

And I would be crazy to not acknowledge God. I love you, Lord. Thank you for never leaving me nor forsaking me. Thank you for granting me favor. Thank you for allowing me to reap plenty in days of famine. Thank you for your protection. Thank you, Lord, for my great health. For without you I am nothing. Thank you for allowing me to impact the lives of millions who don't know your name—JESUS. I love you. God is Love.

PROLOGUE

"No, I'm not coming with you, Kelly. We are over!"

Falling onto deaf ears, he grabbed my wrist so hard that my silver bangle snapped into two pieces and fell to the ground. It was my favorite. As I moved to grab the pieces, he got a hold of the back of my neck and shoved me completely outside of the bowling alley. I was terrified. I had never seen Kelly in such a rage before and I was not about to put up with whatever he was trying to dish out to me.

Spotting a slim framed white guy outside of the bowling alley's door, I stated very calmly, "Please call the police. He's bothering me and I am in fear for my life." And I was! My friends were so far away from me—the lanes which seemed to be miles away were too much of a stretch for me to reach. I repeated again, "Sir! Call the police." He just stood there in shock while finishing up a cigarette. It had become obvious to me that he was an employee of the place. Kelly still held onto my wrist tightly and he was pulling me like a child who had just spilled all of the cans over in a grocery store.

Finally, I got one good jerk in and I yanked my arm free. I started to run back into the bowling alley to get help, but he caught me before I could reach the door. He overpowered me.

"I know you aren't going back in there to your so-called friends. Where are they now? You mean to tell me that you aren't going to come home with me so that we can talk?"

Before I could answer Kelly, he struck me with a closed fist to my face. I felt my jaw snap. "I'ma ask you something. Are you seeing any of those guys in there?" I just held onto my face. He lowered my hand and struck me again. This time I fell to the ground. I screamed for my life, "Somebody help me!" While he started to stomp me out with the bottom of his dirty ass Uptown sneaker, I covered my face with my arms while wailing at the same time. He was clearly fucking me up.

The white guy who was on his break came over to him and yelled out, "Hey! Stop! I'm going to call the police." But his words were no match for Kelly's rage.

He kicked me repeatedly until he saw blood and as I lay on the ground, I could hear a familiar voice. It was Diamond yelling out and running over to him. "Leave Lynn the fuck alone!"

"Yeah. I'm done here anyway," Kelly responded as I lay curled up on the cement, crying out from the pain I was in. He kicked me again, oblivious to Diamond's request. Within seconds, he grabbed my smashed up iPhone and he ran off into the darkness, like a thief in the night. Helping me off the ground, Twin, Reem, and his friend SP came peeling out of the bowling alley, curious as to why we had been gone for so long. Twin took one look at my face and knew immediately what had happened.

SPECIAL NOTE:

Some people can take all of one week to write a book. This book took me three years. It's not perfect, but it's my story. During the original week this book was scheduled to go to print, I was under some extreme spiritual warfare. Words cannot describe what I've gone through; however, I do know that there is a God who sits high and looks low. There is a God who has the final say. I leaned on him two weeks prior to my book going to print. I prayed and fasted that I would write this book in the utmost respect for my clients and for my family. During this time, I refrained from eating from the time I woke up daily until 6pm in the evening. So much happened during that time. My computer crashed one week prior to the book being sent out to print. I was able to recover my book from the computer's hard drive. From there, I borrowed my New Jersey mom's computer (Ms. Debbie) and took an additional week to edit the book once again. Her laptop also crashed. Three days until my book was due to print, I copy and pasted the entire *Diary* into the body of an email and completed the edits.

I don't know why I've gone through so much in my attempt to get my story out, but if I affect just one person's life in a positive way—just one person's life— then I will be satisfied. All I know is that the darkest days appear before the light. The days leading up to my print date have been crazy. Friends have abandoned me; a few clients dropped off the face of the Earth; my computer crashed; and as I type with tears, I know that nothing but good can come out of this.

As my book is being sent off to print, the weight of the world has been lifted off of my shoulders and I am now ready to move on to the next calling God has in store for me, wherever or whatever HE wants me to do.

I hope you enjoy the read.

CHAPTERS:

Chapter 1:
Who Am I?

Wikipedia, the current generation's version of the *Encyclopedia Britannica* for defining all things important or not, defines hip-hop as a culture, characterized by rap, deejaying, hip-hop dance, and graffiti. It is a subculture originated by African-American communities during the 1970s in New York City, specifically within the Bronx.

It also defines a publicist as a person whose job it is to generate and manage publicity for a public figure, especially a celebrity, a business, or for a work such as a book, film, or album. Most top-level publicists work private, handling multiple clients.

However, a publicist is so much more. A publicist is your personal fireman, putting out fires; your personal policeman, protecting you from harm; your personal spokesperson, telling only good stories and helping to clean up all the bad stories circulating about you—all wrapped into one. And when you're a hip-hop artist, your publicist is your best friend.

My definition of a hip-hop publicist's job is multi-faceted. His or her job is to: babysit, keep the calendar, clean boogers out of noses, act as a referee, stand in as a bridesmaid, wipe tears, build self-esteem, act as a spiritual advisor, cook, clean, exaggerate on press releases, make events look larger than life, keep family members away who just want money ALL of the time, and make all clients look GREAT.

That's exactly what I do!

My journey started as an 18-year-old upper middle class black girl with a heart of gold, looking to finally break away from my strict ass father and party like it's the end of the world. I was five foot five with a blossoming big booty, no chest, big brown eyes and a unibrow. I had not been fortunate enough to be introduced to the Koreans to have my eyebrows waxed yet. I had a lot more than that to learn and discover.

I come from one of the most well-respected names in DC history, the Hobson Family. My grandfather, Julius W. Hobson, Sr. was a civil rights activist and well-known politician. As the first Black ever to be on the DC Board of Education, my Granddaddy Julius, was instrumental in desegregating DC public schools. So now there is a "Julius Hobson Day", Julius Hobson Condominiums, and Hobson Elementary School. My family, whether they said it or not, was expecting me to supersede all of the accomplishments they have completed. Child *puhleease*. I didn't have any of that on my agenda, but I did need to get an agenda.

Growing up in DC, I lived with my father and stepmother, Diane. My stepmom's personality was that of Angela Bassett with a Susan Taylor feel. My parents divorced when I was four years old. I am the older of two girls. My mother, Pat, is a retired attorney for the Department of Housing and Urban Development. She to me, is the Black Erica Kane with a splash of Diana Ross fever. My dad, Julius, is comparable to Colin Powell with a touch of the character, Cliff Huxtable. My sassy younger sister, Faye, is eighteen months younger and for most of our childhood, we were attached at the hip.

During my last year of High School, classes seemed to be extra long and monotonous. My sister and I worked part time at Johnson's Flower & Garden Center. Work at the flower shop was uneventful. The flower shop was located two long blocks up from my high school in the Tenley Town section of DC. During our spare time at the shop, we did anything and everything necessary to prepare for the upcoming winter holiday season. And although it was early June, Christmas was a zoo at the flower shop. We never over-prepared for it. To this day, I love flowers. As Gordon, the store's manager, walked over to me, he said, "Lynn, did you make a decision as to where you would like to go to school?"

I replied, "No, not yet. I really want to attend a HBCU (historically black college/university), but we'll see." I had a look of gloom on my face and Gordon could see it. Gordon was a short, white, geeky, cleaned-up hippy who gave up his free spirit to get married and have children. His wife worked in the Arrangements Department. She was a sweetheart.

"Well, if you decide on sticking around the DC area, you are more than welcome to hang on to your job here. You and Faye can stay as long as you'd like." He smiled. Johnson's had become our second home. Though this was our job, it was a huge family-owned business that had fallen in love with my sister and me. For part-time employees, we were spoiled.

Clocking out a few minutes earlier than normal, I caught the bus home. I wanted to relax and unwind a bit before my parents arrived from work because I knew we would be talking about my future later in the evening. As I walked down our tree-lined block of McKinley Street, I could see that my parents had beaten me home. As I approached the steps to my house, I noticed that my dad and stepmom were sitting in one of their vehicles, together. They had matching Maximas. Waving at them, they looked like deer caught in headlights. It was obvious they were having an intense conversation.

I hurried into the house. I changed out of my school clothes. I threw on some sweats and grabbed a cheese slice out of the fridge. By this time, my parents were in the house and in their room changing clothes as well. As I heard their bedroom door creak open, I busied myself with kitchen duties. When my parents headed toward my direction, I emptied the dishwasher. "Hey, Ms. Lady," my stepmom said.

"Hey," I replied.

"Your dad and I would like to speak with you in the living room real quick." She said. I put a piece of Tupperware away and followed Diane.

"Hello," my dad said as I entered into our family's living area. I reciprocated in kind. The intensity was overwhelming for me. "Ok. So Diane and I have decided that you can go to Howard University and live on campus."

"But Hampton is my first choice and I was accepted into Hampton." , I said.

"We know but Hampton stated in their letter that they would not be able to provide you with on-campus housing and we don't think you are ready to move away from home and live off campus at the same time." I was too through, but the idea of going to Howard and living on campus was fine with me.

My translation to their decision was that I was too immature to leave and attend Hampton University so they were playing it safe with me by allowing me to attend Howard University and have on-campus housing. Yeah... I was a little rambunctious and rebellious, so I couldn't blame them.

"Ok. Cool. I'm going to keep my job at Johnson's and work there on the weekends." I didn't even bother to put up a fuss. I just stood up, hugged them both and went on my merry way.

My graduation from high school came and went. I was college bound.

Chapter 2:
Howard University (Fall 1989)

Howard University's "Freshmen Week" would be starting in four weeks and I decided to go with Business Management as a major because it was safe. I was undecided as to what I wanted to do for a career, but I did know that Business Management may be applied in most career sectors.

On the day I was to report to my dorm, my dad and stepmom helped me load my belongings into their car. My sister was not able to ride with us since the car was so packed, but I knew I'd see her the next day because her high school was located right across the street from my college campus and she needed to go there and pre-register for her senior courses.

"Lynn, here's some money. Diane and I have paid for a meal plan as part of your tuition, so you may want to inquire about obtaining your meal card. You may come home every two weeks to wash your clothes. Please abide by all of the dormitory rules. Ok?" My dad preached as my stepmother hugged me for the fourth time. Don't get me wrong. Daddy was strict and calculating; however, he was the most loving and affectionate human being on the planet.

No later than two minutes after they had pulled off, my mom pulled right on up with my stepfather, Eugene. The timing was perfect. Though my mom and dad were cordial to each other, there was always that elephant in the room when they were around at the same time. "Hey baby girl! Mommy brought you some stuff to make your room look nice and cozy." I hugged her and smiled as Eugene parked in a tight space right in front of my dorm. Grabbing an empty "move in" cart, I then pushed it towards my mother's Mercedes trunk.

"Mommy. Oooh wee. What did you get me!?" I was too excited. Mommy always knew just what to get. She was always on point. Eugene greeted me with a hug and then opened the trunk. A comforter set, a lamp, some wall hangings, and more. I was all smiles. Though my dad and stepmom provided the financial basics for my life, my mom accessorized it. As my mom and I hurled everything into the cart, Eugene stayed outside to smoke his cigar. We would need at least two more trips back down to him. Leaning against the car, with his legs crossed, I could tell that he was chillin' and willing to wait no matter the length of time. He had patience when he wanted to. Eugene and my mom were newly married.

"Well... alright. You are all set." My mom sighed. She had done a great job with my side of the room. I had more than enough stuff to make my room feel like home.

I even had a little refrigerator and my own iron with a miniature ironing board. "I had torn out this cute article in the *Washington Post* the other day. It provided me with a little checklist of what a college freshman would need in a dorm room." She smiled.

Walking my mom down to the car, the sun had started to set and Eugene was in the same place we had left him. He was entertained by all of the freshmen and their nagging parents. Though Eugene didn't have any biological children, he did treat Faye and me as if we were his own. "Ok, baby. We are leaving. Do you have any money?"

"I have money my dad just gave me." My mom handed me more dollars. Oh the joys of getting that double portion from divorced parents was a blessing (smile). I thanked her, hugged her, and watched until they drove off. I walked the four flights of stairs back up to my floor since the elevators were crowded with girls moving their belongings in.

Catching my breath at the top of the steps, someone called my name, "Lynn Hobson! Is that you?" Turning my head towards the voice, it was my high school homie, Fani Floyd. I beamed with happiness. I knew that Fani was going to attend Howard, but I had no idea that we would be dorm mates. I was happy to see a familiar face. I hugged her and grabbed her hand to show her my newly decorated room. Equipped with a Hello Kitty comforter set with pillows and other wall accessories to match, she was thoroughly impressed. "Your parents hooked you up girl! I wonder who your roommate will be." Looking over at the other desolate half of my room, I was praying that no one would come. I wanted to have the ultimate freshman pad, but the dream was short-lived when a girl in rollers burst in the room damn near knocking us over just as I was exiting with Fani to check out her room.

"Oh! I'm so sorry." A raggedy cardboard box fell out of her hand and onto the floor. "I'm just glad the box decided to break at its destination," she said. Looking up at us and smiling, she said, "Hi. I'm Shaunda." Reaching for her hand, Fani shook it in a friendly manner. I then followed suit. Bumping in behind, was her little brother and mother. They had all just driven in from New Brunswick, New Jersey. After introducing ourselves, we let Shaunda know that we were from DC. She was happy to know that. "Oh wow. Y'all are from DC? That's great! I don't have to go very far to ask for directions or recommendations for outings." She was formal on the inside, but hip on the outside. I didn't get it. Her personality didn't match her look. It was something that made me go "Hmmmm".

"Well, I'ma get out of your way while you get settled. I'll be down the hall in Fani's room," I stated.

"Ok. Cool. I hope I'm not kicking you out of your half of the room?" she asked.

"Of course not," I replied.

Though DC was my home, I was in a different world. Now, I had to now be political and polite. I was up for the challenge.

Girls and their families filled the hallway. While heading down the long corridor, our RA (Resident Assistant) introduced herself. She was a senior finishing up her Bachelor's Degree in Psychology. She seemed cool. When we arrived at Fani's room, she introduced me to her new roommate, Lauren, who was from Maryland. As the evening went on, we soon realized that we were three locals on a floor with half New Yorkers and half Californians. So for the first weekend on campus, the three of us were like static cling to one another.

Chapter 3:
Hip-Hop

Kim and I met on the very first day of "Freshmen Week" at HU. The two of us kicked it off immediately while waiting in line for our "Welcome Packet" in Blackburn's Auditorium. Kim was mixed. Her father was White (Creole) and her mom, African-American. Kim stood five foot six inches tall and all you could see on her were legs for days. What stood out most for me were her huge door knocker earrings. I had never ever seen earrings so big. In DC, door knocker earrings were the trend, but Kim's were as wide as her face. And her hair—it was cut into an asymmetrical bob with a shag in the back. The 'do was cute, but not cute enough to withstand DC's humidity. I very rarely approached people and introduced myself to anyone, but there was something about Kim's energy that made me feel comfortable. She was approachable, so I introduced myself to her. By day's end, we were friends and Kim's hair was looking like a cotton ball.

Well into the school year, we walked rapidly through the yard of HU's campus. Kim and I shared a huge black umbrella as the rain started to come down onto the pavement even harder. Heading into the direction of our dorm, Baldwin Hall, which was located on the backside of HU's campus, the two of us were chilly and hungry. We had each just copped a "Three Wing Special" with mambo sauce (sweet & sour sauce, ketchup, and hot sauce) from Sarah's Chinese Carry Out along with french fries drenched in ketchup and the sweetest iced teas in all of Northwest, DC

While I was holding the umbrella steadily over the two of us, Kim carried the food. Stepping onto a flyer, which was typical for a Friday afternoon, Kim snapped. "Hold up!" Stopping in her tracks, I looked over into Kim's face curiously. "Back up." Looking at the flyer on the ground, Kim snatched it from underneath me before I could barely remove my foot off of it.

"Awwww snap! We are going to this party! This is Biggie, girl. You know Gucci manages him. We are sooo in there."

"Huh? Who is Biggie?" I asked.

"Don't worry. We goin' and then you'll find out".

As Kim started pulling me by my backpack full of the books I never read or bothered to crack open to study, we continued to our dorm where the two of us began to plot and plan on the outfits we were going to wear for the night. Kim's closet became my shopping mall.

Kim's closet was better than the mall, too. Anything

trendy you could think of, Kim had it—in every color. From shoes, bags, and belts to other jeweled accessories—her room was my one-stop shop. All I had to do was wash it and return it.

The two of us were a match made in "Best Friend Heaven". Kim had the whip, a 1989 gold Volkswagen Jetta and I knew how to get around town. No club, restaurant, or mall was ever off limits to "frick & frack". The old Post Office attached to Union Station was where the party was taking place. Our entrance into the venue was a breeze. Party promoters quickly familiarized themselves with cute freshmen during "Freshmen Week" so by the time the first semester rolled around, we had become VIPs. Why? Because we were young, fresh, and fly.

After all, it was half way through the first semester and we were already two of the more popular freshmen on campus. Getting our hands stamped for entry, Kim grabbed me by the hand and proceeded directly to the dance floor. *Oh uh uh,* I thought to myself. See... I was not publicly outgoing. Kim was extremely outgoing and carefree. I was more laid back and conservative. I found the nearest chair, pulled another chair beside the one we spotted, rested our jackets onto the spare seat and watched the crowd. As the music blared, Kim made her way over to where I was sitting, while still continuing to turn up the volume on her dance moves.

"What you do for me, I will do for you. What you do for me, I will do for youuuuuu," were the words that Mary J. Blige sang on Father MC's song and I mean the party was rockin'!

"Girrrllll! You crazy!!"

As Kim grabbed my arm, I resisted. "Oh. You can act all silly at home, but when we get out you mean you can't even bust a move?"

Winning the tug of war, I landed onto the dance floor by force and bumped into a tall slim thug with a Yankee fitted cap and bomber jacket. "Whoa!" the guy said.

Nervous about the outcome of ramming into the dude, I stared down at the floor and whispered, "I'm sorry."

Grabbing my chin to lift my eyes to his, I looked directly into a kind face and beautiful smile. "Hi. I'm China," the guy announced.

"Oh. I'm Lynn. Nice to meet you." He then grabbed me by the hand, twirled me around a few times and then disappeared into the crowd. Who was that guy? As Kim tugged on me again, the two of us headed to the side of the stage to check out the performance. It was a HU up & coming rap artist by the name of

Tracey Lee who was set to open up for the main performance. With his cornrows parted neatly and evenly towards the back of his head, he tapped the mic and headed onto the stage with an energy that moved the crowd so swiftly that all we could see from our angle were hands moving up and down and side to side. I was in awe of the concert. Never before had I been to a hip-hop concert. Born and raised in DC, I had only been exposed to Go-Go music. You know... Chuck Brown and the Soul Searchers, Trouble Funk, The Junk Yard Band, and many others.

"I was a terror since the public school era," this rapper performed. He was big, dark-skinned, and his energy was hypnotizing. It was Biggie Smalls AKA The Notorious B.I.G. "Puttin' hickies on my chest like Little Shawn and it's on!" he kept going. But when he said that particular line in his rhyme, the crowd went crazy. Another dude with a medium build had come on stage. It actually was this infamous Little Shawn.

There was no denying that this fat rapper came to HU to not only rock the mic, but to leave a huge impression on the minds of future trendsetters and tastemakers—and he did an awesome job.

It was that very night that I fell in love with hip-hop.

Between acts, Kim introduced me to a long-faced HU brother, a sophomore named Gucci from Brooklyn. As he cracked open a grin, he shook my hand, kissed Kim on the cheek and went back to work. The brother had something to do with the show; however, we didn't know his role.

As the night wore on, the crowd started to disperse. "What y'all getting into next?" Gucci asked Kim.

"Oh. We callin' it a night," she replied.

"Oh a'ight. Well, y'all get back safely." Gucci responded.

"Thanks," she responded and we headed to the car. Kim and I were never the ones to entertain after-parties at upperclassmen's cribs. We partied where the majority of people partied and that was it. Besides, Kim didn't know where Gucci was coming from—and though he had good energy we always played it safe.

When Kim and I got into her car to head back to our dorm, I had a slew of questions for her. What was that? How come I never heard of Biggie Smalls? Did you like the performance? Kim just looked at me as if she had just allowed a crack head to cop a ride in her whip. I was psyched. My energy level was through the roof and I wanted answers. She was like, "Dang! Calm down. We will just go to more concerts as they come to town."

Kim had a group of girlfriends that I referred to as the "Gucci Girls". Their entire crew was addicted to those G's. From head to toe, the six of them always wore something Gucci somewhere on their bodies. Two of them, Jill and Kenyatta, were sisters who attended Virginia State, Retha was at Rutgers University, Keisha was at Hampton, Tanya was at UPenn, and Karen, a single mother based out of their town of Freeport in Long Island. I absolutely adored the Gucci Girls. They were fun, witty, and fearless. If they weren't all gathered in Kim's dorm room, then we were waking up from hangovers in theirs on the weekends. There was no party on the east coast that was untouched. We covered the gamut.

The first semester for me at HU was a breeze—all B's and one A. Amen! The second semester was just the opposite. I had gotten too comfortable with those good grades. Courses were a tad bit more difficult this go-around and I definitely did NOT make the grade. Studying was no longer my focus. I just wanted to be in the mix—and in the mix of everything not related to gaining a higher education. Besides, I was majoring in Business because it was safe. My parents had suggested I select a major that would cover the gamut of careers since it was unclear as to what I really wanted to do in life.

It was now the end of our first semester as sophomores, and as I knocked on Kim's apartment door located behind McDonald's at the dorms known as the Plaza, she answered with a sullen look on her face. "What's wrong?" I asked her.

"Girl, my parents are about to make me come home. They aren't happy with my grades and progress in school, so they think I need to bring it on home to cut down costs, buckle down more, and finish." When she said those words, I damn near cried. The thought of losing Kim to a higher education was heart-breaking. Kim was not the type to rebel. She was always listening and doing whatever it was her parents wanted her to do. The two of us packed up her things for the Winter Break and started to push all of her belongings into the hallway. To this day, I don't understand why dorms always made students pack up ALL of their belongings—only to return to the same room in a few weeks. It was annoying to say the least.

Sticking my key into my dad's house during the Winter Break, something was terribly wrong. The key didn't fit. Trying again and again and even taking a step back to make sure I was standing in front of my home, I damn near broke the key off in the door in order to get in. With a jolt coming from the door, my dad answered it.

"Lynn, we are kicking you out. You cannot come home. You've got to figure this thing out for yourself. I'm giving you one year before any other financial assistance will be provided by Diane and me". Looking up at him as if he had bumped his damn head, my dad handed me a bag, some money, and a hug before sending me off. Well... it didn't go down exactly like that, but in my eyes it was a traumatizing experience that went down... just like that!

After being partially kicked out of the nest, my life was so empty and unfulfilled. I flunked out of college—or rather "placed on academic probation". Blah, blah, blah. My dad, the "Money Man", was through with me. He and my stepmom changed the locks on their door and I was on my own—well... not totally, cause there was my mommy!

My mom took me in, laid down her rules—which were few—and that was it. Because there was very little structure in her household, I had plenty of room to figure things out. After all, I had one year to get it together. "Lynn. You better get it together. It's hard out here, and just because you are on Academic Probation at Howard doesn't mean you can't take classes somewhere else," my mom hissed. She was right, but I wasn't about to let her know that. I just wanted her to shut up!

"Oh and one more thing. If you're in my house, then you gots ta go to church," my mom yelled up the steps. Shaking my head, cause I saw the control freak starting to ooze out of her, I agreed—just to keep the peace. I had spent my summers growing up in church. My grandfather, Papa Joe, was a Pastor out of Boston, Massachusetts. He and my grandmother, Mommy Ethel lived, ate, and breathed CHURRRRCH (Snoop Dogg voice)! So I wasn't really too surprised when my mom made the same request, and I didn't know if my mom had a personal relationship with GOD or if she was just used to attending church out of habit. Whatever the case, I just went right on ahead and laid out my Sunday suit, pantyhose, shoes, and purse.

At the time, my mom and step dad Eugene, were attending Metropolitan Baptist Church in the heart of Northwest over by HU. I had heard about the church. It was progressive, growing in members, and I had heard nice things about the Body of Christ. My Mama Carol (Dad's Mom) lived and breathed Jesus. My Mother's parents, Mommy Ethel and Papa Joe started several churches before their passing.

Morning came and we were on our way to church. On a typical Sunday, Kim and I would be waking up in a different state and heading to eat at the hottest breakfast spot before getting back on the road to head back to school. Since the Gucci Girls along with my sister, who was now attending Spelman College in Atlanta, were spread out up and down the east coast, we were always on a mission for the hottest party.

Pulling behind the cars in a single-filed line, we parked our vehicle as directed by the parking attendant. "Whew!" my stepfather yelled out. "You gotta get here early or you won't have a chance at a space or getting into church."

"From the looks of all this, you are right. This is one big production," I responded. My mom just looked back at me, smiled, and gave me the once over—as if to silently say, "Just checking to make sure you don't make me look bad." Whatever Ma. As we entered into the sanctuary, an usher greeted us and sat us fairly close to the front. My stepdad seemed to be hesitant, but me and Ma didn't care. There's always something about sitting up front. Visitors from our church in Boston used to think my grandfather was going to put them on blast, so I guess that must be the same thought for all visitors at all churches. We were used to being put on blast from our church days in Boston.

Handing us programs, we sat down comfortably and then spread out a bit to pace ourselves for the incoming crowd. There was no point in squishing up early in the game. Ya dig? When church started, the program moved along quickly. The music was inspirational and moving. The reading of the scriptures and special prayer was nice and comforting as well.

Pastor Hicks preached a sermon that was out of this world. He preached about leaning on God when you are feeling lost and seem to have no direction, and I could definitely relate because I had NO direction. Everyone around me seemed to know what they wanted to do and be in life, except me. I felt as though I was just being pushed along. By the end of the sermon, I had tears in my eyes. My mom reached into her overstuffed purse and managed to locate a crumpled piece of tissue to hand me. "You should join church with me and Eugene," Mommy wrote on the edge of her program.

I gave her the nod—as if to say, "Ok."

So when the doors of the church opened, my mom escorted me to the altar where I became a candidate for Baptism. I had been christened as a child, but I had never made the decision as an adult to be baptized. At this point in my life, the decision was a "no brainer". I had nothing to lose and everything to gain.

After service, I was assigned a Prayer Counselor who then prayed over me, providing me with all of the info I needed for Baptism and membership to the Church. There was a four-week program required for all new members, which was held on various days of the week.

Leaving church, my mom locked my arm into her arm as we walked over to the car. My stepdad had already gotten the car while I was with the Prayer Counselor.

"Congratulations!" said Eugene as I sat in the car's back seat.

"Thank you!" I replied with the same energy. My stepdad had an energy like no other. He was always willing to do anything different. He was a Research Psychologist for the Department of Employment Services by day and a Suit Salesman by night at Joseph A. Banks in Pentagon City. It wasn't like he needed the money. My stepdad loved clothes and was a snappy dresser. His suit game was tight and his accessories were always on point.

That Monday, I started making phone calls. My mom also gave me a few dollars to get myself back to square one. Lifting up the phone's receiver, I dialed the number for UDC (The University for the District of Columbia).

"UDC. How may I help you?" asked a youthful voice.

"Yes. I wanted to know what I need to do in order to

register for this upcoming semester. I just want to take a few courses."

Tapping me on my shoulder, my mom startled me and whispered, "Just act like you are a freshmen."

"Well. Are you a freshmen?" the receptionist asked.

"Yes." I replied.

"Oh, you just need yo' high school transcripts and das basically it. Come up here by Friday cause we already in the middle of late registration and bring cash or a check. The classes are 250 each. Report to building numba 39. From there, you will sit with a guidance counselor, select yo' classes and din go pay in building numba 37." Oh boy. Was she ghetto or what? She let it be known that she was from "Souf East".

My best friend Kim had been shipped off to New York by her parents where she was going to finish up at St. John's University and reality was quickly starting to hit me. My party buddy was gone. And I still didn't know what I wanted to do with my life. College was just something natural to do until I figured it out. It was better to be productive than to not do anything at all. So when Friday came around, I did everything I needed to enroll in a few classes at UDC. When I enrolled, I made Broadcast Journalism my major.

Though I couldn't write a lick, this major just seemed to be more interesting to me.

Once my school schedule was handed over to me, I headed to the new and improved Union Station where I copped a job at Cacique, the lingerie company owned by the Limited. It was cool. My dad worked on Capitol Hill at Senator Chuck Robb's office so he would often drop by to slip me a couple of dollars. He had gotten the word that I had enrolled in school so he loosened up the purse strings a little. I missed Howard and my friends though. Kim would come down to DC during the course of my new school year and visit on the weekends. We were already one month into the new school year and I was missing my BFF. Kim wasn't feeling St. John's too much either.

"Girl. I'm coming down there this weekend!" Kim called to tell me.

"Oh! Alright," I replied. "What's the occasion?"

"There's a big party going down at Anastasia's in Georgetown and we don't wanna miss it!" she exclaimed.

"Cool! Well, you know I'm here." During this time, I was staying at my grandmother's house in northeast. I had moved from my mother's home in SE, DC because it was more convenient to the subway and bus routes. My grandmother, Mama Carol, was retired and she didn't quite mind Kim coming to visit. I was pretty much on the straight and narrow. My grades were good, I had a job, and I was going to church with her every Sunday.

When Kim arrived early on Friday afternoon, I was too thrilled to see her. Lucky for me, I wasn't on the schedule to work at Cacique until Tuesday. Watching her pull up to the side of my grandmother's house, I bolted out to meet her. It was a brisk winter morning and the sun was shining. My grandmother was excited for me. She could tell I was happier than usual. "Kiimmmm!" I yelled out before she could even get out of her burgundy Nissan Pathfinder.

"Wasss up girl?!"

"I've missed you soooo much!"

"Well lemmee get out the damn car first!" Stepping out onto the street, I ran around to give her a huge hug. I had friends in DC, but none that compared to my relationship with Kim. I missed her and our shenanigans. Helping her get her overstuffed duffle bag out of the trunk, we both grabbed a handle and walked up the side of my grandmother's lawn to the front door. Complaining about us walking on her grass, which was already dead, we just brushed her off by including her in the hugs and kisses. Mama Carol was elated and totally forgot about the crime we had just committed.

The two of us carried on about the latest gossip as we took her bag downstairs to the basement. I had been dating a guy from HU and had not seen Kim since the breakup. I was good though. He had decided to dump me because he wanted to start a new lease on life or was it because I was now going to UDC and he wanted an HU girl? Who knows?

Unpacking her bag, I wanted to see what goodies Kim brought me. I had asked her to bring me some things out of her closet. Clothes were layered all throughout the bag. Tops and jeans were rolled up tightly like Twinkies. She really knew how to pack a bag and make the most out of limited space. While laying out her outfit for the night's party, I was elated. Kim had her outfit mapped out to the T! The color for the night was money green. The top, jeans, boots, and jacket were all green. Her accessories were gold. It was 1994 and the Salt & Pepa phase was still "in". "Wow Kim! That outfit is banging." Her bomber jacket was cropped. It looked good on her as she tried it on for me. Kim was so detail-oriented with her fashion. As I ran my hand down her sleeve, it felt good to the touch. It was suede. Even the bomber's zipper matched her accessories because it was gold too.

"Ok. But now take that off and show me what's in the bag for me!" I never hesitated in holding my tongue with Kim. She just burst out laughing cause she knew that's what I wanted. Kim was, and still is, my best friend. If she had the best, she wanted me to have the best also. So it came as no surprise when she pulled out the exact same outfit for me in brown. The outfit looked great! All I had to do was supply my own belt, earrings, and boots, and I had all of the necessary accessories needed to feel good about the look.

As the day rolled on, the two of us just stayed down in the basement and chatted it up until dinner, which was delicious. We gulped down our food, rinsed off the dishes, started the dishwasher, and then headed down to the basement for a nap. We had a big evening ahead so getting some rest was a must!

Showered, dressed to impress, and ready to party, the two of us gassed up the truck and headed over to Georgetown. As we drove, Kim and I passed by some staple locations we used to frequent. In less than two years, we had created life-long memories. Driving up M Street towards the club, which was located on the southeast corner of Wisconsin Avenue and M Street, the two of us arrived early to start the grind of locating a parking space. Parking in Georgetown, no matter the time of day, was a pain in the butt. We had a strategy though. Kim and I would drive slowly up M Street and while she took the left side, I took the right side. We combed the streets looking for drivers who were looking to dip back into the cars to pull off. "There's one!" I yelled out. Kim was on point. We swerved a double parked vehicle and damn near crossed over the yellow line before we arrived to a white Honda that was pulling out of a space on the same block as the club. "Alright!" We slapped each other a high five and waited patiently for the driver to come out. When the driver pulled out, we were bummed. It was a fire hydrant.

As we began to put the car in drive, disappointed with the illegal space, we saw lights flash on a parked car. It was a lady signaling us that she was about to pull out of her space. She had witnessed our frustration (Who wouldn't feel our pain in Georgetown?). Parking in a lot would've cost a grip. The lady waited for us to arrive closer to her BMW before she got in to pull off. She took a little longer than usual to pull out, but we didn't care. We had a space and that was all that mattered. Waving feverishly goodbye to her, the lady gave us the thumbs up and we parked. Yes! Taking last glimpses of our looks in mirrors, we both added more gloss and got out of the truck.

"We already on the list, girl. So even if there's a line by now, we good," Kim repeated. I just smiled at Kim.

She was hilarious. How she managed to keep up with the HU happenings while living up in New York was beyond me. I had stepped away from the party scene, but not on purpose. Between work, school, and traveling on public transportation, my time and movement was extremely limited.

Arriving at the club's entrance, there was a small line, like four to five people. We opted to not make a big fuss and just moved along. The line was moving quickly and when we got up to the bouncer, he recognized us. "Where y'all been?" he asked with a big smile on his face.

"In school. For real!" Kim replied. Shivering in tow, I nodded as if to let him know I was doing the same thing. I wasn't one for the small talk. It was freezing outside.

Once we got into the club, we found a nook, took off our coats and placed our purses under our coats. The club was nice and small. It was more like a lounge than a club. Lined with leather benches around the dance floor, no matter where anyone sat, a great view of the dance floor was provided for everyone. It was crowded, people were starting to pile in, and we had just beaten the rush. Thank God for that space.

"Oooooh girrrrl! There's that guy!" Pointing over to the

dance floor, Kim pointed out China to me. I had not seen him since my freshman year. Where had he been? I wondered. China was easy to spot and he looked better than he did on the day I bumped into him. Sporting a Yankee fitted cap with a drink in his hand, he was talking to one of my friends, Alecia. Looking at their body language, the two didn't seem to have a sexual attraction towards one another. I could tell that they were engaged in a funny conversation because all I could see was China's left adorable dimple. He's soooo sexy. The night was young so I knew I had time to interact with him.

"I'm going to dance." And before I could reply, Kim was gone, but not too far. She could still make hand gestures to me. Motioning me to go over and talk to China, I held up my hand and waved her off. There was no way I was going to approach him. I didn't have the guts to do such a thing, but I wanted to.

To my left was the bar, so I went over to buy a drink. Kim wasn't much of a drinker so I already knew what to get her. "May I help you?" the bartender asked.

"Yes. I'll have a Shirley Temple and an Amaretto Sour."

"Coming right up," she responded.

"That will be $10.", she said.

Reaching over my drinks to hand her the money, a voice said, "I got it." I looked over to my left and there was China. Lowering my hand, I looked at him with a smile on my face.

"Thanks, stranger," I replied.

"Oooooo so you remember me?" He smiled.

"Yep. I remember you. How are you?" And where have you been all my life, I wondered.

"I'm good. I took a year off from school to explore some other options, but I'm back for the weekend. One of my homeboys got a new place so I came back to hang out with him. I'm moving back here this summer though. And how are you Ms. Hobson?"

He knows my name! My last name! "How do you know my name?"

"A little bird told me. And I mean... it's not like there are a hundred thousand students at HU. It's not rocket science." Giggling at his comment, he followed me back over to our seats so that I could check on our belongings, sit, and sip. China was slim and stood at about five feet ten inches. His chiseled cheekbones and that dimple were what stood out most to me. He was, no doubt, fine!

"Where are you from?" he asked "And how old are you?"

"I'm from DC and I'm 21." I then learned that China was from Brooklyn.

"Oh. Ok. I'm 22. What's your major? How much longer do you have in school?"

"What's with all of the questions?" I jokingly asked him. I was turned on by his curiosity. Though I had been in a relationship, I had never forgotten our encounter. I always used to fantasize about China's personality and I was way off! I thought he was a thug from V.A., but Brooklyn? Oh Boy! From what I heard about those negroes, they were the King of Thugs, but China was intelligent. He spoke in complete sentences, no slang. His mind was alert and he was focused, yes, on me.

Two hours had passed. Kim had come by the table to sip on one of her five Shirley Temples and Alecia had also stopped by to give China the thumbs up. The two were actually cousins. Their family was from Barbados. "What's your beepa numba?" he asked me. "I don't want another moment to go by and I don't have your information." I gave him my beeper number and he gave me his. We also exchanged phone numbers. I had his house number and his brother's cell number.

Cell phones during these days were rare.

China and I chatted until the club lights came on. The club was still packed. Kim came back to the table and the three of us agreed to sit tight until the crowd trickled out. "My man Drake is the promoter for tonight. So nobody will bother us." China's remark could not have come any sooner. Kim and I took notice of how aggressive the bouncers were getting, in an attempt to clear out the club.

Another tall, slim brother came over to us and said, "Gimmee about twenty more minutes. I'm wrapping up in the office now." I assumed that was Drake.

"That's Drake, girl. I been dancin' with him all night. He and China are friends," Kim whispered. "Do you like China? I like Drake."

"Yes," I whispered back to her.

As we waited for Drake to wrap up, I leaned over to China and said, "You going to walk me to the car?"

"Of course," and he leaned closer to me and kissed me on the cheek. His lips were soft and thin, but the kiss was perfect.

"Ok. I'm all done! Let's go get some breakfast!" Drake said with energy in his voice. He must've had a money-makin' night cause it was 4am and I was tired, but not too tired to spend more time with China.

Following the guys to IHOP, Kim and I giggled and cackled like two hens about our encounters with China and Drake. When we arrived, we were seated and since we were all extremely hungry, we placed our orders before the waiter could disappear to get our beverages.

Leaning on me, China removed his hat and I could see his deep black waves shining on my jacket. I had too much of a chill to take it off. I'd rather be hot than cold any day. China was fun, lovable, and our chemistry was electric. When the food came, China and I were entertained by Kim and Drake. The two cracked jokes on each other the entire time. Apparently they had had a chemistry class together and Drake had been trying to talk to Kim for quite some time.

At the end of breakfast, China and I were glued to each other. And from that moment on, we were just that—inseparable.

Chapter 4:
The Agency (Summer 1995)

I fell asleep late one spring night with all of the lights on in our bedroom. It had been one year later and China and I were still together—living together, shacking up, and putting' our families to shame. I was SAVED and I had been baptized, but I wasn't "in" the Word.

We lived together and partied together. The two of us were inseparable. Often times our house was the "crash house" for any of our friends who were passing through DC to attend parties, events, weddings, etc. Our HU brother, Mark Pitts and my BFF Kim were frequent visitors to our apartment. Mark AKA Gucci would often crash in the living room whenever his artist, Biggie Smalls, mostly known as The Notorious B.I.G., was scheduled to perform in the area. To save a few dollars on hotel expenses, he would put his client up in a hotel while he stayed with us. We didn't mind because when we saw Gucci's face, we always knew we were going to have carte blanche at whatever was going on around the city that particular night.

I was reading a book by Terrie M. Williams entitled, *The Personal Touch—What You Need to Succeed In Today's Fast Paced Business World.* China had gotten it for me from his favorite bookstore, Politics & Pros, and I really enjoyed the read. He had gotten the book to inspire me. China knew that I was in need of an overhaul and he was extremely supportive of whatever measures needed to be taken. China was promoting parties and working at a copy center place to make ends meet while he shopped beats by day. He was no longer in school and aspiring to be a music producer.

In addition to the lights, China and I always fell asleep with the radio or CD player on. As I awoke to Lauryn Hill and Tonya Blount's rendition of, "His Eye Is On The Sparrow," I tuned into the lyrics. Though I had heard the song several times throughout my childhood church life, there was something more meaningful with the song since my peers were singing it. As the song played on, I started to mouth the words, "When Jeeeeesus iiiissss my portion, a constant friend is Heeeee. His eye is on the sparrow and I knooww HE watches ova meeeee." Sick and tired of being sick and tired, tears were forming and one managed to trickle down my face. I woke up next to China, looked at him and eased out of the bed quietly to make a phone call. "Hello. May I please speak to Charlene?" I asked.

Charlene was China's sister-in-law. She often came down to DC to visit us whenever Pooh (China's brother) had business to take care of. "Speaking," the voice answered. Charlene was a Brooklyn gal by way of

Trinidad. She had long silky black hair down to her waist. If Pocahontas was alive and well, it would have been Charlene. "Hey Shar. I need a change and I've always said that I wanted to move to New York so what are your thoughts on that?"

Charlene did not know how to respond. She was pregnant with Pooh's child, raising a daughter Christina, and holding down a full-time job. Giving someone advice was the last thing on her mind and by the time we hung up, I realized that Charlene had never answered my question; however, she did state, "Well, if you ever decide to move up here, you will always have a place to stay." That's all I really needed to hear.

Ear hustling at the conversation I just had with Charlene, China rolled over and held his arms out to reach for me. So I walked back over to the bed and sat. "And what is this I'm hearing? You wanna move to my city? Oh, really? Well then you need to consult with me," he said with a big grin on his face. China was good looking. His smile and teeth were immaculate. His Bajan cheekbones were his main feature. I could tell that GOD personally chiseled them onto his face.

"Yes. I wanna move. I don't wanna be no government worker or schoolteacher. And that's exactly what I'ma end up being if I continue to stick around here any longer. I want more out of life. I don't just want to be married with two kids; a townhouse; and a Maxima. I want a mansion, my pick of the day's vehicle, a housekeeper, and I want to be on the "go". I want to be a woman on the move. I want to make an impact."

Nodding his head in agreement, he then asked, "Ok, but what you going to do in New York? What type of job you want? Are you going to finish school up there? Where in New York do you want to live? 'Cause New York is expensive!" China exclaimed.

Shrugging my shoulders as an answer to his slew of questions, I knew I had to do some soul searching. And as Snickers, my tabby kitty started chewing at my feet; I got up to feed her.

Grabbing a chair to sit down at my typewriter, I poured my thoughts out onto paper to this woman, Terrie Williams. One thing was for sure. Once I put my mind to something, it was bound to happen. In the letter, I kept it 'real' by explaining to the lady that I had been working for the past two years at the Department of Defense while simultaneously attending school full-time. I went on to tell the woman about my lack of motivation and my need to dare myself to do something different. Tweaking my already prepared resume for printing, I then attached it to my letter, stuffed it into the matching linen envelope, placed a stamp on it, prayed over it, and headed to the mailbox on my corner. It was done. Now all I had to do was wait for a reply. As the first week passed since my future had been mailed, I became very antsy.

Four days later, I received a call from the Office Manager of The Terrie Williams Agency. "Hello. May I please speak to Lynn?" a voice asked.

"This is Lynn," I responded. She then went on to introduce herself as Sherry Carter. "I'd like to know if you could come up to New York for an interview." I was jumping for joy on the inside. I wanted to yell out and scream as if I had won the lottery or something, but I kept my composure. I agreed to the interview request. Sherry then gave me some date choices and I immediately selected the first date—not even caring about my financial pockets or my work schedule.

At this point in my life, my parents were not feeling me. I had gotten a job and was putting my way through community college at a very slow pace. Calling my dad to ask him for money to travel to New York for an internship interview was not an option. With tears welling up in my eyes, China made an excellent suggestion. "Hey. Since I'm from New York and I know the city like the back of my hand, we'll just drive up and drive right back after the interview." Smiling from ear to ear, I hugged him and we planned the itinerary for that day. It was going to take $26 in tolls round trip, about $40 in gas, and another 20 bucks for McDonald's going and coming back. Rounding up the total to around $70, the two of us scraped up $40 worth of pennies around my apartment. Scooping up the coins into a jar, we then jumped into his car and headed to his brother's place in Maryland to collect additional coins. We then headed to the bank to make an exchange for bills and it was all good!

On the day of my interview, China and I left the house at 10am. My interview was at 4pm so we had plenty of time to burn up the highway. We had filled up the tank of his black Nissan Altima the night before. Rush hour in all directions was over and we were on our way. As we drove up the road, China mentioned, "So. I'm thinking that if you spend the summer in New York, I'll come up on the weekends. 'Cause somebody's gotta hold the apartment down." He was right and I was happy to know that he thought that way. An internship was just a stepping-stone.

Nailing the interview, I was offered the internship on the spot. When I got back to China's car, he was reclining in the driver's seat. He jumped up when he saw my face. He was eager to get every last detail. My face went to a sullen look as I approached the vehicle. His did too. By the time I got into the passenger's seat, I yelled out, "I got the internship!!!"

He burst out with laughter and hugged me. China was so affectionate. We just hugged each other for a good five minutes. Our efforts to just get here had paid off. "Congratulations, big head. I'm so proud of you." I just beamed back at him like a young happy puppy. I was full of energy and excitement. "I called my parents while you were up there. I let my mom know that we were in New York so if it's ok with you, I'd like to stop in and see them before we leave. Is that ok?"

"That's fine with me." I smiled. I didn't care what he had planned. I was just riding high from the interview's outcome. "To Brooklyn we will go!" I yelled out with excitement. I was also happy to be presented with the opportunity to meet China's parents. He spoke highly of them and though we had been dating for quite some time, I had never met them in person.

As we wisped to Brooklyn, we got there in record time according to China. We just beat the rush hour traffic and what was supposed to be a one-hour rush hour drive had turned into a 30-minute commute. Brooklyn was dull, dingy, and hood. As we drove further into the bowels of Brooklyn, I was like, what the hell is going on? It was totally different from DC. Buildings were on top of buildings. People were on top of people and everybody on the street was hustling. For some reason, I thought Brooklyn was the suburbs of the city. I had no idea it would be like this. It just wasn't what I had expected. I was thinking more like, *The Cosby Show*, but as we drove on, I noticed that there were too few blocks similar to the ones Dr. Huxtable and his family lived on.

When we arrived to China's house, my face gave everything away. "What? What's wrong?" China asked.

"Nothing. I'm just a lil' nervous," I responded. He knew I was lying, but he had no time to get down to the bottom of it and I was glad.

Pulling into the driveway, I looked up to a white-gated row house. It was more secure than Alcatraz. There were bars everywhere. All of the houses were like that. China's parents were protecting their assets in the best way they knew possible. It was obvious that I was in the hood. Located on the busy street of Remsen Avenue in East Flatbush, the neighborhood was a mixture of residential and commercial.

As we waited for China's father to unlock the door, the screen door, and then the iron gate, we stepped in. Upon our entry, China waited for his dad to lock everything back up. When he faced us, he gave his father a huge hug. "Dad, this is Lynn. Lynn, this is my dad."

China was the spitting image of his father. He possessed the same chiseled cheekbones as his pops. His father was a lil' stockier and a few inches shorter.

"Oh. Hello." He beamed. And when I reached to give him a handshake, he pulled my arm towards him and gave me a hug instead. Normally, I would've probably hugged him, but I was still on my business ish. It felt good to have his dad receive me the way that he did. "Your mother is in the kitchen," he stated.

China immediately headed to the back of the house and I was right on his heels. As we passed through the glass-mirrored living room, I took notice of the décor. The gold cloth couches were covered in plastic. You know the type of plastic that would mess up your stockings if you sat on a crack? Yeah... that type of hard plastic is what I'm describing. Crossing into the dining room, the china cabinet stood out to me most. It was filled with photos and trinkets from years of traveling. I found it to be interesting. There was no theme to the dining room. It was just a potpourri of everything from antique to modern. The table was already set for four and the smells from the kitchen made my mouth water.

"Mum!" China yelled out as we arrived to the kitchen's entrance.

"Is that my youngest son's voice?" she asked with curiosity. When she turned around from the stove, her face lit up with a wholesome smile. She reached for him and gave him a nice motherly hug. It was apparent she was happy to see him. "And who is this?" she asked.

"Mum, this is Lynn. Lynn, this is Mum." This time I reached out to her and gave her a hug.

With a thick Bajan accent, she said, "It's nice to finally meet you in person." Her look was stern and sincere. There was no warmth in her words and I felt as though my entire being was under inspection. At that very moment, I pegged China as a "Momma's Boy". I hadn't seen the signs earlier and it threw me for a loop. "Dinner is almost ready. You guys can wash up downstairs and then have a seat," she said in her dialect.

Taking my hand, China led me downstairs. The basement had been turned into a plush bedroom, his brother Pooh's bedroom to be exact and it was nice. It didn't match the look and feel of the rest of the house, but it was cool. A half bath was nestled into the room's far corner and the two of us washed up after each other. While China washed up, I looked at some of the framed photos that graced Pooh's dresser. In each of the photos, Pooh posed with celebs such as Special Ed, Little Shawn, Tracey Lee, and Biggie Smalls. Pooh was the man and it showed in the pics. I was impressed and I wanted "in".

"Peanut. What does your brother do?" I asked as China exited the bathroom. He could see me placing one of the photos back into place.

"Uuuuhhhh... what do you mean? What do you think he does?" he asked me.

"I don't know. That's what I'm asking you," I said back to him. I wanted to know.

"Well. For one, he throws parties. He also helps Gucci out with a few of his artists," he replied. "But we'll talk about this later—once we get on the road."

"Ok." But why did it seem like a mystery?

Dinner was delicious. China's mother fixed a whole roasted chicken, string beans, yams, stuffing, and corn on the cob. It felt like Thanksgiving. I ate until I was full. "So. Where are you from?" China's Mom asked me. I could tell she was about to start in with the questions and China started to pick up our emptied plates to move them to the sink.

"I was born and raised in Washington, DC," I replied with a smile.

"Oh. No. I mean where are you from? Where are your parents from?" she asked for additional clarity.

"My parents are from DC as well. My grandparents are from Texas, Louisiana, and Alabama," I added.

China's Mom went from pleasant to strange. "Oh. So you're a Yankee?" she asked.

"What's that?" I asked.

"You ready to go?" China asked me abruptly. By his movement and jittery energy, I could tell that her question or comment may have not been positive.

Getting up from the table, I thanked them graciously for dinner and before you know it, I was in the car and waiting for China to catch up with me. He had handed me the keys to the car before I could even get up from the dinner table. Five minutes later, he was back in the driver's seat. His mom and dad stood in the doorway looking out at us until we backed out of the driveway and pulled off. "Did I say something wrong?" I asked China who had an intense look on his face.

"No. You good. It's just that my moms be sayin' crazy

stuff out her mouth sometimes."

"What's a Yankee?"

"It's supposed to mean someone from the United States; however, to our culture, it means someone who don't really know where they are from," he responded. I burst out laughing. That old lady tried to sucker punch me. I was amused. China looked over to me in amazement. He thought that I would be insulted, but I wasn't. Yeah. It was his mom making the comment, but I was good. I was still riding high from my interview. Nothing or no one was going to knock me off that horse.

I was asleep by the time we hit the Holland Tunnel. And when I awoke, we were parked in front of our building. Knowing China, if I was light enough, I probably would have been carried in, but my ass was too heavy. So I was awakened by a light nudge. "Big head. We home. Wake up," he said in a low voice. When we got in, I was wide-awake. China was exhausted and hungry. While he slept, I whipped up his favorite, salmon cakes. We then ate on the late night tip and dozed off with our bellies full. Snickers was even treated to the leftovers. She was more than happy.

On the day that I was to leave for New York to start my internship, money was nowhere to be found. Everyone around me was strapped for cash. With one hundred and fifty dollars to my name, worrying about how I was going to make it was not even a thought. Deep down, I knew that everything would work out right. I needed to wake my life up and by all means, I was determined to do so. Arriving to DC's airport, all sorts of insecurities set in. What if they don't like me? What if I get lost in the city... etc. I knew that the first couple of weeks would be rough. China was going to stay in DC for the summer, hold down the fort and visit me every other weekend.

"Yo!" China yelled out to me from his black Nissan. "Call me as soon as you get to Charlene's."

"Ok," I yelled back. I then stopped, blew him a kiss, waived, and continued to drag my big bag into the Delta terminal to hop onto the Shuttle. I paid the $75 Student Shuttle fee to New York, and took off.

Landing into JFK Airport forty-five minutes later, I called my friend Charlene. Instructing me to take a taxi to her apartment in Brooklyn, I began to panic. I only had $75 left and the estimated cost was going to be 35 bucks. I was going to have to make something happen on the financial tip immediately. There was no way I could lean on Charlene. She was a single mother of two daughters and her allowing me to stay with them on their living room sofa was more than appreciated.

With the rest of the day left to get myself together for my first day at the agency, Charlene took the kids and me for a stroll around the neighborhood of Bay Ridge, Brooklyn. Pointing to the laundry mat, and local *bodega* (Spanish for store), I was becoming overwhelmed. It was a hot day in May and the streets were crowded with shoppers picking fruits and vegetables from an open-air market. Dragging me, her oldest daughter Christina, and pushing baby daughter Kiearra in the stroller, we walked what seemed like forever to the train station. Providing me with instructions on how to take the train, I was so tired that if I had the option of sleeping on the train bench until the AM, I might have done so... just kidding.

On the first day at the agency, I was one hour and fifteen minutes late. Though Charlene had given me good subway directions, she was unaware that train construction had started that day. Switching train lines several times, it took two incorrect train rides before I had gotten on track.

Apologizing for the lateness, Ms. Shellie Carter accepted my excuse and escorted me around the office with a sullen look on her face. Immediately, I knew that something was wrong. She wasn't the same cheerful person I had met during my interview and the insecurities crept back into my mind. Introducing me to everyone around the office, I was very curious as to which Account Executive I'd be working with.

Upon my office tour, Shellie then called me and the other eight interns into her office. I was eager to hear what she had to say. I was filled with excitement to learn about the entertainment business. As she opened her mouth, I remembered the words and my actions to follow that grounded me as the person I have become. Ms. Carter said, "Unfortunately, I have hired too many interns this summer. We only have enough room for four interns, so I will have to let five of you go."

In a flash, I saw all of my efforts in getting to New York diminish. My world was closing in on me and I felt as if I didn't have enough air to breathe. My palms started to sweat and the room was spinning. In my mind I was like, this can't be happening to me. Why is it that when I get to where I want to be, the world always closes its doors? As she finished her statement, there was complete silence in the room, which seemed to last forever. She didn't seem to have a formula to her removal of the five interns and she was peering back at us as if we needed to come up with the solution.

Raising my hand to make a comment, Ms. Carter called on me. "Yes, Lynn?"

With all of the attention on me, I was horrified. I had raised my hand instinctively and I hadn't a clue as to what to say. "Ms. Carter. How are you going to go about dismissing five of us? I mean, I've come all the way from DC and this is the only time I'd be able to do something like this." After making my comment, I noticed the other interns making the same type of comments. One had come from Canada, another from DC, and the remainder from the tri-state area.

"I didn't come from far away, but I've been waiting on this opportunity for the past three years," said another intern. Josephine Pada was from Tenafly, New Jersey, one of the most affluent townships in the country. She was Pilipino and pint-sized at that. Standing all of three feet tall, she had the aggressiveness of a bull and it showed. "I've always wanted to work in some form with the NBA and this is an opportunity that I refuse to give up," she huffed. Going into the fall, The Agency had inked a contract to work with the NBA Rookie Week and the upcoming NBA All Star Weekend with the Player's Association.

At the end of the day, Ms. Carter called us into her office one by one. As I was the fourth out of nine interns to be spoken to, I had a 50% chance that I was going to be able to stay. Two of the interns had already been told that they couldn't stay and that they were more than welcome to come back in the fall. As my name was called into her office, I knew that it was time for drastic measures. It was already proven that mentioning I had come from another state was not a guarantee for me to stay. So before Ms. Carter could open her mouth, I took over. "Ms. Carter, I know you have to let some of us go, but please don't let it be me. I have never been so inspired to do anything else. I've done average at school and at work, but I just have the feeling that if I stay, it would be an above average experience for me and that can only benefit The Agency."

Smiling at me, she gave a sigh as if she had already heard the same lines from the other three interns, but I just stood my ground. Looking over my resume once again, she said, "Okay. You can stay. I had all intentions of sending you and Lauren home and have the two of you participate in a series of events that would be held in DC"

Shaking my head, "No," I made it clear that I wanted to stay put.

As I headed back home on the train to Brooklyn, I was feeling pretty good about myself. I could hear my Mama Carol's voice state, "Well done. 'Cause if you

don't stand for something, you will fall for anything."
And since the return home didn't entail any travel
detours on the train, I had a moment to relax and take
in the New York scenery. The D Train crossed over to
Brooklyn on the Manhattan Bridge so I was able to
absorb the view. The day was hot and clear. The train
was also packed full of Asian kids in uniforms who had
just gotten out of school. It was June, but school had
not ended yet. And as I came to my stop, I was looking
forward to my four-block walk to Charlene's. Brooklyn
was not the type of New York I was looking forward to.
I was looking forward to just taking an elevator
immediately down to a midtown Manhattan sidewalk;
however, I had no idea that the rent in midtown was
astronomical. Sunset Park was not my cup of tea. Men
and boys seemed to have had a uniform of dress—tank
tops AKA wife beaters; jean shorts; and white Nikes.
Litter occupied the streets and sidewalks while
garbage cans overflowed and were chained to the
outer gates of Brownstones. Rats running from trashcan
to trashcan were the norm.

I was a little homesick. The distance seemed to be
putting a wall up between China and me, but I was
pushing through it. Brooklyn was rough, but I was
having a ball in NYC. I was able to be Rachel's
shadow to movie premiers, photo shoots, basketball
games, luncheons, dinners, and more. Rachel was the
younger, more hip publicist in the agency. With my

stipend of $100 per week, I was also able to pay for my train fare to and from The Agency and I managed to live off of a bagel with cream cheese with a peppermint tea by day and a slice of pizza with a Sprite by night. I was close to my best friend, Kim, and I met a handful of new friends. One new friend in particular was Trina Stackhouse, the new Office Manager. Shellie Carter had resigned shortly after the new interns were in place. She had decided to leave and start a firm of her own. And that is why you strike while the irons hot!

Trina was a tall, dark-skinned sister with a short Halle Berry hairdo. She was an actress who had taken on a job at The Agency to cover the cost of some "new actor" expenses such as SAG fees, headshots, acting classes, and more.

The summer flew by and I absorbed every part of the Terrie Williams Agency. I had come to learn a lot from working there. I didn't want my experience to come to an end. And as summer started to wind down, I was dreading my return to DC The summer was so packed with excitement and new things. I was comfortable and China was coming up for visits faithfully. I loved New York.

Two weeks prior to my return to DC, my spirits were starting to get a little low. My parents had decided to renege on their proposal for me to take a year off of their financial strings and so my only option was to return to UDC. School was just not enough for me. My grades had improved tremendously, but I just wasn't motivated in the classes.

"Girl, did you know that Malaak quit?" Trina asked in a whisper.

"No! Shut up! Why?"

"She has decided to move on and start her own not-for-profit company."

"Oh, wow!" I knew that I wanted her JOB! Malaak was a tall, slim, light-skinned sister who had it all together. She was quiet, fashionable, and stayed in her lane. I knew her prior to being hired at the agency—as she attended and graduated from Howard as well. When I was a freshman, she was a junior. Her best friend's sister was one of my best friends at the time, however, there was never a need for personal chitchat since she was two years my senior. Juniors in college had way more on their minds than freshmen.

As the day moved on, I helped Rachel Noerdlinger and the agency's VP with the Media Credential List for the First Annual Essence Awards Show. Oprah, Bill Cosby, and a host of other elite African-American celebrities were being honored and I was too excited about my "all access staff" badge. So as we sorted the names and placed them into groups via alphabetical order, I thought about my attire for that evening along with my plan of action for acquiring the position.

"Ok, people. Let's take a 15 minute break," JaeJe yelled out. She needed a coffee break. The rest of us looked around, like 'What we gon do?' 'Cause none of us smoked or drank coffee.

"Lynn. Come with me downstairs to the bagel shop," Trina motioned as she grabbed her wallet out of her purse. The agency was located on 59th and Broadway, right in the heart of Midtown Manhattan and I loved it because I had access to everything from Central Park to Starbucks to the subway.

"Ok. No problem." And we left for the elevator. As we started to head out, I felt something weird about Trina's energy. It was a sort of nervousness with her. As we walked into the bagel shop, she ordered some tea and then turned to ask me if I wanted anything, but I just shook my head 'no' and found a table for two. Checking my watch as I sat in my seat, we had 10 minutes left. "Here," Trina said as she shoved a piece of paper into my view. "This is the job description for the Executive Assistant position that's opening up. This will help you get your thoughts together on how you are going to approach Terrie."

"Uhh... How did you know that I was even interested in that position?"

"I wasn't born yesterday and all you keep doing during your spare time is complaining about how the summer is coming to an end. We all know that you ain't tryna go nowhere." I laughed, agreeing with Trina. I folded the piece of paper, tucked the job description into my pants pocket, got up from the table, hugged her sincerely, and headed back upstairs with her. Wow. Was I really that transparent? I knew I had made a few comments about not wanting to leave New York, but I had no idea it was that obvious.

Trina was the agency's Office Manager. Her job was to act as the receptionist, Human Resources, and to basically be a back up for anyone in the office who was facing a crisis on that particular day. At the agency, everyone wore more than one hat. Trina was a trip. We vibed extremely well and though we didn't speak much, we understood each other. We were cut from the same cloth so there was no need for much conversation. Plus, she wasn't a hater. She was a team player. Our birthdays were one day apart and we were truly Taurean sistahs.

Two weeks prior to my last day as an intern at the

agency, I made up my mind that I was going to march into Terrie's office and demand the job as her Executive Assistant. Terrie was not the most approachable person. She was a strong black woman—light-skinned in complexion with a low Caesar cut that sent a message off to me often like, "Don't bother with me." Terrie was not to be played with. My resume was spruced up and I was ready for interrogation. Terrie's office was located on the 10th floor while our main offices were located on the 9th floor. We (meaning the staff) frequently took the stairs up one flight instead of taking the building's slow moving elevator.

With just seven days left at the agency, my stomach was bubblin'. My nerves were bad. Terrie had been interviewing potential Executive Assistants all week and none of them were to her liking. Dressed to impress with my black slacks, newly polished loafers, and fresh button up with ruffles from the $10 store, my hair was neatly placed in a bun, and my lips were nicely glossed. Heading straight up to the 10th floor without even checking in with the rest of the staff, I knocked loudly on Terrie's door. "Come in!" she yelled out. Opening the door nervously, I sucked it all up. "Oh hey, Lynn. You look nice today." Terrie noticed.

"Oh! Thanks Terrie. I dressed for my job interview today," I replied.

"Oh. Ok. I thought you were heading back to DC. Where's your job interview?" asked Terrie.

"With you," I said. "I don't want to go back home, Terrie. I've learned so much here. I've learned more in the few months I've been here than in my three years in a college classroom. So I'd like to interview to be your assistant." Snickering at my remarks, she then motioned for me to have a seat in one of the two chairs facing her desk. I was so nervous that my right foot started to shake uncontrollably on its own.

"Ok. So at least I have an idea as to why you want to be my assistant, but do you know what it entails? And what about school?" she asked with concern.

"I have watched Malaak and Trina handle a lot of assignments so I have some idea. And as for school, I have already called to inquire about City College. They have a program called, 'The Center for Worker Education,' where students who hold down full-time jobs are able to attend school part-time and obtain college credit if they are already working in their perspective fields."

"Mmmmm hmmmm," Terrie replied. I could see her pondering the idea of hiring me as her assistant and my nerves were on ten! She took forever to say anything to me. It was as if the universe had been placed on hold as I waited for her answer. "Well... if you have everything together like you say you do, then you will need to sit with my CFO, Ray Gerald for an interview as well. He is out of town today so I will arrange for you guys to meet tomorrow. Ok?"

"Ok. Great!" I hopped out of my chair with joy. She looked at me as if I was crazy, but I did not care. I was determined.

"Not so fast. I have an assignment for you. Our new client, Charlie Ward of the New York Knicks, is getting married in one month and I need his wedding announcement to appear in the Wedding Section of *The New York Times*. Here is a photo of Charlie and his fiancée, Tonja Harding, along with a copy of his bio. Call *The New York Times*. Get the name of the editor and mail this information along with a cover letter to her."

I nodded to her while accepting the photo and bio in hand. "Don't screw this up. This is important." said Terrie.

The pressure was on. I knew this was a test. Skipping two steps at a time down the flights to the ninth floor, I immediately went to the Bacon's Guides to research the editor's name. The Bacon's Guides consisted of four thick forest green books that compiled lists of all media nationally and internationally. From newspapers and television to radio stations and magazines, the books were the most resourceful tool for publicists. Scrolling through the Newspaper Guide, I turned the pages quickly to the state of New York. I honed into *The New York Times* Editors list to then secure the name and contact for the Wedding Editor. Booyow! I found her. That wasn't difficult at all and neither was preparing the letter and mailing the photo and bio off to her. The challenge was landing the placement.

The next day, Terrie yelled for me over the intercom. I dropped what I was doing, turned to Trina who gave me the thumbs up, and climbed the flight of stairs in lightning speed. With some shortness of breath, I knocked on Terrie's door and then entered. Seated in one of her visitor's chairs was a distinguished African-American gentleman wearing an Armani suit and Ferragamo shoes. "Lynn, this is Ray Gerald. Ray Gerald, this is Lynn Hobson." He then stood up to shake my hand. He looked a lot like my dad with his full beard and mustache.

"So I hear you want to be Terrie's assistant," he stated. It looked as though he was trying his hardest not to crack a smile. He looked at me as if he was a proud father who was commending his daughter for daring to stand up for what she wanted and believed in. "I read your cover letter you mailed to Terrie this past spring and I knew you'd end up being more than just an intern for this company," he added. His comment let me know that the two of them had their eye on me from day one and I loved it. This was exactly what I was striving for. I worked hard. I did my part and I was also a team player. The internship had its challenges, but I loved every minute of it. "We are going to start you off with a salary of $25,000. That should work, right?"

I had calculated prior to the offer that I would need to earn $30,000 per year in order to maintain things on my own in New York City. "I was thinking more like 30 k," I counter offered. "New York City is extremely expensive." We agreed to $28,000 and I got the job! Thank you, Jesus!

When I got the job, I was like, 'Where the hell am I going to live?' I'll start with Trina because staying with Charlene and the girls long-term was not an option.

Hopping happily down the two flights of stairs back to my desk, I bumped into Trina in the office's foyer. "How did it go?" she whispered.

As Lena, the agency's accountant walked past, I gave her a thumbs up and skipped back to my desk. I was too thrilled. I then jotted down a note asking, "Do you know of any apartments in Brooklyn near you?" Handing her a note, I then awaited her response. I immediately picked up the phone to call Kim to share the good news with her. She was elated. She was happy to know that my stay in New York would be permanent. We made plans to celebrate with each other and the other Gucci Girls. The remainder of the day flew by. We were busy preparing for the first Annual Essence Awards. Oprah Winfrey, Bill Cosby, Angie Stone, and more were scheduled to appear and it was the Agency's job to put the finishing touches on the magazine's production. Printing out the press badges, ordering the red carpet, ordering the Step & Repeat and several other formalities kept us holed up in the office until at least 11pm. It was too late for me to even attempt to trek it back to BK alone so Trina offered to let me stay at her place. And though I didn't have a change of clothes, I planned to pick up some Hanes and a toothbrush at the CVS Pharmacy down the street just before jumping on the train. I was in "grind mode". I no longer cared if I was being seen in the same outfit as long as I was clean.

Once we copped a few toiletries from the store, we hopped onto the C train and headed to Brooklyn. Trina lived in the Clinton Hills / Bed Stuy section of Brooklyn and I was glad that I would be checking out the neighborhood at night. That's when I could really tell if it was the hood or not. "Tell me about the neighborhood, Trina."

"What do you want to know?"

I didn't know how to put it, so I just came straight out
with the question, "Is it ghetto?"

"Oh. It all depends on what you mean. To me, my
neighborhood is part hood and part hip. There are
hoodlums hanging out on the corner and then there are
hippies walking their dogs as well," she said with a
frank look on her face. I felt her honesty and when we
arrived to the Clinton/ Washington stop, she was right.

As soon as we climbed the stairs to the night breeze,
brothas were damn near blocking the exit. "Excuse us,"
Trina said politely as we moved quickly past their dice
game. The hood side had automatically been revealed.
Catching a quick glance at one of the guys, I could see
him staring right back at me. He was handsome. He
was my height, which is short for a guy, but his smile
and lips were gorgeous—the LL Cool J feel. And though
light-skinned brothers were not me, my eyes locked
into his and I couldn't help but to smile back as we
moved through the bunch. I was starting to like
Brooklyn already. "Girl. Did you see that guy looking
at you? He was going to rip your face off with that
intense look." Trina laughed.

"I know," I responded. It had been months since a guy
had paid me any attention. China was still in DC and

though he had committed to coming up on the weekends, the visits started to become far and few. He was down in DC working and hustling. I estimated that I probably wouldn't even see him until Thanksgiving. I was starting to suspect that he was cheating on me, but I was too busy focused on the future of my career to investigate.

Walking down Washington Avenue, we made a right onto Gates Avenue, walked three brisk blocks, and arrived two brownstones into the block on Grand Avenue. Opening up the gate that set the perimeters to her place, we climbed the stucco steps to the tall oak door where she reached for her keys to unlock it. The door screeched loudly when she opened it. The hallway was brightly lit. After I entered behind her, she closed the door tightly and locked it. Heading 20 feet down the hallway, we approached another tall door that she then began to unlock as well. "This is my apartment," and as she said that, she slid the door into a compartment and we stepped into her pad. It was a studio—one large room. Turning on the light so that I could see more clearly, the 20-foot crown molded ceilings are what I admired first. Trina had the place neatly sectioned off into areas. Though it was a studio, there was a bedroom/sleeping area, a living area, and a dining area. The kitchen did have its own nook and so did the bathroom. The only door belonged to the bathroom, which was a nice size. Other features in

Trina's apartment were the two windows that stood from floor to ceiling. They were amazing. I could only imagine the amount of sunlight that would beam into her place. There was also a working fireplace with framed photos that adorned the mantle. "This is so nice," I said. There was no holding back. "Your apartment has character and it's cozy," I added.

"Thanks, girl. I'm always so busy at the agency that I barely ever have time to enjoy it. I'm either asleep or in the streets for work," she said. But it was all good. I could tell that Trina loved her job also. Handing me a huge white tee, I thanked her. Motioning that I would change in the bathroom, I was able to catch a detailed glimpse and it was nice as well. The tile was laid neatly onto the wall and though the appliances were not updated, the bathroom was clean. That was important to me. The bathroom's linen rug and shower curtain were also color-coordinated. Slightly used scented candles lined the back of the toilet and along one corner of the bathroom floor. I could tell that candle lit baths were definitely a part of Trina's routine. While in the bathroom, I rinsed out my underwear and hung it neatly across the tub for drying. Though I had picked up some fresh undies, I didn't want to carry dirty ones with me the next day, throughout the day.

Peering out of the bathroom, the apartment was dark and Trina had white candles lit throughout. If I had not gotten to know her as well as I had in recent months, I woulda thought she was trying to seduce me. As the candles danced, Trina passed me a mug filled with tea. "This is how I normally end my night," she stated. "I wash off the day, sip, and meditate." She smiled. I could dig it. Our days were long and complex. There was always something crazy going on at the agency, but in a good hectic way. I was tired. Trina and I didn't talk much after she handed me a comforter. I lay across her futon and fell quickly to sleep.

Waking me at 7am with a gentle nudge, I was blinded by the sunrays that filled her place. "Good morning." She smiled. I just looked at her and smiled. That was my salutation back to her. A mist came from her bathroom door and it was obvious that she had just jumped out of the shower. "I left you a towel and washcloth on top of my sink," she said. I then rose up, folded the blanket, smoothed out the futon's cover, collected my clothes, and headed to the bathroom for a shower. I slept really well. Turning on the shower, I stepped into the hot water and wet my body. Grabbing the bottle from Bath & Body Works, I lathered up my cloth and washed. The country apple gel awakened my senses. And as I began to rinse, I thanked God for my job. I dried off, slathered lotion on, got dressed, and came out into the apartment. Trina had fixed us some bacon and heated up some frozen waffles. Shoving them down my throat, we were out of the apartment and on our way back to work within the hour.

"How did you sleep?" Trina asked.

"I slept so well. I felt so at home in your home." I smiled. As we walked up the block back to the subway station, Trina greeted her neighbors with waves and nods.

Stopping us to speak was a short, dark-skinned brother. "Hey, Ms. Stackhouse. How are you?" he asked. His pearly white teeth stood out to me and he did seem to be very familiar with her.

"I'm good J.R. How are you?"

"I can't complain." He smiled back. "And who might you be?" he asked me.

"This is Lynn, J.R. She works with me at the agency. Lynn meet J.R."

"Hello," I responded with a smile. Reaching for my hand, I met his and we shook. He was a polite brotha. He wasn't tryna kick it to me or Trina. He just seemed like an all-around good dude and I liked his energy.

"Matter of fact, J.R. Do you know of any apartments available around here? Lynn was just hired at my job and she's in need of a place."

"Yep. There is a one bedroom available on Cambridge Place." As I looked up at the street sign, I saw that we were standing on the corner of Cambridge and Gates.

"Ok. We are rushing, but can you show it to her? She needs to secure something soon."

"Yeah. Give me your number Trina and I'll call you later with a date and time for you guys to see it. We're looking at possibly tomorrow or the next day. I can get you in right away," he said with a smile.

"Ok. Cool." Trina spewed out her phone number while J.R. jotted it down. "Call me later and let me know." I then thanked him and we sped up the pace on our walk to the train. "It normally takes 30 minutes for me to make it to the Central Park stop, but I always give it an extra 30 minutes since it's rush hour. Anything goes during rush hour coming from Brooklyn girl." I could relate because the ride from Sunset Park often turned from a 60-minute ride to a 90-minute ride. We didn't speak much once we got onto the train and I didn't mind. I was too busy looking at the faces and checking out my surroundings. New York was unpredictable and it was important for me to stay on guard.

"Lynn. You are more than welcome to stay with me

until you find an apartment. I know Bay Ridge is a hike for you. And besides, I may need a roommate anyway because I'm thinking about leaving the agency and pursuing my acting career full-time."

"Oh. Wow. That sounds great! The part about me being a roommate and the part about you pursuing your dreams—I'm down with both," I stated.

"Well, say no more. My rent is $600 a month. We can split the bills down the middle until you get your own place."

"Deal!" I moved in two days later. I would've moved into her studio apartment sooner, but I needed time to organize my belongings that started piling up over at Charlene's.

Thanksgiving was coming and I was excited about seeing China for the upcoming weekend. I had not seen him in a month. Though he wasn't in school, he was working at a copier company and making beats while holding down the apartment in DC He wasn't quite ready to move back to New York; however, it was a goal of his to do so. It had been almost three months since I had taken on the position as Terrie's Executive Assistant and I was worn out. A break was much needed. China and I had our weekend all lined up. After eating Thanksgiving dinner with China's parents, we had planned to party with Gucci and Pooh and then head to upstate New York to his family's "getaway home" in the mountains. I had been up to the home on several occasions. Every other weekend that China would manage to make it to New York, we would go upstate with his parents at least one of those weekends out of the month and it was so relaxing. We would often wake up early on Sunday mornings to head back to Brooklyn before church traffic started up. We would make these trips like clockwork. With a consistent travel routine set in place with China and his parents, I had grown to become extremely close to them. I no longer needed China in order to communicate with his parents. I had established my own personal relationship with the two.

On this particular Thanksgiving night, I was too excited. I was eager to see all of my friends from HU that were coming into town to party. The flyer was packed full of HU notables and China was excited too. We had shopped the day before to make sure that our gear was in order—and it was.

"Y'all be careful tonight," China's dad stated as we headed out the door. Dinner was delicious as usual. And instead of driving the Maxima, we upgraded and drove his dad's Pathfinder. It was a much better look. While walking down the steps to the driveway, I looked and pointed at a couple who had on matching camouflage jackets. I liked their style. It was corny, but cute. I smiled at them and yelled out, "Happy Thanksgiving!" They looked up at us as if I had spoken a foreign language and kept it moving. They didn't even reply.

"I don't even know why you speak to people on these streets, Lynn. Ain't nobody checking for you. I know you are trying to be nice, but everybody is not as nice as you," China stated. And as he talked, I watched the couple cross at the light. There was something about them that made me want to speak to them. But oh well, it was over and done with. You would think at times that China was my father. He always made sure that I was on point. And it wasn't because he didn't wanna look bad. He genuinely cared about my wellbeing and that's what I loved most about him.

When we arrived to the party, it was packed. Everybody was there. Though China and I were happy to see everyone, we were a little tired from the workweek, shopping, and eating. "Hey, Fruity. It's entirely too packed in here. Do you want to stay?" China asked. I was hoping he was ready to leave.

I smiled. "I'm good. I'm ready to go. I'm beat, too." The two of us grabbed hands and then made our way through the crowd and to the venue's entrance. When we arrived to the door, we could barely exit. Gucci was arguing with security. People were pushing and shoving to get in and as we squeezed our way back out into the midnight air, the fire marshal was parking, so it was about to be a wrap for the party anyway.

"Hey China!" a voice yelled out. We both turned. It was his brother, Pooh. "Y'all headed back to the crib? Y'all wanna go grab something to eat with me at the diner?" he asked.

"Nah, bro. We tired. Plus, we heading upstate with Mum and Dad in a few hours. Dad wants me to drive, so I'ma lay it down for the night."

"Oh. A'ight. Cool. I'ma grab something to go and then I'ma see y'all at the crib." I then waved to Pooh and we headed to the car. It took all of our energy to stay awake. China even had the window down in an effort to keep his eyes open. The radio was blasting and I was engaging him in light conversation during our drive from the city back to Brooklyn. Upon our arrival home, we started to perk up. We were happy to have made it back in one piece. As China reached to the back of the truck to grab the club to lock up his dad's steering wheel, I grabbed my purse and looked around for any other belongings such as my hat, scarf, and gloves. When we exited the car, China and I walked to the front of the vehicle. And as he started to unlock the garage gate, a gun was cocked to our heads.

"Hands up," a voice stated with authority. What the hell is going on?! As we both raised our hands in the air, my purse was taken out of my hands. "Now. If you don't want to get killed, I suggest you listen to me and do exactly as you are told. That way, no one will get hurt," he said. "Unlock the door my man," a voice said to China. Trembling, China took the key and began to unlock the padded garage door. China and I often entered from the basement if we were ever coming home on the late night tip. His mother was a light sleeper and we didn't want to wake her.

"A'ight. I'ma open the door, but my parents are in the house sleeping. They are elderly so please do not harm them," China stated.

"Cool. And if they get out of line, then you will handle them. Like I said, you do what I say, and no one will get hurt." China and I still were not able to get a look at the gunmen. I had estimated that it was three to four of them. And whatever the case, we were in hot water. When the door opened, it screeched extremely loud. Normally, China would have stopped the door prior from doing that, but he was under pressure and was just going through the motions. Once the gate was opened, the main gunman then instructed everyone to step inside of the gate. "You stay here with her. And if she gets out of line, then shoot her," he said to another gunman. He was providing instructions for the person who was holding the gun to my head. They had me face a wall while China and the gunman who had him entered his parent's home.

"Please don't shoot me," I said nervously to my gunman who seemed to be poking my head with the gun even more.

"Well, if you keep quiet and your man don't pull no dumb sh** while he's in the house with my man, then no one will get shot," the voice answered. Oh snap, I thought to myself. My gunman was not a man, but a woman. My body twitched and shifted some. I was starting to gain a bit of confidence once I realized I was being held hostage by a chick. Besides that, I realized she was short. Her arms were starting to get a little tired from holding the gun up to my head. As I stood there, I tried to strike up a conversation with her. "You know, you don't need to rob people to make a way."

"Shut up. I don't need you to tell me what to do. Y'all getting robbed cause you have too much. We going to lighten up the load a little bit," she responded in a cocky manner. I mean... I'm not from the hood, but I've watched enough movies to know that she was NEW at this and that is what worried me. It's the NEW crooks that always screw up.
  "A'ight. Cool. But can I shift a little bit? 'Cause I have

a cramp in my leg," I said. I was scared out of my mind. It had been several minutes and I heard nothing from the inside of the house. I was worried about China. Shifting me around in a 180, I was then facing the garage's gate. I looked up. The moon was full. I prayed in silence, "God. If you really do exist, please help China and me. Please don't let these people harm us. I will always follow you if you let us go free." I remember saying those exact words in my mind while time just seemed to stand still. It was freezing outside. It was a cold November Thanksgiving and my body was starting to get cold and so was hers. The adrenaline kept me warm. My stomach ached and it took everything I had to not throw up.

A loud thump came from the inside of the house. I whimpered. Something seemed to be going terribly wrong in the house. So many thoughts started to cloud my mind. As the door squeaked a little, a gunman came out of the house and said to the girl, "Let's go, babe."

"What about her? And how did you make out?" she asked boldly.

"I didn't get what I was looking for, but we good for now. Let's just get in the car," he said. "Walk her out with us. I'm thinking we should hold on to her for what we really came for." Nudging me to walk with them, I

was like, *Oh no the hell they ain't taking me with them.*
I then tripped and fell to the ground. The gun fell out of
the girl's hand and instead of grabbing for her weapon
or me, the two of them ran to the car and got in it, and
drove off. While on the ground, I was able to get a
great look at the two. What I thought was three to four
gunmen turned out to be the matching camouflage
jacket wearing couple I had waved to earlier. My jaw
dropped to the ground when I peeped them. They then
sped off in China's Maxima. I just hugged the asphalt. I
was happy to be alive. I bruised my knee on the tumble
to the sidewalk, but I didn't care. As I began to pick
myself up, I could feel someone grabbing onto my arm.
It was China. I hopped up quickly and hugged him
tightly. I didn't know if he was dead or alive. I was just
happy to have him holding me.

"Hey, Fruity. Are you alright?" he asked with a slight
smile on his face.

"I'm good." As I looked him in his eyes, I then saw
blood begin to trickle down his face. I was horrified. As
China stood there, I said, "Baby. You have blood all
over your face and head." I was trying to remain calm,
not wanting him to change his demeanor.

"I'm ok. He banged me over the head with the handle
of his gun because I wasn't moving fast enough for him.
I'ma need to go to the hospital though." And that's

when I noticed a huge gash in his head.

"Ok. Let's get you inside so that I can get some help."
As we turned to walk into the house, all of the house
lights were on. Pooh was also pulling up. Noticing us
looking crazy on the sidewalk, I think he jumped out of
his truck before realizing he had not placed it into park.
As soon as Pooh approached us, China collapsed. The
blow he had sustained to his head caused him to pass
out. Running back to his truck, Pooh grabbed his cell
phone to call 911. We then picked China up and as we
started towards the house, I immediately began to
regurgitate everything that had transpired. Pooh
looked on and listened with very little expression on his
face as he took on the majority of his brother's weight.
We brought China into the house and laid him onto the
sofa.

China's parents were wide awake. It was now five in
the morning and they were scurrying around the house
looking for items and trying to get themselves together
for our bi-weekly "get away"—oblivious to what was
going on. Thank God.

It wasn't until Pooh started bouncing around the house
frantically that they took notice of me holding an ice
pack to China's head and that something was terribly
wrong. "What is going on!?" their father yelled out.
China's parents were up in age. They were older than
my grandmother. The two had decided to become

parents later in life so all of their faculties weren't as sharp as the average parent to 25-year-olds. As their pops started towards me, he approached to check out China lying in my lap. I started to tell him the story. China came to enough to nudge me—as if to say, "Tone it down with all that talk." So I just said that someone tried to rob us outside while we were coming into the crib. Their parents were mortified. As the paramedics arrived and got China up onto the gurney, his parents and the police received a watered down account of what actually happened. After that nudge from China, I knew what position to play.

While China's mother rode with him in the ambulance, I rode with Pooh because he needed a detailed account of what happened, only thing was—I didn't know everything since I was kept outside of the house during the entire robbery. It would be almost a month until I would return to spend the night at his parent's house. By that time, all of the locks on the house were changed and a top-of-the-line security system had been installed. From that day forward, my street senses were heightened. I had become very observant. I had inherited an innate ability to sniff out trouble and proceed to an exit on too many occasions to name after that, and my instincts never failed me from that day forward when it came to my security.

Months after the robbery, China moved back to New

York. After that incident, he felt a strong need to be with his loved ones. As I continued my work at the agency, China would run the streets with his brother and shop his beats. Landing a placement on Foxy Brown's multi-platinum album, *IL NA NA*, his royalty checks afforded him the ability to continue to hone his skills full time as a music producer. Our careers were beginning to match and we were on the road to becoming the power couple we aspired to become. I was starting to feel fulfilled in my life and that was a great thing, but I wanted more out of life. I wanted to do more.

"Lynn, you have a call on Line 1," the receptionist blared over the intercom. Picking up the phone, I said, "Hello, this is Lynn."

"Hey girl. It's Leota."

"Hey! What's shaking?"

"My birthday is coming up and I wanna put something together real quick. Puff is giving me a few days off and I wanna have a party." Leota was the Executive Assistant to Puff—whom everyone now knows as Sean "P.Diddy" Combs.

"Ok. Cool. What you doing after work? I can make a few phone calls so that we can take a look at a few venues real quick." Having access to venues was never a problem.

"That sounds like a plan. Come to my office when you get off."

"Cool. Lata!" I hung up.

After meeting up with Leota at the Bad Boy office off of 5th Avenue, we hopped into a cab to check out the first spot.

"So tell me what you want your party to be like?" I asked.

"I just want it to be a cozy fun environment for my close friends and family. I don't want it to be stuffy. I just want good music, good booze, and lots of fun."

"Ok. I hope you like this spot I'm taking you to. It's on 8th and 28th. The spot just opened and they are only doing private events prior to opening up to the public."

"Oh. That's hot. I like the thought of that," Leota beamed.

Leota was a dark-skinned stylish sistah who was always about her business. So it was a pleasure for me to throw the party together for her. She was always catering to others so I wanted to show her that she was deserving of being looked after as well.

Arriving to a quaint spot on 8th Avenue, Leota and I were immediately sold. Located in the heart of midtown and less than two blocks from Penn Station, no one would have any excuse as to why they wouldn't be able to make it to the party. The venue was under new management and the manager couldn't wait to get something going. The venue was free of charge. "I will keep all of the monies made from the bar," he said as stern as he possibly could. "Ok," we both said in unison. And even though he said that we could charge guests at the door, we stuck with the theme of "Invite Only". Leota just wanted to party and not worry about hassles at the door.

Less than one week from the party, the RSVPs were rolling in heavy and the anticipation was growing rapidly. Leota's party was becoming the talk of the town and it was apparent that it was going to be rockin'. Ordering her birthday cake from Aliyyah of "Make My Cake" in Harlem, I quickly started to knock things off of my "To Do List". Even staff members in my office were starting to inquire about the party.

"Lynn. What's good? Can I come to the party tonight?" one of the interns asked me. "What party?" I responded. Rolling her eyes, she then opened her mouth to respond, but her words were then swiftly interrupted by Terrence, the mail clerk. "Stop it. You know good and well what party she's asking 'bout," Terrence said with a huge grin on his face. "Invited or not, I'm coming," he continued. He knew that I'd never turn him down for anything. Terrence had saved my ass plenty of times in and around the office. He was the official clean up guy for me. Covering my tracks was more of his full-time job. And I am forever grateful for him.

Terrie had come in from out of town today and I was required to stay later than usual of all days. Heading home from the office, Trina had already been out of the shower and out of my way. I was still staying at Trina's and I was comfortable there. We shared a studio, but it was our palace. Upon my arrival home, I was expecting my godsister, Erynne, to also be there. She was contemplating a move to New York to pursue a career in modeling, so I offered to let her crash at our pad for a few days.

"I already knew that you would come bolting in here like lightning," Trina stated. "I just need to put on my clothes and then I'm ready to rock 'n roll."

"Oh. Great!" I came into the house ripping off my corporate gear. I barely said two words to Erynne who sat on my futon, waiting patiently for us to get dressed.

I hugged her and kept it moving to the shower. Erynne's mother and my mom were best friends. The two of them met while attending Howard University's Law School and just as they had been inseparable, we had been too. Erynne was beautiful. She was five foot seven with long, light brown, curly hair and bright green eyes.

I then jumped into the shower, lotioned, and hopped into my party outfit. Sporting a black, tight top and a white and black cow print skirt, you could not tell me I wasn't FLY. "Trina. Are you almost ready? 'Cause China is picking us up at 8pm. I gotta be at the club early to set up." Stepping in my way to show me she was ready, I then gave her a friendly shove.

Arriving on time for once, China pulled up in his father's Nissan Pathfinder. "I got here on time and you still ain't ready," China commented. "I'm really proud of your efforts, Fruity.

I was growing so much and China wasn't even taking notice of me anymore. He was too engulfed in his own world and endeavors. It was "ok" for now though I really wasn't ok. I had too much at stake and I had to keep it together.

On too many occasions to name, my weeknights were spent looking for China. Too often, he was missing in action. I was a new New Yorker, naïve, and in love. Over time, the sting of his infidelity started to wear off on my heart, so I fought fire with fire. If China wasn't available to spend time with me, then I began to explore other options. After five years of faithfulness, there was no way I was going to stand on the curb of loneliness and not enjoy my 20s. I had gotten too tired of turning a deaf ear to girls in bathroom stalls at parties, talking about his packaging. My pride wouldn't let him go though and besides, I really loved him. I wasn't about to give up on the possibilities of us, but I wasn't going to be no dummy either.

As China pulled off to begin driving to the party with Trina and Erynne riding in the backseats, my mind drifted for a minute as we drove up to the corner of Grand to then head down Fulton towards the Brooklyn Bridge. The night before had been an amazing experience for me. Two months back, I had met a guy on my way out of the subway station. His name? Pumpkin. He was that light-skinned brother with a beautiful smile and caramel complexion I noticed the first time I had spent the night at Trina's. What stood out most about him were those muscles bulging from his light-weight jacket. He was sexy as all hell. For two months, he met me coming out of the subway each and every weekday evening and walked me home. Though the NYPD had done an amazing job at ridding robbers, I welcomed the security guard God had employed to watch over his favorite child each and every evening. With each lengthened ten-minute walk from the Clinton/Washington subway stop to the stoop of my brownstone, Pumpkin and I always took the time out to share our very different worlds with each other. And in two months time, Pumpkin had become my undercover lover, my friend with benefits so to speak. The night before had been our first physical episode and I just got lost in my thoughts of what took place during the entire ride to the city while China, Trina, and Erynne chatted it up.

When we arrived to the front of the club, the girls climbed out of the vehicle. China was a gentleman when it came to parking. He would always drop me off to our destination in the city and then looked for parking each and every time. Now I realize that it just gave him extra time to place phone calls to his fans.

"What's good, Fruity? You alright?" China asked. "You were quiet during the entire ride."

Smiling back at him, I replied, "I'm good." I then reached over to kiss him on the cheek and let him know that I would see him inside.

As I entered into the club, Trina had already begun to meticulously place the balloons and streamers around the venue. Setting up was a breeze. The venue was very classy and it had the character that needed little to no additional décor; however, we did place balloon clusters strategically throughout the venue.

And needless to say, the night went off without a hitch. The cake was fabulous, the DJ was on point, and Leota was on cloud nine. Every well-respected industry head was in the house. Bad Boy staff members along with friends and family of Leota's rocked out to the continual play of Biggie's latest single, "Hypnotize". The song was off the chain and Biggie's presence made the party even more hype! The Bad Boy staff kept asking the DJ to bring the song back and he did just that—all night. And I didn't mind because the party brought me back to the night I fell in love with hip-hop when I saw Biggie performing at HU.

The party was flawless and my first independent NYC event was a success. "Lynn. Thanks so much for helping me put my party together. It was better than I had imagined," Leota gushed at the night's end. "I had a blast and I owe ya."

"Ok. I'ma hold you to it," I replied jokingly. The whole party-planning experience really brought Leota and I closer together. We had become two peas in a pod and I was excited about my new friend. We started to attend all of the album launch parties, movie premiers, and award shows together.

More than a month had passed and the Soul Train Awards in LA were quickly approaching. "Lynn. You comin' wit me to the Soul Train Awards, right?" Leota asked.

"I'm not sure. I don't really have the money to fly out there like that. Not to mention, I gotta take care of my hotel, car rental, and food," I said to her in a calculating tone of voice. I wanted to continue hanging out, but there was no way I could pull off a trip to LA on my salary. I couldn't even front if I wanted to.

"Well tell ya what. Pay for your plane ticket and I'll cover the rest. You can stay in my room. And I gotchu on the food and transportation. Ok?"

"Deal!" I had only been to LA one time before and I was extremely excited about the adventure. The three weeks leading up to my trip with Leota sped by quickly. With my vacation notice placed into Terrie's Office, I squealed with excitement when the wheels of the plane went up into its compartment.

When I arrived to the hotel, I grabbed the spare room key Leota had left for me at the Concierge Desk. I then rushed upstairs, greeted Leota with a hug, freshened up and we quickly got into the LA flow of things. Leota had more than a mound of work to do, from scheduling car services to the award show, booking flights for staff members who wanted to fly out last minute to booking studio time for Biggie and other Bad Boy Artists who were in town. Her schedule was packed with parties and that is what I was looking forward to most.

"Tonight, we are going to head out to Malibu and grab a bite to eat with some friends of mine," Leota yelled out to me as I showered.

"Ok. Cool. You know I'm down to eat." I never really asked too many questions when I was with Leota. She was often too busy so I just observed and would quickly obtain answers to my mental inquiries usually within an hour of my curiosity.

"When you get dressed for dinner, just get dressed for the night because we are going to go straight to the VIBE Magazine Party to make sure everything is in order and organized for Biggie and Puffy's arrival."

While relaxing a bit before getting dressed, I picked up the phone to dial China's number to let him know that I had arrived safely. "Hey, baby. I'm here in LA. I made it safe and sound."

"Oh. Ok. That's good to hear. I'ma need you to check on my brother while you are there. Apparently, Pooh was jay walking and a car hit him. He's going to be alright, but he's in the hospital with a broken leg. He may need surgery."

"What!? Are you serious? That sounds crazy. Ok. Just hit me on the two way with his hospital information and I'll check on him in the AM." China sounded frustrated and drained. I could hear his parents in the background badgering him and questioning him for updates on his brother's health. I could hear the concern and worry in their voices.

Dressing in a halter top and leggings, I then put on some light makeup and put my hair up into a french roll with dangling bangs. I was looking too cute. As we piled up into our vehicle, Leota, her assistant, and I took a nice drive out to Malibu where we ate at a beautiful ocean front seafood restaurant called, Gladstones. Upon our arrival, we were seated with other BadBoy staff members and an up and coming comedian. Rapper/ music producer Dr. Dre was also spotted enjoying a meal with his family. As we ate Dungeness and King Crab legs, Leota kept getting the play by play of the awards show via two-way pager. "I want to time our arrival to the after party with the ending to the awards show," she stated, but as the food and drinks started flowing, it became increasingly obvious that we would be running late.

The entrance to the Peterson Automotive Museum on

Wilshire Blvd. in Los Angeles Museum was packed, but thanks to Leota's clout, we never had an issue about entry. Upon admission, it was evident that the party was fully under way. Of the hip-hop world: Busta Rhymes, Heavy D, Da Brat, female rapper Yo-Yo, music producer Jermaine Dupree, and several others including Biggie and Puff were on hand to party in peace. In no time, I was passed a glass of champagne and began to join in the festivities. The party was rockin'! Not too long after I started to get my pallet wet, the fire marshals came in to survey the capacity and soon after shut the party down. I was pissed. I was just starting to get into the groove of things. "C'mon. Let's get out of here," Leota said to me. "Let's try to beat the crowd outside and get to our vehicle before people really start to move out."

"Ok," I responded. And as we turned towards the entrance, I saw Leota double back to speak with her Bad Boy staff members. I assumed she was giving them the same suggestion to leave quickly from the looks of her tone and body language. Out of the staff, Leota was the "Mother Hen" of the crew. She made sure everyone was in line and on point. She did her best to protect the interests and integrity of the label. When we arrived at our vehicle, we climbed in and headed directly to our hotel room. Since the party was over, Leota thought it best that we turn in early to get a great jumpstart on the following day. I agreed.

As we hopped onto our beds and began to peel off our shoes and clothes to swap them out for PJs, Leota's phones started going off like crazy. Her two-way pager was signaling like an alarm and the hotel room's phone started to ring, so I picked up the phone. "Hello."

"Oh my God, Leota!" said the voice on the phone.

"Oh. This isn't Leota. This is Lynn." And before I could turn to take the phone to the bathroom door, Leota was already standing over me, grabbing the phone out of my hand. "Hello. Who is this?" she asked. To this day, I don't know who she was on the phone with, but all I remember is hearing her scream at the top of her lungs, "Nooooooo... Are you serious? Nooooooo." She then hung up the phone and started to get dressed again. I followed suit. As she began to throw her clothes back on, I moved even faster. It was a long ass seven minutes before I would hear the news that Biggie had been shot. As Leota and I sped off into the night to Mount Sinai Hospital, we could see a huge crowd outside. Police officers were attempting to move the fans back and upon arrival to the hospital we received the news that Biggie had been pronounced dead. The bullet-riddled vehicle was also there, taped off for the impending investigation. Leota was devastated and so was I. The young man who made my heart pump for hip-hop was gone and I was heartbroken. With no time to openly mourn, Leota began to work. Gucci was whaling in the street, crying profusely over the news about his artist and friend. Every Bad Boy staff member that was in LA was now at the ER entrance crying and screaming aloud about the death of the Notorious B.I.G.

Needless to say, my trip was cut short. Leota was thrown into serious work mode while juggling her very own emotions, but through it all, she remained strong for her team. Changing and scheduling an entire staff's departure back to the East Coast while also coordinating the flight of Biggie's body back to Brooklyn was no easy task. She handled everything like a pro. "I just want everyone else that I'm concerned about to get back to New York safely and that means you as well." She then had my flight changed and I was unable to even get through to Pooh at the hospital. His cell phone and pagers didn't seem to be working, but China didn't mind me flying immediately back home either, so I did just that.

Biggie's music touched me and his death baffled me. I remembered having nightmares for well over two weeks after his death. In life, whenever a tragedy would hit, I always came up with some sort of rationale about the whole thing. In the case of Biggie's death, that reasoning never added up. Searching for answers, I couldn't come up with any. I even turned to God whom I had forsaken since I had moved up to the Big Apple—only to get the silent treatment.

Upon arrival back to Brooklyn, the questions flew out of everyone's mouth that had gotten word that I was even in LA when the shooting had occurred. Random knocks on the door by neighbors wanting answers filled my first evening back at the crib. Trina and I lived on Grand and Gates—two short blocks from where Biggie's block, St. James, was located. I had no answers for anyone. My questions weren't even answered.

Opting to go right into work, I canceled my remaining two vacation days. Sitting at my desk with a glum look on my face, Terrie peeped it and asked, "So did you know Sean's artist? Did you see him get killed?" And before I could answer the questions, she simultaneously barked out a "to do" list to me. I just grabbed a pen, sucked up my feelings, and kept it moving. That's all I could do. The older generation wasn't into the hip-hop movement and several of them at the time thought of it as silly.

Immediately after Biggie's death, I started to take notice of the disconnect between my generation and the older generation. As my generation started to come into its own, the older generation turned a deaf ear to anything pertaining to our views and philosophies. It was after this realization that I set a goal to open up the doors of my own public relations firm, geared to my peers of prominence. I started to map out my plan. I started to slack off at work. Calling in sick to do research on building my own company to halfway finishing the assignments Terrie had given me became the norm over a 30-day period.

To top it off, China and I were on the outs. I had caught him the previous weekend cheating red-handed with some random chick. When he was supposedly heading down to DC to handle some business, some girl managed to get a message to me that she had plans to rendezvous with my man while he was down for the short visit. So I raced it to DC on the Greyhound bus one hour behind him to catch his ass. While I didn't catch him in action, the evidence was overwhelming. Besides, what was I really going to do at this point? Nothing. So I headed back to Brooklyn without my confrontation. At this point in my life, I was not a happy camper. People in general were beefing so clubbing was subsided. My man wasn't faithful. I was sooo over my job and I wanted a change of pace, ASAP.

"Lynn. It's Terrie. I know you aren't sick so I expect you in my office no later than 3pm today." That was the message that Terrie had left on my voicemail.

Five minutes later, I received another phone call from

our office intern, Joy King, "Lynnnnn... girl... you in trouble. Terrie found out that you aren't sick so she's pissed. She's up here in the office tryna iron out the kinks to the upcoming Essence Awards and you ain't here. It ain't looking good." Click.

Joy was the new intern at the agency. Fresh off the bus from North Carolina, this wet behind the ears southern bell had too much energy than a lil' bit. Standing at all of five foot two with a big chest, petite frame, and a kool-aid smile, Joy was the new energy in the office. With my wanting to exit, her excitement about her new internship annoyed the hell out of me. One month into her stint, Joy greeted me every morning with questions and dialogue about our current clients that made my skin crawl. Terrie had taken a serious liking to Joy—the same familiar liking she had taken to me when I had replaced Malaak. But I was too engulfed in making my exit to even give her the time of day.

"Oh snap!" I'm in big trouble. I had gotten fed up with all of the annual event properties. The company had become a well-oiled machine and I was bored. Hip-hop was calling my name. But damn, I didn't get a chance to prepare my exit like that. I needed some numbers outta that rolodex.

I was already dressed comfortably in sweats so I just threw on some sneakers and hiked it to the C train on

Fulton and Washington. The day was cold. It was the end of April. The air was brisk and the sky was clear. Sliding my Metro Card through the turnstyle to enter the station, I started to imagine what Terrie would possibly say once she saw the braids in my hair.

Creeping into the office, with big black sunglasses on, I removed the shades quickly to find that no one was in the office. Where is everyone?

"I sent everyone to lunch. I'm back in my office," Terrie yelled out. She had ears like the Bionic Woman. How did she know I was in the office? I mean, I didn't bump into anything. Picking up the pace, Terrie looked at me in disgust. It was so evident what I had done on my sick day. I had gotten my hair braided at Afrigenix on 72nd Street in light brown silky twists. It took too long and it was too expensive for me to take the braids out and pretend I was indeed sick.

"Well, I knew this day was coming. So I'ma be blunt. You gotta go. You ain't gotta go home, but you gotta get the hell outta here. I love you like my own daughter, but it's time to kick the baby bird out of the nest. You have wings. You can fly now. So soar and excel in whatever else you wanna do. It's just you ain't going to continue to do it on my dime and my time." She grinned. My heart sank into my chest. I was fired! Bam! Just like that and that's the way it is! But there was no love lost. Terrie was right. I was fed up. I wanted to do something more exciting. Showing me one last time to my desk, Terrie had already packed up my personal belongings which entailed photos; notepads; and a few of the Media Placements I had obtained for the agency's clients. Handing me a box and cab fare, she hugged me with the most sincere hug and said, "That money is for you to take a cab home cause there's no way you getting to Brooklyn with all this stuff."

"Ok. Thanks," I replied. Then she turned and walked out. As the doors to Essence Communications damn near scuffed up my heels, I was not all there. Holding back the tears, I was able to hail a cab and get in it before the first tear came rolling down my cheek. A chapter had ended. I was now on my own.

Turning the key in the door of our studio apartment, I felt like a super LOSER. "Oh girl, please. Don't come in here looking for a pity party cause that ain't happenin'. Go down to unemployment tomorrow and file. That will give you at least six months to figure out your next move." Trina laughed. She always looked on the brighter side of things. Throwing my box from the office onto the middle of the floor, Trina just sat on the couch and shook her head with a smirk on her face. Charlie and Tonja Ward's *New York Times* wedding announcement had fallen out when the box hit the floor. That was my first placement out of several. It fell out for a reason. I had come a long way and I was really all grown up now. "Don't just sit there and let this situation get the best of you. Take the rest of today to plan and then move forward tomorrow."

Chapter 5:
Iron M.I.C. Entertainment

Trina was right. I took a long hot shower. Showers always seemed to help me center and focus on my priorities. Showers were also spent talking to God— letting him know what I wanted and needed. So I didn't hesitate to start belting out my long list to Him before stepping into the tub. As the water moistened my body, I began to wash once over with Dove soap and then I rinsed. Doing it once again, I then began to get some clarity. While lathering up my washcloth to start my second round of washing, I began to map out the next day. I would go and file for unemployment first thing in the morning. Rinsing again, I then picked up my favorite body wash and lathered for the third time. The nice cucumber smell awakened my senses and I began to relax more. I would apply for unemployment and then start my own business, a Public Relations company for my peers of prominence whose voices were often misunderstood and/or misinterpreted. Bam!

Drying off, things were much clearer. Deciding to open up my own business immediately made me start plugging away at getting things organized. I didn't want to waste any time. I felt like Jerry Maguire... on a mission all by myself. Little did I know, I would have a lot to learn about myself and the business.

Finding out the key elements to starting a business, I got up the next day on a brisk morning to walk down Fulton Street to downtown Brooklyn to apply for unemployment and secure a business certificate for my company. At the rate of just $120, I knew that money had to be recouped quickly, 'cause that's all I had!

The unemployment line was actually kind of short. I thought it would be a multi-day affair; however, it only took me four hours to stand in line, speak with a Counselor; and apply for unemployment. "Ms. Hobson, it will take four to six weeks for your unemployment to kick in. You will be receiving the maximum weekly payment, which is $402. You will need to call this number once a week to report in for unemployment. You will be required to look for employment daily. Keep and track a log of your efforts to find a job," said the Counselor. She was extremely informative; she never looked me in my eyes—weird. Whatever, I was one goal down for the day and ready to move on. Signing some forms, she then handed me an envelope full of papers and I was done. I thanked her for her time and bolted out of the office.

It was a beautiful spring day and summer was right around the corner. The day had started to heat up. The sun was out and the pavement was packed full of people on their lunch breaks. I was starving. The hot dog stand was crazy busy so I opted to keep it moving.

As I climbed the stairs to the Kings County Clerks Office in Brooklyn, my fingers were crossed. I wondered if the company name I wanted would be available and I also hoped and prayed that the certificate wouldn't cost too much money. Entering the building, I then walked through a metal detector and then asked the officer for directions. "Excuse me. Where should I go to obtain a business certificate?" He pointed in the direction to which I was to go. I thanked him and headed to that office.

As fate would have it, the name HobbieCom was available. Yippee, and it would only cost me less than 50 bucks. I had chosen the name, HobbieCom because Hobby is my dad's nickname and a portion of my last name while the Com part was going to be short for "communications". As I paid the fees due to obtain my paperwork, I became so excited. I felt accomplished and it felt great! Walking home with my business certificate in tow, I kissed the envelope, and stopped at the hot dog stand. Grabbing a lunch special, which consisted of a hot beef sausage with mustard, some BBQ chips, and a Welch's grape soda, I sat on a Brooklyn bench and ate. While collecting my thoughts, I began to gather a mental tally of the things I'd need in order to start my company. Though it wasn't much, it still cost money and I was lacking in that department.

I was always taught that I should never give up, cave in, or quit. The music industry was like musical chairs and I couldn't stomach the thought of getting caught out there again without a chair once the music stopped. So what did I decide to do? I decided to build my own chair, a mahogany one, one that would withstand the tests of time. That way the music would never stop on me again. I could enter the game at my own risk, take breaks, and even re-invent myself—thus the birth of HobbieCom, Inc. a full service Urban Public Relations Company. Getting up off of that bench, I was determined to make it.

Finishing up my lunch, I threw away the trash and started the long walk home up Fulton Street. Engulfed in my thoughts, I then heard my name being called, "Lynnnnnn!!!!" Then I heard a horn honking hard while my name was being called repeatedly. It was Jackie Rowe, Mike Tyson's sister who was a client of the agency's. Beeping her horn again as I turned to acknowledge her, she waved for me to come over by her car. I remember her words: "Hey Lynn. How are you? I actually called the agency today and when I asked for you, they told me that you are no longer with the company."

Clinching my teeth at the embarrassment of not being a

part of the agency, I replied, "No, I'm not with the agency anymore. It's time for me to move on and explore other options in entertainment."

"Well, I'm starting my own company, Iron M.I.C. Entertainment (IME) with my brother and I would love to have you help me get the company off the ground." She smiled. Suggesting that I come over to her Brooklyn apartment in a few days, I agreed. Taking a pen and paper out of her purse, she jotted down her address and phone numbers. "How's Monday?"

"Monday is cool," I responded with a happy smile on my face. From what I had already known about their family, I was taught that you really do get what you pay for and if you want great service and you don't want to stand in line, waving money around does help. In a city such as New York, there are always people who want to be catered to. Everybody is somebody. As I turned to continue my walk home, Jackie asked me if I wanted a ride. I politely turned her down. Though a ride in her whip would have been nice, I was hoping to bump into Pumpkin. When I arrived at the top of my block, all eyes were on me. Pumpkin immediately walked over to me. "Yo, didn't I tell you not to walk this way? You are so hard-headed," he stated with an agitated look on his face. Though I was not his girl, you couldn't tell that I wasn't. He was so protective of me. The guys had gotten to know my face and my safety was no longer an issue. But still in all, it was obvious that Pumpkin didn't want anyone else to lay their eyes on his prize.

"I know. It's just that I hadn't seen you in a while." I smirked. He gave me a boyish grin and walked me home. It worked every time. I didn't have a phone number or beeper number on him, but whenever I had an urge to see him, I just channeled my energy in thought to him and he would appear. I knew nothing personally about Pumpkin, nor did I care to know anything about him. I was still in a full-fledged relationship with China, so less was best. I didn't even know if Pumpkin had a real job other than standing out on the corner. I knew he had a girl. He did keep it funky with me about that and I did with him as well. When we were together and alone, nothing mattered.

After we finished pleasing each other, Pumpkin jumped in the shower. I entered into the bathroom as well to use the toilet. We were so comfortable with each other. You would've thought we had known each other for years. While he finished showering, I straightened up and picked up his stretched out wife beater. Reaching for a fresh pack I often kept on hand for him, I laid one out and threw the worn one away. I wouldn't dare mix his dirty tee in with my laundry, so trashing it was the only option.

Stepping out of the bathroom, he reached for his boxers, then his jeans, then his socks, and then his Timbs. I handed him his fresh tee. He smiled. He loved it when I did that and I know it made him feel special. Walking over to my closet, he grabbed my secret deodorant where he glazed his underarms and then rubbed lotion up and down his muscular arms. Reaching for me, he hugged me tight, kissed me passionately, and left. Shortly after, Trina came in. The two always missed each other. Pumpkin's timing was always impeccable.

The night before I was to meet with Jackie, Trina and I prepped for my meeting with her. Trina stated, "Lynn. Don't over talk. Just let them know you can get the job done and just do it." I was nervous—to think that Mike Tyson would be my first client was amazing! At this time in Mike Tyson's career, he was clearly not on top. He had just lost the fight where he had bitten off a piece of Holyfield's ear and the media made him out to be a monster.

When we arrived to their Brooklyn flat, my stomach started to act funny. I was super nervous. Trina and I had cabbed it to Flatbush. Buzzing the bell to a neatly tucked away tenement building located in the middle of a quiet brownstone-filled block, we pushed the door inward and walked into the lobby where Jackie's son, Prince, greeted us and led us up to their apartment. It was summertime and the hallway was heated. Entering into their lavishly decorated four-bedroom flat with the latest in home décor, the inside was nothing like the outside. From the black cherry hardwood floors to the crown molding that hugged the ceiling's rims, the cool place was ghetto fabulous.

As Prince seated us in the living room, Jackie greeted us in a long luxurious house robe while carrying a lalique tray of various fruits, cheese, and crackers along with a matching pitcher of homemade lemonade. As she laid the tray down on her ottoman, we stood up to greet her with hugs. Jackie was soooo over the top. You couldn't tell her she wasn't either. Her personality was extremely energetic, yet aggressive. As she sat on the loveseat opposite of where we sat, Jackie poured our drinks and got right down to business.

"So basically, Mike and I remembered your work and diligence while you were at the agency and we would like to hire you as our publicist. The two of us are starting our own label, Iron M.I.C. Entertainment and we will be focusing on two acts—one of them is my son, Prince. He is a rapper."

Nodding, smiling, and sipping as we listened attentively to her words, Mike walked in and took a seat next to his sister. Waving to acknowledge us, he did not want to interrupt the meeting, but sat quietly and listened. The opportunity sounded very exciting. "So to start, we are doing a talent search or a talent showcase. We are looking for new talent and we want to scout for locations that would house up to three hundred people. We will have Mike, Foxy Brown, and a few other celebs come in weekly to judge the talent." There will be a general admission fee charged at the door for anyone interested in coming in to be entertained. Jackie had a plan and it sounded really good. "So what are your fees going to be for helping me do this?" she asked. And that's what I liked. She was straight to the money.

With the showcase slated to happen once a week, I said, "Fifteen hundred a month sounds reasonable to me," I replied to Jackie. Mike looked up at me as if I was crazy, but I held my ground. I didn't know if I had insulted him with the rate and my heart started to race.

"That sounds fair," he said as he got up and walked over to Trina and me. He then shook our hands and as he walked out of the door, he turned to Jackie and said, "Write the check." I was overjoyed.

To this day I am forever grateful for Jackie and Mike for providing me with an opportunity to launch my business and I didn't let them down. Over the months, the showcases proved to be a success. Celebs from all walks of life showed up to judge the talent. After the stint, artists were signed to the company and my tenure had come to an end.

During the quarter that I had the privilege of working with Mike and Jackie, I was able to really see for myself that the media had Mike pegged completely wrong. He was made out to be a beast, but in actuality, he was a cub. Over time, I had come to learn that Mike was completely misunderstood. More than anything, he was not the angry maniac that the people pinned him out to be, and folks were always targeting him. It still isn't too often where anyone can go into the hood and still see, touch, and speak to a celeb such as Mike. He stayed connected to the hood. He embraced his home in Brooklyn and gave back any way possible. The media didn't see him paying people's rent, purchasing cars, awarding youngsters for staying out of trouble and excelling in school. Those things went unnoticed and unrecognized to this very day.

The Iron M.I.C. account was so hectic that I had failed to seek out additional clients. Juggling was something I needed to begin perfecting. Though I was still on unemployment, I wanted to be financially stable by the time my unemployment had ended. Even though HobbieCom was underway, I was still open to the possibility of an industry job. With the experience of having IME under my belt, I saw that I still needed more experience and structure to solidify my career.

It was now the early fall of 1998 and my pager went off. It was Leota. I hadn't spoken to her in a while so I picked up the phone to call her. "Girl. I just got offered a new position at a label. I will need to hire a publicist. You down?"

"Heck yeah!" I exclaimed.

"Cool. I will fill you in on everything in a few. Lemmee just put in my notice here. Gimmee about two weeks."

"Cool. And thanks! I'm already excited."

As the two weeks flew by, I didn't just sit around and twiddle my thumbs. I still kept on the hunt for additional clients. I was not about to put all of my eggs in one basket. I couldn't afford to take any chances.

Two weeks to the day I last spoke to her, Leota called, "Hey Lynn."

"Hey, Lee. What's up? How you doing?" Often times, I would call Leota, Lee.

"Blessed. I feel really good," she replied. And she sounded good. "Soooo, I'm really going to leave Bad Boy."

"Really? Are you serious?"

"Yeah. I'm out of here. It's cool here. I'm just ready for some growth. Do you know Un?" she asked.

"No. Who's that?"

"He was Big's partner for the record label they had together. The label was called Undeas. You know... with Junior M.A.F.I.A."

"Oh yeah. Right!"

"Well... he has gotten another situation and he is starting a fresh label at Epic/ Sony. He just hired me to be his GM. The salary is really good. The work load won't be as heavy, and besides, it's time for me to take a step up that ladder."

"I feel ya. You know, I'd be honored to do all of your executive publicity if you'd like me to. My contacts with Billboard and other industry publications are still pretty strong."

"Actually, I'd like for you to do something else," she stated and filled me in on the plan she had for the budding label.

Chapter 6
UNTERTAINMENT

Weeks had passed and I had not heard from Leota. I was getting anxious and I was bored. But before I could reach for my cell phone, it rang. It was her.

"Hey, Lynn," she said.

"Haaayyyy," I replied.

"I will be in Brooklyn all this week working at Un's apartment. Can you stop by here tomorrow for a quick interview and introduction?" she asked.

"Yep. I sure can," She then gave me a time and the address, which was three long blocks from my apartment.

"Ok. See ya at two o'clock," I replied. Hanging up the phone, I then threw open my closet to begin figuring out what I was going to wear. Yeah yeah, yeah, I know I had been determined to build my empire with HobbieCom, but the opportunity that Leota was granting me was a no-brainer. So for now, provided that I'd get the job, I decided to put my business on the back burner and go back in for more experience.

I opted to wear some slacks and a button-up, hoping that it wasn't too dressy. Knowing that I had an interview at a hip-hop label, I didn't want to burst up in there wearing a full-fledged suit. That would have been way too over the top. I even figured that attire would be somewhat of a "turn off" to them. Can you imagine walking in to an interview and wondering if you are dressed too conservatively for the job? LOL! That's hilarious! But I was worried. For hip-hop, I was considered too conservative.

When I told China the news of my interview, he seemed to be happy for me, but a little hesitant about it at the same time. There was a hood element to working at a rap label and he clearly didn't think I was equipped to handle it. "I'm happy for you, Fruity. Just work hard and watch your back. I gotchu, but just tread lightly," he stated.

As China was speaking, Trina interrupted. "Girl, please. Go head with all that. You will be fine. God's got yo back." And that was the end of that conversation. Trina was always good at looking on the bright side of everything and I counted on her for that. She would always attempt to ease my mind before I got into deep thought. I was an overthinker, always weighing the pros and cons to everything. Though that wasn't entirely a bad thing, sometimes, it would hinder me from making any type of decision. So often times,

Trina would do her best to nip shit in the bud.

When I arrived to the Washington Avenue building, I rang the doorbell and was immediately buzzed in. Grabbing for the heavy door before the buzzer stopped, someone reached for the door to assist me. It was a heavyset dude. "I got it," he said with assurance. "You goin' to see Jacob?" he asked.

"Umm... no. I'm going to see a friend. I don't know a Jacob."

"Oh, I'm sorry. Wrong person. I thought you were the new girl here for an interview." he said. And in my mind I was like, how he know what I'm here for if I'm taking the elevator inside of a tenement building?

Letting down my guard just a bit, the two of us stepped into the urine scented elevator and we proceeded to the same floor. "I am actually here to meet with Leota. You know her?"

"Yep. I'm Dre." And he extended his hand to me for a quick hand shake and I followed him off of the elevator to the apartment door. Banging on the door, it was immediately opened by another dude who was swollen from head to toe. With a goofy grin and broad muscular shoulders, he introduced himself as Justice and led me over to a bedroom turned office where

Leota was seen working behind a wooden desk. When I was just about to reach over and hug her, she extended her arm for a handshake. Oh snap. I get it. We are not friends in this environment. Ok. Cool. I just need the job.

"Hi, Lynn. How are you?" Leota asked.

"I'm doing well. Thanks so much for having me come in for an interview today," I replied.

And before Leota could get into the meat and potatoes of our interviewing process, three more big guys squeezed into the office/bedroom. "Lynn. This is Buck, Jacob, and Un. Buck is our VP of Promotions of the label and Justice, who opened the door for you is the VP of A&R. Jus is also Un's younger brother. Jacob is the President of the label and last but not least, this is Un." All of them stood in the doorway looking extremely proud of their titles and accomplishments thus far.

"Hello everyone," I said, smiling.

The guys were huge. The smallest was Jacob who stood at five foot five and weighed about two hundred twenty pounds. He was dark-skinned with a small afro. "Oh. So you are the publicist Leota has been raving about?" he asked in a cocky manner.

"Hi, Lynn. Nice to meet you," said Justice who stood at six foot two with a large frame and friendly grin." Justice had great energy. Rocking a short Caesar cut with a bronzed tan complexion, he stepped out of the room after shaking my hand. Buck, the promotions dude, didn't even speak. He just looked at me and kept it moving to the back of the apartment.

Looking me up and down as if to inspect the make up of me, stood Un. I didn't know if I was there for a model's audition or a position in publicity. He then smirked at me, went into his bag to grab his soda and cigarettes, nodded at me and then walked out of the room. It was as if he had chewed me up and spit me out with his eyes. What was all of that about? I wondered. I just nodded back at him and turned back around in my seat to face Leota. "Well, alrighty then," she said. The energy between Un and me was weird. It was as if he was an angry ex who had no choice but to hire me.

As Leota walked me towards the front of the apartment turned office, my mouth hit the floor when I bumped into Pumpkin! Oh my God! "Oh. This is another one of our execs. He is an A&R for the label as well. You will hardly ever see him because he works late at night in the studio with our artists." The gulp in my throat could've given me away.

Looking directly into my eyes, he didn't even crack a smile. He didn't even acknowledge that he knew me. "Oh. Hi. How are you?" It was weird. Our paths had crossed on a whole nother playing field. The energy was off and awkward. I felt uncomfortable and I was glad the exit was closer than it was.

Turning to Leota, I thanked her for the opportunity and we made arrangements to meet again. When the elevator door closed behind me, I gasped. Mixed emotions clouded my mind. I didn't know whether to gag or giggle. The guy I had been seeing was now my co-worker. Go figure.

At the end of the day, this business is all about relationships. On several occasions prior to landing my job with Untertainment, I had come through for Leota and she had come through for me. It was just a no-brainer for her to consider me for the job.

I jumped right into my position as Director of Publicity for Untertainment. Long days at the office turned into longer days as Un requested that all employees spend quality time at the studio to keep the artists motivated and to stay connected to our product. McDonald's Happy Meals and pizza slices became the norm. I would always grab one or the other before climbing the stairs to the infamous Hit Factory Recording Studio on 54th Street.

Every night, I would head to the studio and cop a squat in the corner. Pumpkin and I stayed far away from each other. He would occasionally throw pieces of paper my way as a signal to wake up whenever I napped. Though closing our eyes was forbidden, I would still slip off into a subtle sleep until the bass in the studio speakers became unbearable.

On top of our jobs, it was always mandatory for us to keep up with Un and his ideas. So on the weekends, we often played the role of Video Production Crew. Shooting videos over the weekend, Un pursued his passion of directing. "Lynn. We all have to be on set tomorrow," Vickie peeped in my office and whispered one fall Friday. Vickie was Director of Production. "I'ma make sure you are there too. I'ma pick you up 'round six. Ok?" I often had excuses as to why I couldn't make it to the extra stuff. It wasn't in my contract and I was already drained. Besides, the weekends were all I had to spend time with China.

"Six am!" I just shook my head and waved her off. My personal life was suffering with China and the label was taking up all of my time. Vickie, on the other hand, was newly married and expecting her first baby. My thoughts on her were, if she can do it, then I have no choice. Vickie was a tall, dark-skinned sister. She had a large chest with a thick frame. She often rocked a sleek long clip on ponytail that fell all the way to her lower back. She had a warm smile and a bubbly personality. The two of us clicked instantly because she, like me, was not from Brooklyn. Vickie had migrated to New York to pursue a career in music by way of Alabama.

Ringing my doorbell, Vickie arrived right at 6 am. Lying on the bed fully dressed, I grabbed my jacket and headed out. Greeting her with a sleepy grin, I said hello and asked, "Who is the video shoot for today?"

"Un is directing Aaliyah's "Hot Like Fire" video today," she replied.

"Oh wow. That song is really poppin' on the radio," I replied. Aaliyah was a young female coming out of Missy and Timbaland's camp. Their sound was new and different. When we arrived on set, Un delegated the day's responsibilities. While Vickie oversaw the Kraft Services Department (food), I was put in charge of the "Holding Area" (extras casted for the video were placed between scenes). During two of the scenes, the staff was even requested to act as extras when a parade of hot red luxury vehicles cruised through a block in Red Hook, Brooklyn. I was hired to do publicity, but filling in the holes was an unspoken but understood part of the job description as well.

On hand for cameos were celebs such as Brice Wilson, Changing Faces, Lil' Kim, Junior M.A.F.I.A, Missy, and Timbaland, to lend their support to Un and Aaliyah. The finished product of the video was nice! Un did his thing.

"You are whack, Lynn," Un burst out and said in front of the entire staff one day as we were discussing the idea of having a party. "You just have no confidence about yourself. Whenever I ask you a question, you just give me this goofy confused look. What's up with that!?"

I was speechless. I couldn't believe he just said that out of nowhere. I didn't even reply. I just looked him up and down and walked out because I didn't want the staff to see me cry. I hated to be around Un because he had a mouth on him and just the thought of having to see him in the office every day made me sick to my stomach. I was scared of him. To me, he was the big bad wolf. Walking back to my office, I decided to cut my day short and leave. I was starting to shut down my computer, when Vickie walked in without knocking. "Girl! Are you ok?" she asked.

"Do I look like I'm ok, Vickie?" My face was beat red for a black girl.

"Don't pay Un no mind and don't leave. All that will do

is prove his point. UN thinks you are soft. Most publicists are aggressive and seem to have a stronger level of confidence about themselves." Vickie said.

"But I am confident, Vickie! Just because I don't go around popping off at the mouth and talking loud doesn't mean I'm not thorough."

"Just don't leave. We can talk about this later. Grab a notepad and pen and come back into the meeting. Everyone thinks I went to the restroom so hurry up." She then left my office and closed the door.

Grabbing a notebook and pen, I gathered my thoughts and left my emotions behind. Taking Vickie's advice, I then rejoined the meeting and began to give input into what would potentially be our "Cigar and Brandy" label launch party. As the meeting rolled on, I could sense Un staring at me because the side of my face was burning. He had it in for me. I held on until the end of the meeting, and then got out of there.

When I got home, I let it all out. I burst into tears. As I grabbed a wad of toilet tissue to blow my nose, Trina walked in. "What's wrong!?" I belted out so much information while sobbing at the same time. She could only gather bits and pieces of what I was saying. "Girl. Get a grip! I can't understand half of what you are saying, but all I know is you've got to grow some balls.

There's no way you will make it in this industry if you ain't got tough skin. I can't believe you are crying about this crap. As much drama you've gone through with Terrie, I can't see you not being able to handle this, Lynn!" Trina was furious and disappointed on me. I was tired and drained. I was tired of Un always picking with me. Every time I passed him in the office, he always had something slick to say. I thought I was his verbal assault punching bag.

"This job is different, Trina," I belted out. "This job has a street element to it. I don't want to do the wrong thing or say the wrong thing. These are hood dudes with corporate money. I'm afraid to pop off at the mouth, Trina. They will gag me and have my body bound up in duck tape!"

"You don't have to pop off at the mouth. Defend yourself! Do it with class and no matter who it is, don't let nobody disrespect you. Now stop all that damn cryin' and get ready for work tomorrow." Trina roared.

As the next three weeks moved by quickly, the "Cigar & Brandy" Party came and went. Located on 21st Street on Manhattan's west side, the chic warehouse turned club/lounge was where we held the event.

At the "Cigar and Brandy" party, we smoked cigars and sipped on brandy. China accompanied me while

Pumpkin's girl accompanied him. Our lives were now becoming too complex. And with one long glance of non-verbal communication, we both knew it was over between us. From that day forward, we never saw each other again.

From the glimpse of things at the label, you couldn't tell any of us anything. We were sitting on top of the world. Executives such as Puffy, Chris Lighty, radio personality Ed Lover, and more were on hand to toast to the launch of our label along with newly signed rappers, Cam'ron and Charlie Baltimore.

Hiring a photographer, I had the photos placed into magazines and newspapers. Announcements equipped with every executive's headshot showed up in the "Executive Turntable" section of *Billboard* magazine. The buzz was out. I was a part of the action and it felt good.

Trina was also excelling in her career as an actress. She had landed a reoccurring role on *New York Undercover*. Her role as a prostitute kept her out of the house most of the time and on set. I would often stop by her tapings to check her on the way home from work since we lived as two ships passing in the night. My other BFF, Kim was also doing well. She was now in a long-term relationship and she worked in Pharmaceutical Sales as a rep. Though our lives were extremely different, we still managed to link up at least once a month to catch up over lunch, brunch, or dinner.

As the holidays were just around the corner, Un came through with our holiday bonuses. Though we had not released the label's first project from Cam'ron, the new year was looking promising for the label. Knocking on my door and barging in, he said, "Here. Here's your holiday bonus. Merry Christmas. And if I had a box of singles, I'd pay you that way."

"I just smiled. I knew he was partially serious, but I didn't care. I didn't take it personally either cause it was still money and that's what I wanted. The office was filled with holiday festivities. Food and beverages were floating around the office and it was evident that our vacation was starting sooner.

"What you doing' for the holidays, Lynn?" Vickie asked. "If you are in New York, I'd love for you to join me as my guest at my church."

Wow. Church. I had forgotten all about church. It had been almost two years since I had been to church. "Oh. Ok. What kind of church do you go to?" I asked. "And where is it?"

"I attend a church called CCC The Christian Cultural Center in Brooklyn. The Pastor is awesome. He delivers a great word every week. I always understand what he's talking about and he always takes that extra time to explain the scriptures.

"Oh. That sounds great. Yeah. I'm down. Just hit me up the night before service to confirm, but for the most part, I'm down. I haven't been to church in a very long time"

"Girl. You need the Lord in this industry. I don't know where I'd be if it weren't for God. I woulda strangled someone in this office by now. Trust me on that." She smiled.

That was exactly what was missing in my life. I had gotten so engulfed into my career that I had forgotten all about my spiritual life. At so many different points in my life, God was so important to me, but now my spiritual life was nonexistent. My relationship with God is what provided me often times with balance and I was definitely in need of Jesus. "You know. You should also check out this young preacher on BET. His name is Creflo Dollar. He teaches a good word also. He comes on every weekday morning and I often watch him before heading out to work."

"Oh really? Ok. I will check him out," I replied.

"He just has a way of teaching the word with simplicity and understanding and I love that," Vickie said.

At the start of the New Year, I dreaded going back to work. The two week vacation was needed by the entire staff. During my break, I did attend church with Vickie and I loved it. I also tuned in to Pastor Dollar each morning and I was totally down with his method of teaching all about Jesus Christ. I was happy to be getting that balance back in my life—as I was in need of it. I was working hard. The entire staff was working hard and that outlet was exactly what was needed.

We had been grinding hard. However, upon my return to work, the atmosphere was different. The environment was more intense and everyone seemed to be uptight, including Vickie who was normally the more cheerful one. Knocking on Vickie's door during my lunch break, I asked, her. "Hey girl. How was your Christmas vacation? And why is everyone looking so glum in the office today?"

"Girl. We are spending too much money before any results are shown. I do know that we've got to cut down on our spending and get Cam'ron out the gate and running. You feel me?" I understood. I just nodded my head. Since Vickie was the Director of Production, I knew she knew what she was talking about. Easing back out of her office, I then dug in to finish out the day until I heard Jacob's voice through my office wall in Vickie's office. His tone sounded strange so I locked my office door and leaned my ear up against my wall to ear hustle.

"Something is going to have to give. I gotta let Lynn go today" Did he just say what I heard him say? Were they firing me? My heart sank. I know I heard him correctly and I tip toed back to my seat, I hit my foot on the desk and damn near toppled over. Catching my balance, I couldn't even scream. I just held it in. Gathering my thoughts while massaging my foot, I picked up my cell phone to dial Trina's number. She didn't pick up. I didn't know who I could call and vent to. Kim was at work and it wasn't an environment that was conducive to personal calls. So I just began to pack up my belongings and get rid of anything that looked remotely like trash.

Why was I being let go? Was it my performance or was it them? I had been at Untertainment for well over six months and no matter what the reason, it wasn't working for me anyway. I had garnered as much exposure for the Label, its executives, and the artists that I could. I couldn't help but wonder if it was the quality of my work. That moment, all types of insecurities kicked in. I couldn't even pick up the phone to dial Leota's extension. Ever since she had become my boss, our friendship had become strained. We didn't hang out anymore and I cringed at the thought of bumping into her outside of staff meetings. We no longer kicked it or updated each other on our personal lives and that was disappointing. Still I was appreciative of the opportunity. My position had turned into a job. At the moment my career turned into a job, I knew it was time to exit. At the end of the day, everyone should love what they do. If it doesn't add up, then do some soul searching. Ask yourself what it is that you enjoy doing most, and then just do it. Make it happen. Don't worry about the money. It will come!

When close to 6pm had rolled around, my desk had been completely cleared off and out. I had created a checklist of what I had accomplished during my tenure at Untertainment and it was impressive. I was not going to allow anyone to attempt to inform me that I had not done my job. My personal belongings were put away neatly into a small duffle bag and I just sat and waited. There were 15 more minutes left in my day when a faint knock came at the door. "Come in!" I lashed out loudly. It was Leota and I was shocked to see her.

"Can I speak to you in the conference room?" she asked sternly. I just nodded, got up, and followed her. While waiting for me at the door, she did take note that my office was bare. As we entered the conference room, Leota stated, "I'm going to have to let you go today, Lynn."

"Aight." I stood up, shook her hand and exited the

room. I quietly got my belongings and left the building. I didn't bother about saying Goodbye to anyone. I was over it. I felt a sense of relief and I was ready to move on.

Not even two days had passed before my college colleague, Mark Pitts and his cousin Wayne Barrow called to hire me as an Indie PR person for their label, ByStorm Entertainment. With this agreement, I was able to negotiate an office within their label, a small monthly fee, and the ability to run my business HobbieCom within their operation. My future was looking good—real good.

I know one thing, I may have been fired from Untertainment, but if it weren't for that job, I would have never grown the balls to stand up to the people and situations in not only business, but life that I would come to encounter. Whether he knew it or not, Un toughened me up to prepare me for the years ahead.

In a male driven industry, you have to have balls. Before I walked into the doors of Untertainment, I didn't have balls, but I had them when I walked out.

Chapter 7:
Don Pooh (1998)

"Lynn. What up? I need some help with my company. What you up to?" Pooh asked as he peered into his brother China's bedroom. It was the weekend and the two of us were camping out at his parents on a typical Friday night so that we could take that trip upstate for a "get away".

As China and I lounged around, exhausted from the workweek, I responded. "I'm just working on a few independent projects. What do you have in mind?"

"I need a few things. I need to get my office in my new spot organized and I need some publicity on myself," stated Pooh. Pooh was a tall, dark-skinned heavy-set guy with a smile that fit his name. He was a quiet guy and often a hard read. Though it had been almost one year since Biggie's death and his accident, his leg was still in the healing process.

It was August of 1998 and all of NYC was abuzz about Pooh's upcoming birthday bash. Pooh had blossomed into a well-known and respected music executive. His annual parties became the "who's who" in New York City. In a four-month agreement, Pooh had hired me to conduct some PR services for his entertainment company. His first artist, Foxy Brown, had heated up the rap charts with her debut album going Platinum. *BRE* magazine; *Billboard* magazine; and several other publications featured Pooh as an up and coming executive on the rise. Watching the clippings come in boosted my confidence. As the clippings started to roll in, so did the clients.

Figuring out an outfit for the party and a hairstyle was a day's worth of preparation for this affair because it was necessary and mandatory that I would be FLY. As Erynne, Trina, and I trained it from Brooklyn to the West Village of lower Manhattan, we first stopped at the infamous L'Impasse store on 8th Street where I selected a simple but elegant red dress. After purchasing my dress purchase, I stepped down into the shoe store, Petit Peton, where I copped a pair of high heels to complement the look. Erynne picked out a pair of hot red pants with a skimpy top to complement her shape while Trina accessorized a beautiful long form fitting powder blue dress for the summer festivity. During our day of shopping, we recognized other industry notables who were also shopping for the party. Some were talking to their girlfriends who stood on the opposite side of the dressing room while dresses were being tried on. Some were cackling about the party while checking out the heels in the shoe store. Nonetheless, the party was the talk of the industry. It was estimated to be one of the hottest parties of the year.

After shopping, the three of us joined the long line outside of BBQ's Restaurant on 8th Street where we waited patiently for 20 minutes for the opportunity to chow down on barbeque chicken, fries, baked potatoes, and huge Texas style drinks. The three of us were seated at a table for four, and we used the additional seat to pile our purses and shopping bags while we grubbed and speculated about the party. It was a hot summer evening and the summer was in full gear. We had worked up an appetite from shopping.

Hopping on the train back to Brooklyn was an ease. The train approached the platform as soon as we arrived into the West 4th Street station, so we quickly moved onto the train, stood and rode all the way to our Clinton/Washington stop. I loved the C train. It was simple for me.

As party time rolled around the next day, the three of us dressed with just enough time to wait on the car service that always seemed to take forever. As our Myrtle Avenue car service arrived. Trina gave Erynne and me a glance over. "You guys look soooo lovely." We both thanked her and returned the compliment. It wasn't in our budget to grab a sip of something prior to our arrival to the party. We were just happy to be able to afford the ride.

"What's the address again?" the cab driver asked as we started to approach the World Trade Center. Whether you were a New Yorker or not, the streets were always kind of tricky down in the Financial District. As I let him know the address for the 50th time, Trina pointed to the building.

"It's right here sir," she said as he looked into the direction of her finger. "As a matter of fact, give me your cab number so that when we are ready to go, we can ask for you. We don't wanna be standing outside, waiting on a cab that may get lost. It's better that we just get you again." Nodding to agree, we handed him the money while he handed us his card complete with his name and car number. As we stepped into the night's summer breeze, we could see people heading into the building. The party was held at Windows on the World Restaurant located at the top of the World Trade Center's North Tower. While the line was long for entry, the three of us were immediately escorted into the party by Big Joe, security for Foxy Brown. Boy it sure felt good to not have to stand in line. "Thanks Big Joe," I shouted back at him.

"What y'all drinking"? Dee asked us as he spotted us walking over to the bar. In unison, we all said, "A Cosmo." Lol! It was too obvious that we were the three musketeers. Dee was one of Pooh's partners in several ventures and he was always a gentleman when we saw him. Handing us our first round of drinks, we toasted to the night, thanked Dee, and walked around to take in the restaurant's décor before the party really got crowded. The Windows on the World Restaurant was hot! You couldn't get any better than this. This was a real boss venue. The place was breathtaking. With windows from floor to ceiling, I was able to see amazing views of the Manhattan Skyline, Liberty Park, Ellis Island, and the Verrazano Bridge. The lights sparkled in the night air like diamonds. I was in awe of the city's beauty. Though I now lived in New York, I took in the view as if I saw it for the first time.

In no time, the party was popping! It was packed minutes after our arrival and I'm glad we got there when we did. The DJ spun all the latest hits such as Lauryn Hill's "That Thing"; Faith's "Love Like This; Dru Hill's "How Deep Is Your Love"; and Jay-Z's "Can I Get A". The crowd yelled out every time a hit came on, and just as the DJ was bringing back the Jay-Z song again, you saw nothing but hands in the air. The drinks were flowing and there wasn't a dry lip in the building. Everybody was sipping on something.

As the DJ cut the music, everyone took notice of two females brawling in the middle of the dance floor. Bottles and glasses were being thrown. Nothing but pure pandemonium broke out. Looking for the nearest exit, I could see Mike Tyson being hurried quickly to the restaurant's kitchen. He was out of there and I couldn't blame him. It was truly in Mike's best interest to get the hell out of dodge. Fans were always quick to slap him with a lawsuit just for being in the same room with them. Mike smelled and looked like money and people were always looking for a quick come up. While the three of us pushed towards the exit, we opted to step back into the venue and onto a booth to elevate ourselves for safety. Peering into the direction of the fight, I was able to get a glimpse of the two fighters. A ponytail was on the floor. Contents from a purse were strewn onto the dance floor and there was broken glass everywhere. Just like that, the party was over.

So many celebs came out for the event that I just knew Pooh's party would be heavily talked about the next day; however, we had no idea his party would show up in headlines on Page Six of the New York Post for the drama that ensued. "Awww man, Lynn. They have my name in the paper about the party, but it's negative. I don't want to be known for having a fight at my party," Pooh stated in a concerned manner as I walked into his office the next day.

"Oh paleeease. That party was the hottest ticket in town. Don't worry about it. You've had plenty of events before and nothing else has ever happened. So don't be too hard on yourself," I encouraged. "Besides, publicity was obtained whether you wanted it or not.

Your name was mentioned in one of the hottest gossip columns in the world. Trust me. You are good money," I smiled.

I could then see Pooh rolling the positive side of things around in his head and from that moment on, he didn't let that particular incident get to him; however, it would be a while before Pooh would throw an event of that magnitude again.

During the months that I worked on the Don Pooh Entertainment Account, I learned a lot about Artist Management from organizing his files. Contracts such as endorsement deals for Foxy to Performance Contracts, were at my perusal and I absorbed it all. While organizing his paperwork, I took the time and opportunity to read any and everything I could get my hands on. I was like a sponge during this pivotal point in my career. Learning the terminology and lingo written in Rider Agreements, by the time my tenure with Pooh ended, I had even tightened up the Rider Requirements for his artists. Rider Agreements are the contracts that all artists use when booking appearances and/or performance dates with promoters and organizations. Each artist had their own requirements from white lilies and Evian water in the dressing rooms to Grade A sound systems equipped with the best lighting for stage performances. In addition to those things, I also communicated with contractors for Pooh's new townhome in Jersey, created a media kit for his company, and obtained placements of Pooh's accomplishments in music trade publications.

I started to learn more about my field and grow more into my career as a publicist. It didn't take long before realizing that each client brings something different to the table. For Pooh, it was the grind of it all. We spent hours in Pooh's vehicle running around, taking meetings, and networking with people. Keep in mind that emailing, texting, and the type of technology we have today was way more costly. Most of the day was spent maneuvering through traffic, which meant a lot of the day was spent listening to music. From Biggie Smalls, Total, 112, Busta Rhymes, and Missy Elliot, each song that hit the airwaves on Hot 97 managed to continually motivate me to keep pushing. There is something about hip-hop music to this very day that stirs my spirit. First it would be the beat and then the lyrics. If the beat was hot, I always listened attentively to the words. Every time a hot song would come on, Pooh would blast the radio and rhyme with the MC featured on air. As I would also join in to spew out the words, I would often feel empowered and invincible. One thing was for sure. I was always sitting on top of the world and feeling exhilarated once a hot song had just been heard.

Rolling around NYC with Pooh to attend meetings was always a part of the day's plan and it felt good. The day would start at noon and end at midnight, but I loved every minute of it. When the account came to a close, Pooh had inked an executive position at MCA Records and I moved on to the next client. This account afforded me the opportunity and the flexibility to do everything I wanted and needed to do for my client—no questions asked.

Chapter 8:
Ruff Ryders Records (1999)

It was the fall of 1999 and as I was starting to make my way as an independent entrepreneur, I was called over to Ruff Ryders Records to be interviewed. Leota had actually referred me to them. When the receptionist from Ruff Ryders called to see if I could come for a meeting, she mentioned Leota's name. As soon as I heard her name, it was the confirmation I needed to know that I in fact had done my job at Untertainment—and that left a nice warm feeling down in the bottom of my stomach.

The problem was—I was broke. I didn't even have the round trip train fare to make it to midtown and back to Brooklyn. My assistant, Katani, who worked weekends at Bloomingdale's had more money than me and I was stressed out.

"Good morning!" Katani greeted as she entered into my studio apartment. Trina often left the apartment door unlocked after leaving out for the day, so hearing Katani slide in was of no surprise to me. I was still in the bed with no desire to even peak my head out from the blankets that enveloped me. "Why are you still in the bed Ms. Thang? Don't you have a meeting today at Ruff Ryders Records?" Katani asked.

I was beyond embarrassed at this point. So, I told her, "I don't have money for the train," I mumbled with my mouth hanging off of the pillow. She caught what I said the very first time and laughed so hard I had to sit up because I thought something else was going on in the room.

"Ok. I mean I know it's probably funny, but is it really that funny? I asked.

"Girl. You are just sooooo dramatic. Get up and get dressed. It's so obvious that you are not a New Yorker." At that rate, I knew Katani had it figured out so I just got up, made up the bed, and hopped into the shower. Preparing my thoughts and getting my business mind together, I focused on the upcoming meeting and not my finances. Katani had that part covered for the day.

While getting dressed, I took the time to thank GOD for another day. I also powered on the TV and tuned into Pastor Dollar on BET. After Vickie had referenced him as a good teacher of the word, I started watching his programs faithfully. Though I had been watching the program for a while now and reading the Bible, my faith was still not to the level where I wanted it to be. I still had work to do in the spiritual department.

Putting on a conservative sundress and some fancy flats, I grabbed my purse, notebook, and keys and left out with Katani in tow. It was a nice summer day in early September. It was hot, but not muggy. A nice breeze soothed me as we walked. Money was back on my mind. Arriving to the train station, Katani had me follow her instructions. "We are going to wait one staircase up from the station until we hear the train coming. Ok?" I just nodded. "When I say "go" just run right behind me. Stay as close as possible behind me and we will get through the turn style together with my fare card. I just nodded again. I was speechless and scared. Not even one minute passed by and the sound of the train started to get closer. My heart was beating so fast, I thought it would jump out of my chest. I was scurd!

Before I could even catch my breath, Katani and I were through the turn style and on the train. Thank you Jesus! After three stops, I could talk. Between damn near hyperventilating and laughing hysterically, it took several minutes before I could speak.

"We are looking for someone to coordinate and organize the video management component for our entertainment company," said Joaquin Dean, more commonly known as Wahh, The Co-CEO to Ruff Ryders Records.

Katani and I sat in the lower level of the company's evolving empire and she took notes while his assistant/girlfriend, Keisha elaborated on the exact scope of work that needed to be executed. "We have some new video directors that we will be signing on and we are in need of press kits for each of the directors," she stated.

Since I had grown accustomed to encountering the hood inside of record labels, I did go into Ruff Ryders Records with my guard up. As the Yonkers-based family was known for their street credibility, I was more equipped this time around to deal with the hood aspect of the business; however, to my surprise, nothing of that nature was displayed.

When Wahh opened his mouth to speak, he was extremely focused. He had direction and a vision. He had the eye of the tiger and it inspired me and Katani to want the business.

Katani complimented me. It is always a blessing to have a right hand to balance things out. As a budding entrepreneur, I was hyper and eager. Katani, though she was five years younger, was more laid back, relaxed, and mature. She had an old soul. And often times, she was my voice of reason.

As Keisha opened her mouth to speak, she was poised and precise in her wanting the best for her man and their business. Her mane was tight and her nails were nice. "I understand that you are independent. However, we would require that you work at least one day a week from our office. Is that possible? I just want to maximize this business relationship and have you get a weekly taste for how we operate. I want our vision translated to the best of your ability," she remarked.

"That shouldn't be a problem," I replied. "Tuesdays work for us. We can come in next Tuesday and interview all of the video directors for the creation of their bios." I actually loved the idea of coming to their office once a week. Besides, I did still come into the city during the weekdays to work out of the ByStorm Offices. I could be in a different loop and have my ear to the ground of other happenings instead of relying on my own research. As soon as I replied to Keisha's question, she whipped out the check and handed it to me. I accepted the payment, stood up, shook their hands, and left out humbled and happy. Thank you, Jesus!

Landing the account at the rate of one thousand dollars per month, the two of us walked out of the office with check in hand. "You did it, Lynnski!"

"We did it!" I replied in a loud childlike manner. Heading to the subway, I had a sense of how it was going to go down so I went with the flow. Upon our arrival back to BK, we stopped at the bank, deposited the check, and went back to my place to make some lunch. Today was a great day!

Less than one week into the account, most of the director's bios were already written and things were underway. As Katani and I entered into the Ruff Ryders offices, Wahh approached us with a stressful look on his face. "Hey, ladies. Please tell me that one of you knows how to braid hair."

"Katani knows how to braid. Why? What's wrong?" I asked.

"Eve has a video shoot today and we can't seem to locate her stylist. Keisha is making calls, but so far, she has no luck in finding anyone." Wahh replied.

"I'll do it!" Katani didn't hesitate. She jumped right in and volunteered. Whatever it took to make the dream work, we were definitely down for team work.

"Yes!" Wahh exclaimed. "Lemmee go get Eve now."

Not even five minutes had passed by and Eve was standing in the doorway. She was quiet, polite, and humbled at the thought of everyone chipping in to make sure she looked right for the video. Sitting silently into a chair, Katani braided her hair in less than one hour. Completed in a neat and timely manner, Wahh and his camera crew were back on schedule. We began the hike to Brooklyn where the majority of the video was shot at the classic Grand Prospect Ballroom. From the early afternoon 'til the wee hours of the night, the Ruff Ryders video team worked tirelessly at perfecting each shot.

While on set, local press was invited to come and interview Eve and the crew during breaks and film changes. The setting was nice, smooth, and professional. It was refreshing to be in an environment where the workers were from the hood, but didn't act hood. I was impressed. The Ruff Ryders team was too focused on getting a job done rather than getting a job done rather than getting caught up about minor setbacks.

Once the music video was completed and in heavy rotation, my tenure at the label had come to an end. As the music video started to make a lot of noise, so did the label's Music Video Department—thus my job was done. The media kits had been completed and this made it easier for them to communicate with the media and potential clients moving forward.

It felt good to start an account, work it, and then leave with a bang. To top it off, I may not have been the person hands on to get Eve's hair done, but because Katani was an extension of me, I did make it happen. Filling in the blanks is often times what a publicist does and I loved it.

This account was the crowning moment when I knew that holding a typical 9-5 was never going to be me again. Having the luxury of creating my own schedule and to maneuver around with flexibility while working and having fun was priceless. I wouldn't trade that for anything.

Chapter 9:
Sister Souljah

During the spring of 1999, I received yet another referral from Leota when she introduced me to Political Activist/Rap Artist/Author/Motivational Speaker, Sister Souljah. At the time, Souljah was burning the candle at both ends. By day she was the Executive Director for Puffy's non-profit organization, Daddy's House Social Programs and by night she was an author who was about to release her first novel, but second book entitled, "The Coldest Winter Ever".

I remember the day clearly when we met. Entering into my office walked a strong black woman with the most beautiful dark brown skinned complexion. Rocking two ponytail puffs on each side of her head, she walked over to me with poise as Katani introduced us. With big brown eyes like mine, I immediately made her my very own sister in my head.

She was so serious. Even a joke made her barely chuckle, so as the years have gone by, I was always determined to poke a hole through that tough skin. In my eyes, Souljah was carrying the weight of black women's issues on her back and I always wanted her to lighten up her load a bit, especially when she was around me. So I would always have something outrageous to share with her.

"Sooooo... Leota speaks highly of you," she stated. "And I just need to know if you can do the job." She was straight to the point, no chaser.

"Well of course I can do the job," I answered.

Published by Simon & Schuster, Souljah hired me to do supplemental and grassroots PR for her newly released street novel. She hired and paid me out of her own pocket. As the list of things "to do" was spoken to me, my assistant Katani jotted down everything while I began to mentally categorize my assignments from easy to challenging to most challenging. Souljah was no joke. Her presence commanded respect and attention. She was no ordinary client. She was extremely specific about the assignments and tasks that I was to accomplish.

I was a procrastinator—especially when it comes to the most challenging things. "As a part of my needs, I need you to book panelists for me. I want to have a dais where celebrities speak out and give words of encouragement to our lost little sistas," said Souljah.

The Book Launch Party was being held at the Atrium located inside of the Sony Music Building. Handing over to me a list of celebrities, I nearly passed out. How the hell am I going to get these people? I wondered. Slipping the list into my portfolio, beads of sweat started forming on my head. "Handle this Lynn,"

Souljah looked at me with her big brown eyes. "I won't accept 'no' for an answer," she went on. "I need to have at least five of the ten celebrities on my list to be present for this panel," she went on.

A celebrity presence for Souljah's panel was important. Souljah knew the impact celebrities made on the minds of young adults. As the head of Daddy's House, Souljah was too often able to get a glimpse into the minds of female teens. Because her book was based on the shortcomings of a female living the fast life and doing whatever it took to get by, she felt that celebs would be the best mouthpiece to convey her message in the book.

Only God knew how much of a challenge it would be to produce an event for such a well-known activist. Wrapping up our initial meeting, it ended with her handing over my first payment and a list of all of the celebrities she wanted to have on her panel discussion during her event. She wanted her book event to not only become a success, but a forum for young adults struggling to make it in their drug infested communities as well.

As I subway'd it home, my mind started to organize and picture the book extravaganza. I couldn't sleep. I was presented with an opportunity to not only shine, but to make a difference—and that was important to me. Creating a uniformed letter upon arriving back to my office the next day, I then began to address each letter relative to the names written down on the list Souljah had handed over to me. Reaching out to Jamie Foster Brown of *Sister 2 Sister* magazine, she agreed immediately. "I'd do anything for Souljah," Mrs. Brown responded. Securing her at the time was extremely important. She was the senior on the panel and the print media component needed for such a panel.

The celebrity twins, Tia and Tamera Mowry who at the time were very visual and influential in teen publications and television were then asked through my colleague, Sharon Paige. One by one, through the grace of God, five celebs were secured. Despite their busy schedules, Tia and Tamera Mowry; actor Malik Yoba; Jamie Foster Brown; former talk show host and VJ, Ananda Lewis; and multi-platinum Grammy Award-Winning artist Mary J. Blige were secured as celebrity panelists. I did the damn thang!

The event was a success and despite Souljah's initial hesitation on hiring a young publicist such as myself, I could tell that she was just as happy for me pulling the event off than for herself. She was thankful and I was honored. "Lynn. Girrrrl. You did it. We did it. I was a little nervous, but the event was a success. Thank you." Souljah beamed. I loved to see her smile. Whenever the world gets the best of me, I pull out the autographed poster she gave to me from the event and read it. Inscribed, "There will always be challenges in life. Thanks for taking on this challenge." It reassures me that I have the power to conquer the tasks that are given to me.

And needless to say, authors and publishers from all walks of life have since hired me for various aspects of their book releases. But, there's nothing like the first.

Over the years, I have had very few female clients. And it's not that I don't like having female clients. Males have always been more focused on putting the spotlight on themselves. However, having Sister Souljah as a client over the years has been a real jewel to my life and career.

Ten years later, her novels are making huge waves in the book industry. From the hoods of Harlem to the bowels of Brooklyn to the bright lights in Japan, Souljah's stories have become a force to be reckoned with in not just street literature, but literature in general.

Chapter 10:
LIL' MO

In 2000, I was working on the HitCo Music
Publishing/Windswept account through my former
colleague Shakir Stewart. I met Shakir through Val
Bisharat, an LA based music publishing executive who
worked with QD-3, a well known producer. Shakir and
my sister Faye attended college together, Faye at
Spelman and Shakir at Morehouse. The two were close.
When I met Shakir, I was also simultaneously working
with his good friend and my client, Kenlo Jackson who
owned a t-shirt line called Player's University. The t-
shirt line was off the chain. Impressed by the way I
handled my B.I., Kenlo strongly suggested to Shakir
that I do PR for HitCo as well. At the time, there were a
lot of hits being generated.

Additionally, I was writing for XXL where the Editor,
Datwon, afforded me the opportunity to write
occasionally for their "Executive Turntable" section of
the publication.

Since my work with HitCo was going so well, Shakir
then introduced me to Jaha Johnson. "Lynn, I know you
are doing your PR thang, but I really want you to meet
my dude Jaha," Shakir said. I was in Atlanta for the
weekend visiting him and his girlfriend Michelle. Shakir

was in the middle of producing a huge mansion affair at the time called, "Beautiful Skin". The party was the most highly promoted exclusive event on the East Coast for the summer and everyone from Babyface and Janet Jackson to TLC and Usher were expected to attend.

"Ok, I'll meet him, but what's up?" I asked him. Shakir had an energy like no other. Keeping up with him was damn near a full time job, but he radiated a presence that demanded attention at all times. Anything Shakir had cooking was nothing but positivity, so I obliged him. When the party got under way, the two of us rode around on a golf cart until we came to a stop. Almost rolling over a short black skinned brother with pearly white teeth, Shakir jumped out of the golf cart.

"Yoooooo... what's crackin!!??" Shakir belted out at the dark skinned dude. He was cute. He didn't have muscles, but his swag was on 10. His name—Jaha Johnson. He was so black, all I could see was his teeth and style. He could dress. His sneaker game was on point and his grin had a look of mischievousness on it. His personality was a little more mellow than Shakir's and his demeanor was attractive. Extending his hand out to me instantly before Shakir could even make an introduction, the two of us hit it off immediately.

"Well... it's nice to meet you," Jaha said as I extended my hand to shake his. "Shakir has mentioned a lot about you so I definitely would love to pick your brain a bit to see if you'd be interested in running my management company!" stated Jaha.

"Ok. Cool," I replied. We exchanged information and scheduled a time to meet once we both got settled back up in New York.

At the time, Jaha was shifting from A&R at Def Jam Records to the President of Def Jam UK in London. Since it was not in his best interest to manage singer/songwriter, Lil' Mo, he brought me on board to assist with the transition. "I think you and Mo would be great together. I'm taking this job and I will not be allowed to manage any other artists while I'm under contract, so I think you should take over where I started with her," he stated during our lunch meeting at Mike's Diner in Clinton Hills, Brooklyn.

Not even 30 minutes after those words came out of Jaha's mouth, Lil' Mo came pulling up in front of the diner in her brand new Volkswagon Beetle. Is she serious? I wanted to burst out laughing, but I held my composure. I didn't know if this was a joke or if Lil' Mo was serious about her new whip. And as she cracked the biggest grin, damn near 50 pearly white teeth snapped back at me and I knew we would be a match made in heaven.

With so little time to explain everything to me, Jaha just pushed Lil' Mo off on me, gave me very few instructions on how to handle her, wished me luck, packed his bags, and was off to London. Being handed an artist was like someone dropping a newborn baby off to a doorstep. Left with NO instructions, I skimmed through a few books pertaining to Artist Management—particularly how a Manager gets paid and the main role of a Manager.

Calling my phone the very same night we met, Lil' Mo spit out a laundry list of needs. "Hey, Lynn. I'm sooooo excited. First things first. I really need a hairstylist," she mentioned. "Who does your hair?" That was easy!

"This young girl by the name of Yazz does my hair. What you tryna do with your hair though?" I asked. Earlier in the day, Mo pulled up wearing a dainty hat a la Cindy Lauper. So I had no idea what her hair was like.

"I'm not sure, but I need to establish a new look for myself." she said.

"Ok. I will call Yazz and schedule a time for you guys to meet." I replied.

"Ok. Great. I'm available anytime after 5pm this week. I'm a night owl so I don't wake up til about three or four."

Jotting down the other things that needed to be handled, Mo gave me explicit instructions for each assignment.

• Call My A&R Jay Brown to introduce yourself and schedule a meeting

• Find a hairstylist

• Call her attorney regarding her paper work with her Production company

• Call her publishing company Warner Chappell about getting her some additional writing gigs

Mo gave me the run down and schooled me quickly about each task and each person I needed to contact. She was patient with me. Describing the role of each person, it felt good to know that she was on top of her business but didn't want to do it "day to day".

In time, we established our own groove and got the hang of things.

At the time of our meeting, Mo's career was at the start of some wonderful things. It was 1999 and Missy's song, "Hot Boyz" featuring Lil' Mo had set a record while ruling the #1 spot for 18 weeks on the Billboard Hot Rap Singles Chart. Less than one month into working with Lil' Mo, I had already secured a new glam squad for her, and in less than six weeks, we were already shooting the video for "Hot Boyz". From sun up to sun down, she sang the mess out of that hook while on set. Scene after scene, she gave it her all. Nas, Eve, Q-Tip, and even Mary J. Blige gave Mo her props. When it was all said and done, the song ended up in the Guinness Book of World Records.

Within a month of working with Mo, I was in total "hectic mode". She was the most sought after songwriter in the industry and all of the music producers wanted a piece of her. From working with Missy writing for other artists to working on her very own album on Elektra Records, she had very little time for herself.

Mo's personality made her extremely easy to work with. We both could smell bullcrap coming from a mile away and whenever it was time to make an executive decision, she respected my opinion. Very rarely did we have a disagreement. Her personality was comical. Addicted to Martin Lawrence's sitcom, *Martin*, Mo would often refer to the show for inspiration, lyrical ideas, and more.

What made our relationship really sweet was that her

family was based outside of my hometown of Washington, DC in Maryland where her father was stationed as a photographer in the military. One thing I remember most about Lil' Mo was that she was not a man, but she was a provider. She made sure that her family had the best of everything and I rocked with her on that. "Lynn. I wanna do something at my house for my bday," she mentioned to me. As her birthday drew near, Mo explained to me how her birthday was often over shadowed by the Thanksgiving holiday.

I often peeped how Mo held it down for her family and close friends and rarely saw anyone do anything for her in return. Noticing a short list of her wants, I aimed at acquiring one of the items on the list—a miniature Yorkie.

Driving up to Puppy City in Maryland, I immediately spotted the pooch I wanted to cop for Mo. Pulling over to the side while my mom parked and stayed in the car, I asked the clerk, "How much is that doggie in the window?"

Pointing at a quiet, sleeping puppy Yorkie, I knew he'd be perfect for Mo and her lifestyle. This puppy was cool, calm, and collected. He was fighting for attention like his other peers. He had a swag about him that stated, "Yeah... I KNOW I'm cute." Lol! So dishing out my last fifteen hundred dollars, I purchased the puppy for almost a stack while I used my remaining dollars in my pocket to purchase food and accessories for the pup. God put it on my heart to do this, so I did it without question and I enjoyed every moment of witnessing her surprised reaction to the pup.

"Awwww man!! Lynn, you shouldn't have," Mo repeated happily. "I love her! But oh! Wait a minute. Is it a he or a she?" she asked. To tell you the truth, at the time, I wasn't even sure. Flipping it over to the genital area, Mo confirmed that the pooch was a "he". "It's a boy!" she exclaimed. "And I'm going to name him Jigga." How ironic. We all laughed. Mo and rapper, Jay-Z had just completed a song together called, "Parking Lot Pimpin" and Mo was a huge fan of his. Working with him was a dream come true for her. So naming the puppy "Jigga" was no surprise to any of her friends and family members gathered at her new townhouse in Maryland to give her birthday love.

Sliding on my sneakers to head outside, I was beat. Lil' Mo was definitely a night crawler. She worked best at night and I worked best during the day. Even though we stayed in close proximity of each other, with everything that needed to be accomplished, we were still like two passing ships in the night.

For almost three months straight, we took the drive out to producer Eddie F's studio out in Closter, New Jersey.

There, Lil' Mo worked on several projects—one for herself, some things for Missy Elliott, some stuff for Darius Rucker, formerly of Hootie and the Blowfish, as well as songs for R&B crooner Donnell Jones. Eddie F and his partner Darrale Jones are well known music producers, who have produced hits for the likes of Pete Rock & CL Smooth, Heavy D, and more. The two made it happen.

Whenever Lil' Mo would pick me up in Brooklyn for the evening to head out to Eddie F's mini mansion, I would be dressed for bed. I would literally climb into her SUV with a baggy tee and sweats. I would immediately find my regular spot on the sofa's studio. By sunrise, I would awake to hear her latest recordings and provide my feedback to her skillfully written masterpiece.

Lil' Mo was a work whore. She would work her butt off. She was the prime example of someone who absolutely loved what she did for a living. Standing at all of five feet, she could belt out tunes to beats that needed life. Her songwriting skills were that of a painter. The beats were like blank canvases that called for color and formation.

Very often, Lil' Mo would commit specific stints of time to dedicate to a music producer in efforts to sell the catalogue of songs they worked on together. Once that stint passed, she would then move on to the next producer.

Barry Salter's bedroom in Queens quickly became a recording spot for us—and one of our favorites as well. A lot of well known songwriters graced the room where the recording booth was the bedroom's closet. As Lil' Mo often sifted through Barry's tracks, she would always take the lower bunk to stretch out and write while I dozed in and out of sleep on the upper bunk. We were truly on grind mode. If there was a hot music producer somewhere, anywhere, we were there.

Barry was not your typical music producer. He had the swagger of a drug dealer and the words of a scholar. His beats were beautiful, melodic, and packed full of unpredictable changes. Though we would often move on to the next producer after completing a catalogue of songs, we stayed longer at Barry's spot to hone in on Lil' Mo's own singing career.

If you were from Queens, then you were definitely hitting up Barry for beats. On more than one occasion, Barry stopped the session to let a local rapper listen to beats. "Lynn, Mo, this is 50 Cent," he mentioned as a heavy set dude pushed into the bedroom/recording room. As the rapper waved, Mo and I immediately knew who he was. Industry news traveled and 50 Cent was recently involved in a stabbing at a local studio in

Manhattan. He would often come in, grab a CD from Barry and bounce. "Sorry, ladies. I just had to slip him some beats. I just have a feeling that he is going to be alright with this music shit and I just wanna be a part of his growth," Barry explained.

"We understand. That's why I'm here. I know you believe in me," said Mo.

During the winter of 1999, Lil' Mo's A&R, Jay Brown, called. "Hey, Lynn, y'all about done with Eddie F and Barry?"

"Yeah. I think she's ready for the next producer," I replied to Jay Brown.

"Well, I have a suggestion. How 'bout LA? I have a few producers out here that are starting to get a buzz and I think Mo would be a great fit with them."

"Oh really?" I asked.

"Yeah. And they are young too. Their names are Brycyn Evans and Troy Johnson. They are signed to QD3." QD3 is Quincy Jones III. QD3 is the son to the legendary music icon, Quincy Jones. Quincy Jones to date is a musician, composure, TV producer, arranger, conductor, philanthropist, and more. His work within the music industry spans well over 50 years. His innate ability to create music fused together artists such as Michael Jackson, Ice T, Miles Davis, Dizzy Gillespie, Ray Charles, Queen Latifah, Melle Me, Shaquille O'Neal, and numerous others. His son, QD3, has followed in his footsteps to become a well known music producer, television producer, and more.

"Oh. Ok. Lemmee ask her and I'll let you know what's up? I just need you to begin to work on where we would be staying."

"Ok. No problem. You guys can actually stay at QD3's place or my place. It's up to y'all."

Hanging up the phone, I began to weigh the pros and cons of going out to LA for a few months. At this particular time, I had my rent squared away for the next few months. However, LA was expensive and it was something I had not factored into my finances. It would be a struggle, but the opportunity was priceless. After discussing the pros and cons of going out to LA to work, we decided to take the trip in two weeks time.

Gearing up for the long west coast stint, Mo and I took the 14 days to pay bills, have follow up meetings with label A&R's in New York City, tie up loose ends, and pack for our trip. I didn't have too much to worry about. Other than my rent and cell phone bills, I had very little overhead. Trina and I were still roommates and she was going to hold it down without a doubt.

"Please place your seat back in its upright position and lock in your tray tables to prepare for landing," the flight attendant announced. Mo and I were landing into LA for an indefinite period of time.

As the hot LA air hit my chest, I was happy we made the decision to come. "Well, I know one thing, I don't miss that New York winter." I laughed.

"Me either," Mo sheepishly replied. It was 11:30am when we landed and she was not used to being awake this early. Jay Brown, Lil Mo's A&R was from LA. He and his wife lived in the valley and the two made sure we had everything needed to have a comfortable stay.

Picking us up from the airport, Jay Brown began to immediately spill out the plan of action for Mo. We knew that Troy and Brycyn, the music producers were young but we had no idea that they were in school—high school that is. "They are what!?" she asked.

Rolling her eyes at Jay when he stated that the boys were 16 and 17, we were both too through!

"Don't knock 'em til you try 'em," Jay replied in a cool calm and collective voice. "They have already worked with artists such as Ray J, Tamia, and Tupac." Jay had a demeanor that would drive Mo crazy. Mo's energy was always on ten and her patience as the schedule grew even more hectic was starting to wear thin. Jay always had a tactic or strategy to cooling off the room whenever hot air was being blown around. Parking at a meter, we headed over to Fat Burger and got our grub on. From that moment on, Denny's, Fat Burger, and Roscoe's were our daily spots. No one had time to cook.

As we pulled up into QD3's driveway in Northridge, we spotted two boys grabbing book bags out of the car. "Oh. Great. They are here already," Jay blurted out. Looking even more irritated after spotting the youngsters, it took Mo almost 15 minutes to peel out of Jay's car. "C'mon Mo. Trust me, you won't be disappointed."

After an immediate introduction to QD3 most affectionately known as Snoopy, we chatted it up with him for a bit to get a feel for his energy. His vibe was great. His tall thin frame was equal to his personality— quiet and humble. You would have never known that he is the son of music icon, Quincy Jones. His home was welcoming and inviting. We felt at home right away. Then we met Brycyn and Troy. Brycyn barely had balance when he stepped up to shake our hands. Troy on the other hand was tall frail and firm with his shake. The two immediately had one thing in common. They both had tape wrapped around a part of their eye glasses.

"Let's get to it," Mo said.

"Ok. Brycyn and Troy, you may take the ladies upstairs." Following the guys up the steps, we entered into the studio. Brycyn and Troy began to turn up the lights and power on the equipment. With not much to say, they spoke to us without even looking at us. With their heads bent down in a slump, they put the first dat in and began to play the first track. As the track began to play, Mo's eyes lit up. One foot started tapping and then the other followed. Her head started bobbing and she immediately started belting out amazing harmonies. As the track ended and the guys moved on to the next, she did the same. By night's end Lil' Mo had referenced four songs. The chemistry between Mo, Troy, and Brycyn had become undeniable on our first night of recording with them.

Hands down, Troy and Brycyn had talent like no other producers we had worked with. Lil' Mo was amazed. The boys had opened up and their nerdy disposition had turned into two teens with confidence and clear direction. As time rolled forward, six weeks had passed by and we had managed to record a catalogue of well over 36 songs. "Ladies Man" a single sang by R&B duo, Changing Faces, was one of the hits that came out of the batch.

Exhausted from the day, it was 4am before we would check into our hotel at the Le Montrose in Hollywood. Mo had snubbed the idea of staying with anyone she worked with and I was all for it. With a long-term stay reservation, the two of us made ourselves at home. The hotel was well known and highly respected by industry insiders. Nestled mid block off a residential neighborhood, the hotel could have easily been mistaken for a condominium complex. Mo was paying out of pocket. One of her royalty checks had come in so we were good on our additional living expenses for at least one month.

The one thing we both learned most about this experience was to never judge a book by its cover. Who would've thought that Brycyn and Troy, from the look of an eye could kick out hits they did. The trip was amazing and it paid off. As a result of our hard work, my managerial and publicity skills started to shine and someone was taking notice of it. Val Bisharat, an executive at Windswept Music Publishing, would often stop by QD's studio to check on Brycyn and Troy's progress. In fact, Lil' Mo ventured out to LA several more times after meeting Brycyn and Troy to complete songs with the dynamic duo up until Brycyn's untimely death. Slipping into a diabetic coma at the young age of 21, Brycyn will never be forgotten.

While I enjoyed my time with Mo, management was not my cup of tea. It was time consuming and the schedule was way more unpredictable than being a publicist, so I moved on. The stress of the grind outweighed the financial benefits, so I hung my hat. I began to get some balance I began to get some balance between my business and personal life back. I moved in with China to an amazing one bedroom apartment in Boerum Hill Brooklyn. Our exposed brick walls and high ceilings was cozy and convenient to shops and the city.

Just as I hung my hat with Mo, the call for potential clients began to roll in. While I was jotting down a potential list of clients, my cell rang. I didn't recognize the number. "Hello," I answered.

"Hello. Is this Lynn Hobson?" the voice asked. It was a deep dark voice on the line.

"This is she. How may I help you?"

"My name is James Ellis and I was referred to you by Lil' Mo. She told me you are a good publicist and I'm in need of your assistance." At that moment, I just started to laugh. I knew exactly who James Ellis was. He was an emerging manager in this business of entertainment.

We met a few months prior in a midtown Manhattan Studio. During that time, Lil' Mo had been laying down a hook for Ellis' artists, Redman and Methodman. They were two of hip-hop's most influential rap artists at the time.

"Hey, Ellis. How are you?"

"I can't complain. Listen. I just signed an author to my roster and I'd like to sit down and meet with you about doing some publicity for her book. When are you available?" he asked.

"I'm free on Monday," I replied. It was now Thursday and the rest of my week was packed with New Business meetings. I was eager to meet with Ellis though, but I didn't want to squeeze him in. He seemed to be very successful with his current roster so I wanted to schedule out a block of time so that I could absorb questions that I actually had for him pertaining to his own career and business strategies.

After a long and productive meeting, Ellis hired me to conduct publicity for Ellis Entertainment, where I publicized his company and his clients, which at the time consisted of rapper Redman, Grammy Award-Winning Music Producer Rockwilder, and Best Selling Author Teri Woods for her book, *True To The Game.* This account afforded me the ability to spread across the gamut of entertainment. Working with Ellis Entertainment, I was able to be a part of history as the film, *How High* had become and is still the highest grossing film in hip-hop.

Chapter 11:
Vital Marketing Group (2000)

In 2000, I wanted to expand HobbieCom. I wanted it to be a real company with employees. I wanted to print out paychecks and offer benefits.

"Hey girl. Wanna go out tonight? Derek is having something and I want to go out." It was Trina typing me on my SkyTel Pager. I hadn't seen her in well over a week. Though I still lived in Brooklyn with China, the two of us were extremely hectic. The Black Diamonds Event was promoted by Derek Corley. He and I had attended HU during the same time. I often frequented his weekly events because they were the more upscale events for the urban chic.

As I began to get dressed, my cell phone rang. It was Kim. "Hey Girl!" I answered.

"Girl! Are you sitting down?" Kim asked while skipping the greeting.

"Ummmm yeah. I'm sitting down. What is it Kim?" She was starting to scare me a little.

"Girl. I'm pregnant!"

"Are you serious? What are you going to do? Are you going to keep it?" I asked. And lord knows I had to ask because Kim was definitely not the motherly type. However, she had been with her boo for well over five years and the relationship was starting to get serious. I knew Kim had feelings for the dude when she turned Gucci down months prior while we were at an HU Party in NYC.

"Yes. I'm going to keep it." I was happy to hear those words come out of her mouth because taking a trip to the ABC (Abortion Clinic) was definitely a form of birth control for a lot of our girlfriends.

"Oh wow!" I exclaimed. "I'm so happy for you! Are you happy?" I just had to make sure that my feelings lined up with hers—and they did. Kim was expecting her first child and I was too excited for her.

"Do you have a preference? Do you want a girl or boy?" I asked her.

"I want a boy since Jeff has Shanelle." Shanelle was Jeff's daughter from a previous relationship. "But overall, the health of the baby is what's most important to me."

"Well if you are happy, then I'm happy," and as I

looked around for my black pumps, I could see China in the cut, trying to figure out who I was talking to on the phone. Guys crack me up. They act like they don't want the scoop, but they always actually want it more than females. Congratulating Kim again, the two of us ended the call.

"Honey! Kim's pregnant!"

"Oh, wow! Ok. That's what's up," he responded as he made his way back into our bedroom. Though the apartment was nice, the apartment didn't feel like my home and China sensed it as well. "The other day, I road into Jersey with Mike from the store and I saw this newly built apartment complex on the Hudson River. It's off da chain. Anyway, here's the brochure. Lemmee know your thoughts. The lease is up in a few months and I was thinking that we should probably move. We need more space." I was surprisingly shocked at the strides China was making in our relationship. He was starting to become more consistent. And though his actions were what I had longed for, I was growing too busy with my business to bask in that aspect of my life. I had things to accomplish. I was on the move.

"Ok, honey. I will check it out when I get back, but from the looks of the brochure, it looks amazing. So if we can afford it, I'm with it! Trina and I are going to hang out tonight. I haven't seen her in a while. So can we talk about this more tomorrow?" I asked.

"Yep. We sure can." Sundays were always our day to relax, listen to music, take a walk, or check out a new movie. Sundays were the best days for us.

"Oh. And don't forget that my sister's wedding is coming up. We need to talk about that. The wedding is in June and I really want you to be there with me," I stated. I had to put my bid in for China's time early. He was often on the road with his brother Pooh and Foxy.

"Cool. We can talk about that on Sunday also," he replied. We were clearly growing up. Our friends were all starting to get married and settled down. China and I were starting to make our own strides as a couple as well. After all, we had been together for almost 10 years. It was time to either poop or get off the pot.

Kissing China on the lips, I left to pick up Trina. Cruising in my lavender Saturn coup, which I had purchased during my last visit to DC, Trina was already on the stoop of the brownstone waiting for me to pull up. I could tell she was excited because it wasn't often that she was dressed and ready to go anywhere on time. When she got into the car, we hugged, laughed about the color of my car, exchanged updates on our lives personally, professionally, and just yapped, yapped, yapped until we arrived to the city. Only the concentration of looking for a parking space broke up the chit chat, but as soon as we located the perfect space just three blocks from the venue, we were back at it again.

Trina had just gotten back from a long stint in Los Angeles. She loved LA, but her acting opportunities were more rooted in New York. While she was in LA, Trina received so many calls to audition in New York that she opted to move back. I was glad she did because I missed her.

Heading over to the bar with Trina, I spoke to a tall handsome guy that I would often see at Derek's events. "Hey. How ya doing?" I asked.

"Oh. Hey. I'm good and you?"

"Oh. I can't complain," I replied.

"I saw you on the news the other day. What exactly do you do?" Joe asked.

"Oh. I'm a publicist. You probably saw me on TV in the backdrop with Sister Souljah. She's promoting her new novel, " *The Coldest Winter Ever*".

"Oh. Ok. Well my name is Joe by the way. I have a small marketing company based here in the city called

Vital Marketing Group. We are actually in need of a publicist."

"Oh really? Cool. Well I'm the one." I smiled.

"What's your schedule like on Monday? Can you stop by my office around 3pm?" Joe asked as he handed me his business card.

"That will work. I'll see ya then." I shook his hand and then walked back over to Trina where she was in conversation with another mutual friend of ours.

This would be great. 'Cause I could sure use a new client if I'm ready to hire a new staff member.

My initial meeting with Joe and his partners Kwad, Garnet, and Shawn was a success. We worked out the logistics of our business arrangement and began working vigorously on combining our clients and efforts to generate revenue.

As days turned to weeks and weeks turned to months, I loved working with Vital Marketing. The guys were always vibrant; positive; and full of energy. Their passion for marketing matched mine for PR. In March of 2001, one year after working as a team, Vital Marketing acquired my firm. Meeting Joe and the guys at VMG was the boost I needed to take my business to the next level. Joe's marketing tactics, Garnet's gift to make numbers work, Kwad's great business acumen, and Shawn's hustle was a match made in heaven for my desired future endeavors.

Hooking up with them, as a team, we locked down a chic office space on 34th street and Madison Avenue, and rocked out on accounts such as Posner Cosmetics, *VIBE* magazine, Adidas, the FORD Motor Corporation, Remy, and more.

While we had Madison Avenue status, we didn't have Madison Avenue money, but we made it look good— so good that *Black Enterprise* magazine came knocking in the summer of 2001 and nominated our firm for "Up & Coming Entrepreneurs Award" as a growing business.

Our accounts came from great accredited businesses. However, they would always expect us to work miracles with their tuna fish budget and caviar dreams—and that's just what we did. Joe never turned down that dollar. From our marketing wings and my public r
elations mouth, to the outdoor media's muscle, we strong-armed the best of them. And when we did it, we did everything in fun. We loved going to work and we enjoyed what we did for a living. Loving what you do is important. We never had a dull moment in the

office.

One of our most memorable events was our fusion of two accounts, Remy and my client, music producer, Rockwilder of Ellis Entertainment. Remy hired Vital Marketing to brand their product within the music industry elite. We merged the two for one night to create a star-studded event entitled, "Remy Rocks with Rockwilder." This event introduced Rockwilder to the world as an emerging music producer while Remy garnered the platform to hob nob with tastemakers and trendsetters. At this red carpet affair, celebs such as Kelly Rowland of Destiny's Child, model Tyson Beckford, Redman, and several others came out to congratulate Rockwilder on his upcoming nominations for his production of "Lady Marmalade" featuring Pink, Missy Elliot, Lil' Kim, Mya, and Christina Aguilera. The event was a huge success.

Business was really picking up and in the midst of everything, China and I needed a new home. Our lease was up on our one bedroom apartment in Boerum Hill, Brooklyn known for its' restaurants, brownstones, and boutiques, but we wanted a change of pace. "I wanna get us a place where it's a perfect combination of the suburbs and city life," China stated.

"Ok. But where?" I asked him.

"I'ma start looking around more. I'll ask Danny or Mike tomorrow at work." Danny and Mike were China's employers. The two were both married with children and living in the city's suburbs. While Danny lived out on Long Island, Mike lived right outside of the Lincoln Tunnel in Weehawken. They were always helpful to us. We looked to them for advice on our relationship and finances when needed. China was working as a Jewelry Salesperson within New York City's diamond district by day, while he sold his beats by night.

Chapter 12:
Rockwilder (2001)

It was 2001 and business was booming. Clients were signing up left and right. My staff of two had grown to a modest staff of six. Each Account Executive handled an average of four accounts. Music Producers Rockwilder, Bink Dogg, Bryan-Michael Cox, HitCo Music Publishing, Windswept Music Publishing, and more signed on to get a taste of good publicity and I really started living.

Our work with Remy was still going. Though Trina was still acting and temping, I would often pull her in to help me with special, big events. During a brainstorming meeting, I could see Trina through the conference room glass. She was leaning over the receptionist's desk and I knew she was asking for me, so I picked up the phone and called her to come into the meeting over the intercom. Looking over at the glass, she smiled, entered, and greeted me and the guys. "Hellooooo. How's everyone this fine afternoon?"

The guys just gushed as she placed her bags on a separate table and took a seat. If I were working at a conservative corporation, there would have been no way Trina would've been allowed into my meeting. Besides, the guys and I were just brainstorming so we needed another mind. After all, the five of us were starting to think alike. Having a different perspective on the matters we needed to accomplish and discuss was refreshing.

China and I moved from the Brooklyn brownstone apartment into a plush carpeted two-bed room in West New York, New Jersey. The Riverbend Complex was situated right on the Hudson River where we had a Manhattan view that was breath taking and priceless. We really moved on up—just like the Jeffersons, to a deluxe apartment in the sky high. I mean, there was no way you couldn't tell us that we hadn't arrived. Our apartment was nice! Don't ask me how we got approved cause our credit was shot! Not only was the apartment nice, but many of the up and coming "Who's Who" were living in the complex as well.

On the actual day China and I moved into our apartment, I bumped right into Joy, the former intern who witnessed my untimely exit from the Terrie Williams Agency. "OMG! Lynn! How are you girl? Long time no see!"

"Oh. Wow! I'm doing great. My boyfriend and I are actually moving in to this building today. Do you live here?" I asked.

"Yes! OMG! We are going to be neighbors! Gimmee

your numba girl. I live on the fourth floor."

"Ok. Cool." I then informed her of my apartment number, we exchanged two way pager numbers and scheduled a time to catch up over lunch once China and I got settled into our new home.

In May, for my birthday, China took me out for a nice walk in the village—something he only liked to do. But even though it was my birthday, I didn't pull the "It's my birthday card." Lol! I just went with the flow. "Hey, Fruity. Do you want a Caramel Frappucino from Starbucks?," China asked.

"Yeah... why not? I could go for one." The day was warm but cloudy. The sun was trying to peek through the clouds, but it was a 'no go' for the day. As China stood in line to order our drinks, I grabbed two seats by the window. I jumped at the opportunity to take a rest. Walking around downtown Manhattan was a Sunday ritual for China and I needed ever break offered in order to keep up with him. When he arrived with our drinks, I also seized the moment to run to the ladies room. "I'll be back. I'm going to go use the restroom." China just nodded, took a seat, and whipped out his freshly purchased *New York Times*.

Returning back to the table, I noticed China on the floor. Wondering what he may have dropped, I sped up to help him—only to realize that he was down on one knee with a ring in his hand. I gasped! "Fruity. Will you marry me?"

"Oh my God! Yes! Yes. I'll marry you." Tears started gushing out of my eyes. I was in shock. I had been nagging China about making a commitment for so long that I had given up on bringing up the topic more than three months prior. Placing the round diamond onto my finger, he then stood up and held me tightly. At that moment, nothing mattered. We just held on to each other until we were ready to let go. Starbucks wasn't very crowded, so no one even seemed to notice China's proposal and I loved that. It was just the two of us. As we sat back down at the table, I must've stared at my ring for well over 20 minutes. I also took the moment to pick up the phone to call my mom who was extremely happy and then my Dad. "Congratulations B," my dad replied once I delivered the news.

"Thanks, Daddy!" and putting my stepmother Diane on the phone thereafter, she also congratulated me. Hanging up from them, I began to inquire about a wedding date from China.

"Let's look at the summer of 2002 for our wedding," China suggested.

"Ok. That's fine with me." After all, I had too much

lined up on my plate already. It was May of 2001 and my year leading up to NBA All Star Weekend in 2002 was already placed onto my calendar. "I'd love to look at some of the restaurants on the waterfront over by us. The Chart House would be a dream for me. Their view of the Manhattan skyline is amazing!" China just smiled at me. China often smiled when he started to think about the financing. He smiled whenever he started to get overwhelmed so I just dropped the subject—for now.

"You ready?" China asked as he finished up the last drop of his coffee, placed his newspaper into his man bag, and wiped the table with the left over napkins. "I wanna go into this sneaker store for a minute." Greg was a shopaholic. You would think it would be the other way around, but not in our case. I didn't care if he wanted to check out some sneakers. I had just been proposed to and I was happy. I could not have asked for a better Birthday.

Just four days after my birthday and engagement, I received a call from Jeff. "Hey Lynn. The baby is here! Kim gave birth to our baby boy today!"

"Oh. Wow! I didn't even know she had gone into labor! Wow! Congratulations Jeff! How are they doing? What are you guys going to name the baby? How much did he weigh?" I was too excited. I had too many questions. Jeff couldn't even answer them fast enough, but he took his time and responded to each one.

I was elated. I asked him to have Kim call me once she had some energy, wished them well again and hung up the phone. I immediately called to share the news with Trina and China. If there was Facebook; Twitter; or even MySpace at the time, I would have blasted it because I wanted the world to know that I was officially a Godmom. Jaeden had been welcomed into the world.

August rolled around and I was honored and humbled to be awarded with the prestigious 2001 "Network Journal's 40 Under 40 Award." This award was created by the Publication known as *The Network Journal.* Other recipients were clothing Designer Maurice Malone, my elementary school buddy /Actor Laz Alonzo; Fubu's CEO Damon John; Publisher Keith Clinkscales; and more. My hard work was paying off and I was basking in the glow of my success. As I was handed the award during the ceremony, a brief video clip aired of me on the ballroom's big screen. Photos and a narration of the work I had accomplished was seen. And when the clip ended, I was recognized with a standing ovation. Everyone loved the quote I provided, "When all else fails, burn the bridge. Burn the bridge so you won't have the option of giving up when you've crossed the bridge and obstacles are in your way. Deal with the issues at hand and everything will be alright."

One of my favorite clients, Rockwilder, had been nominated for a MTV Award for his rendition of "Lady Marmalade" featuring Mya, Missy, Christina Aguilera, Pink, and Lil' Kim. And though Rockwilder had been nominated for an award, this was a MTV Music Video Award show. While he created the music, there was no level of respect established with MTV because he was an up and coming music producer. "Lynn, we can only accommodate the artist and the video director for Orchestra seats during the Awards," a talent executive at MTV told me when I called to request prime seating for my client. I was furious—as I was damn near 90% sure that Rockwilder's record would win at least one of the six nominations for the hit re-make. "We have actually sold out of all of the tickets on the mezzanine level, Lynn," she went on to state. I was pissed and embarrassed.

"We are going to have to make something happen," I hissed at the lady over the phone. I was not willing to take, "no" for an answer. Rockwilder had been working his ass off all year and he was continuously taking the backseat to the recognition he so deserved. Hell... I was starting to take it personally. I had been by his side all year through the ups and downs of his career and I wanted to see him win.

"Lynn, we will try our best to get at least two seats for him but I can't promise that they will be on the mezzanine level," she stated. "How many tickets were you looking to obtain?"

"Four," I answered. I then hung up the phone after providing her with my full name and phone numbers. I then picked up the phone to call Rockwilder's manager, Ellis to deliver the news. "Hey, Ellis. So here's the deal," and as I began to give him the run down on the ticket situation I could tell that he was tight as well. Before I could even finish my last thought, the other line rang and it was MTV calling. "Hold on, Ellis. That's actually MTV now."

"Hello. Lynn Hobson speaking," I answered.

"Hey, Lynn. So we are able to provide four tickets to Rockwilder. However, they are in the balcony. Should the song win an award, we have him seated by a stairwell that would shoot him directly down to the Orchestra level so that he can collect the award." As she talked, I could feel the blood rushing to my face. If I were a white girl, I would have been as red as a beet. A flashed glimpse of Rockwilder running down four flights of steps and down on to the stage horrified me.

"That's insane. Can you imagine me explaining the scenario to my client?" I asked the Talent Executive. It just sounds crazy. Plus Rock ain't no little dude. He's six foot four inches tall and diesel. He'd be completely out of breath before hitting the stage to even deliver a thank you or wave to the crowd.

"Ms. Hobson. I'm sorry, but that's the best I can do." I paused for so long she had to say my name again to ensure that I was still on the phone. What was I going to tell Ellis? What the was I going to tell Rock?

On the day of the Awards, Rockwilder made sure he had on his fresh throwback with matching Nikes. He was looking fresh ta def and it took all of my might to keep my energy level at ten. It was my job to always look on the bright side of things, even if we were going to be seated four flights up from the stage.

Upon arrival to the red carpet, Rockwilder exited his chauffer driven SUV and stepped onto the Red Carpet where I hugged and greeted him. Walking solo as expected, there wasn't too much fanfare with Rock. As I guided him to each Media Post, Interviewers were very much intrigued with his look; stature; energy; and name. No one turned him down for an interview. He was as humble as they could get.

The Metropolitan Opera House was packed. And even

though Rock was already prepped and aware of our messed up seating arrangements, it broke my heart for me to have to guide him up three flights of stairs to our nosebleed seats amongst the fans. I wanted to cry. I felt like I had failed him. With my head hung low as we climbed the stairs, Rock placed his hand on my shoulder and continued the climb with an energy like, "I'ma make it to that stage. Don't even stress it," and at that moment, my spirits lifted.

As we watched celebs such as Britney Spears, Justin Timberlake, and a guest appearance by the one and only Michael Jackson grace the stage, the intensity grew as we continued to laugh at Jamie Foxx's jokes. "Do you think we are going to win Lynn?" Rockwilder asked.

"Hell yeah," I replied with a positive smile on my face.

"And the nominees for Video of the Year are…" And as the Presenter started to call off all of the Artists in the category, Rockwilder got up out of his seat and started the three-story trek down the stairs. The Presenter had not even announced the winner, but Rockwilder was gone and I couldn't blame him. You gotta call things that be not as though they were, in order to have the things you want in life manifested. "Moulin Rouge! Featuring Christina Aguilera, Pink, Mya, Lil' Kim, and Missy." As the ladies got up out of their seats to grace

the stage with their notes of thank yous, Rockwilder
arrived to the stage just as they mounted the staircase
to the podium. I sighed the biggest sigh of relief. I
sighed so loud that a fan shooshed me but I didn't care.
I was just happy in the moment I was in. As the ladies
and Rockwilder exited the stage, I knew they were
heading back to the Media Room for post winning
interviews so I left my seat and started to track down
Rockwilder's driver and SUV. By the time my phone
rang, I had located the vehicle and parked on a
discreet corner so he would be able to locate us.

Climbing into the SUV, he yelled out, "We did it!"

"Yes! We did it!" I shouted. Rockwilder was happier
than a kid in a candy store. "We are going to head
over to Club 151 on 51st Street. Ok? Mos Def is giving
Beyonce a surprise birthday party and my friend Shakir
invited us." I mentioned.

"Aight. Bet," Rock responded. "Michelle is waiting for
us with our passes in front of the club so all we have to
do is jump out upon arrival."

We had a ball at the party. Celebrating was definitely
in FULL affect. I can't even remember the last time I
partied that hard. My client was happy. He was a

winner and the weight of the world for this day, had been lifted off of my shoulders.

Following the days after the MTV Awards and partying every night from the week prior, I had decided to take the week off from city commuting to the office. Realizing that Dr. Dollar would not be preaching this particular morning on BET, I flicked the television off with the remote and closed my eyes. I wasn't sleepy, but my body was just tired. A feeling of restlessness was starting to overcome me, but instead of just getting up for the day, I attempted to force myself to rest. Just as I was reaching to pull the sheets up onto my body, my cell phone rang. Looking at the caller ID, it was my friend and neighbor, Joy.

"Hello?"

"Lyyyyynnnnn," Joy inquired. "Is that you?"

"Uh Joy. Who else would it be?" I asked.

"Girl! Turn on the TV!" she yelled.

"Why? What's up Joy?" I was kind of annoyed cause I really wanted to get more time in to rest before the day's drama began. I would always set out to do one thing, but my day was always re-mixed into something else.

"Turn to channel four!!" She didn't care that I sounded half sleep.

Flipping on the TV, to that particular channel, I watched in horror as NBC News showed barrels of smoke emerging from the Twin Towers. "What?!" I yelled out. "What the hell is going on?"

"Girl! I have no idea, but Logan and I are going outside to see what's going on." she replied.

"Ok. I'll meet you in the lobby," I said and hung up the phone. Reaching frantically for some sweats and sneakers, I looked at the television again. The camera lens from the NBC News' helicopter seemed fuzzy. As I watched, it was unclear as to what was happening. I reached for my cell phone to call China and got no answer. "Damn!" It was so typical of him to not answer his phone—especially on his ride to work. He absolutely loved taking the ferry to Manhattan, and referred to it as his time of solace.

Our complex was located directly on the Hudson River Waterfront. It was a prime location and we had the convenience of living across from New York City. So when I got to my elevator, I pressed the "down" button and waited. The elevator took forever, so I opted for the stairs—after all, I only lived on the second floor.

When I arrived in the lobby, Joy was ready to go with baby Logan strapped securely into his buggy. As we headed to the water, we could see all of our neighbors stretching out their arms and pointing their fingers toward the Twin Towers. The sight was horrific. Everyone watched in horror as an even larger cloud of smoke appeared. The black smoke was so thick that we couldn't even see the buildings. The thickness lasted for hours. It was obvious that something was terribly wrong and fear came over me. "Trina! Oh my God! She works in the towers!," I yelled out. "I want to go back upstairs and watch the news Joy. I have to know what's going on."

She nodded and we headed back up to my apartment. Our cell phones were not working. We couldn't even get through to 911. A fast busy signal was all that we received after pressing the "call" prompt on any phone. The news reported the towers had fallen, but to the naked eye we couldn't tell because of the smoke. Joy and I just sat in silence. She rocked Logan to sleep while I just stared at the wall in my living room.

It would be hours before China made it back home—11:30pm to be exact. As he turned the key to our apartment door, he came in the house talking, "I had to stand on line for the ferry for over ten hours. I'm beat, but I'm glad I'm home." He looked beat and tired too. He went on to mention that once they had gotten word the towers had fallen, the diamond district closed down and everyone had gone home— only thing was that all bridges and tunnels had been shut down as well. Millions of people were stranded that day.

Two days passed by before I was able to reach Trina. Trina was now the lone ranger in our Brooklyn studio apartment. I managed to still have our old landlord's phone number. Mr. Francis happened to be in the building so he knocked on Trina's door and handed her the phone.

"Trina!" I yelled.

"Yes, Lynn. I'm fine." she wimpered.

"What the hell!? Why you ain't call nobody? Yo mom is even looking for you! Why haven't you called anyone?" Before she could even go on about anything else, I immediately started making three way calls to her family in Trenton who were worried. Trina explained that she didn't have a cell phone and, her home phone was physically broken.

After Trina finished explaining herself to everyone, I convinced her to pack a bag and come to Jersey for a few days. I needed the company. China was working long hours now in the midst of developing his own line of watches. The rest of the month was basically a wrap and the city was a ghost town. No one had any desire to go into the city. My staff and I worked from home, but as the days went on I started to have no desire to work as hard as I did. So many people had lost their lives. There I was busting my butt for a dollar when so many lost so much. It was officially "tone it down time" for me.

I was working myself into the ground and as a result of the stress, I had developed a skin condition called Vitaligo. Michael Jackson also had this type of skin discoloration. This disorder consisted of white patches appearing on my face and hands. It became discouraging to walk outside and attend functions with this happening to my body. Makeup now became the norm following this diagnosis. To date, doctors are still researching a cure for the disease.

One morning after dropping Trina to the airport for her to visit a relative in Texas, I woke up sneezing. My apartment was filled with dust. It had been a minute since I had actually done a serious cleaning of our home. Looking out of the window, I could also see the pollen blowing off of the trees and into the wind. My window seals were actually dusty from the pollen as well. So I brushed my teeth, wiped my face and got the cleaning products out. Starting with my bedroom, I wiped down everything. I dusted the nightstands, our bed frame, TV stand, and lamps with orange scented

Pledge. I changed the sheets and dumped any and all dirty laundry into the hamper. I was on a roll. It was my goal to have our place in tip top shape within the next two hours. Grabbing the vacuum cleaner, I began to snatch up every piece of dirt and crumb that hid within the crevices of the bedroom's carpet. As I eased the vacuum under the bed as far as it would go, something kept bumping up against the rim of the vacuum. Powering it off, I got down on my knees and looked under the bed—annoyed at what could possibly be messing up my cleaning flow. It was not just one empty Heineken bottle, but several empty bottles of beer and liquor from Heineken and Coronas to Hennessy and anything you could name. I stood up onto my feet in shock. What the hell was all of those bottles doing underneath my bed. And who the hell put them there? Walking to the kitchen, I quickly grabbed a trash bag and began to move our huge bed out of its position. As I began to grab each empty bottle of brew or liquor, I became overwhelmed. The bottles filled up one and a half large hefty trash bags. Was I living with an alcoholic? Why wouldn't China just throw the bottles away after using them? When did he find the time to drink all of this liquor? I was stumped. My entire day was consumed with my findings. I was living with a stranger and so was he.

As I continued cleaning the remainder of our apartment, I was in deep thought. I felt as though I was living with a man that I really didn't know. We had been together for almost twelve years and here I was discovering something new and not so pleasant about him. Thinking about his whereabouts, I checked the time. It was now 7pm and I had not heard from China so I sent him a Skytel message that read, "Where you at?"

"I'm in the city looking for a spot to throw my next weekly party. I'll be home in a few." China had been looking in Manhattan to have a weekly "after work" event. He had just completed the launch on his new line of watches and he wanted to find another source of revenue while waiting to get a return on his larger investment. The man was a hustler. He always had the ideas to keep it moving.

"What's a few? What time?" China never liked to give me specifics, but I wanted to know.

"Within the hour," he responded, and I was cool with that. For now, I hid the bags in the guest room/office closet. China rarely went into that closet and I needed to keep the evidence for my confrontation with him.

I began to prepare dinner, something I had not done in months. Turkey spaghetti with a tossed salad and garlic bread was going to be the dish for the night. I even pulled out a bottle of wine. I needed to relax. I rarely drank at home. I was only a social drinker. I would only drink if I was out at a party or lounge with a client. Setting the table with place mats and cloth napkins, the table looked romantic and pretty. I wanted to throw him off, switch things up a bit. China and I were starting to disconnect so I wanted to spice things up a bit.

Within the hour, China was home. Greeting me in the kitchen with a hug and kiss, he stated, "Whaaat? You cooking? Well if you want a new bag or jewelry, I ain't got it."

"Boy, I don't want anything. I just wanted to surprise you."

"That's thoughtful, but I'm not hungry. I ate a slice of pizza while I was out, but I'll sit with you until you are done." I couldn't even get mad at him. Grabbing something before coming home had become the norm for both of us. I was slipping.

"Oh. Ok." I was a little disappointed, but he did sit down to keep me company. In the apartment's entrance way, I could see China's belongings placed neatly onto our coat rack. His jacket and Louis Vuitton back pack hung on a hook. A brown paper bag peered out from the side pocket of his LV book bag. It was a bottle of something. I stared so hard that China turned to the direction of our apartment door.

"Faye's wedding is in a few weeks. You need to get a

suit and we need to determine how we are getting to DC"

"Oh, wow. It seems like yesterday when she got engaged!" He said. "Ok. I'ma pick something up on Friday after work when I get paid."

"Cool. I'ma meet you in the city to go shopping with you."

"You don't have to meet me. I'm good," he answered. This wasn't like China. I was always welcome to go anywhere and do anything with him. Now he was shutting me down. Shit was definitely different and I was so engulfed into my own life that I had stopped paying attention to him. So now, I was at full attention with him. Finishing up my food, China got up to grab my plate and started to the kitchen to clean up. I was impressed. He never lifted a finger to do anything domestic in the house. Taking out the trash was his only designated chore, but that didn't' bother me too much.

After finishing up in the kitchen, China grabbed his brown paper bag out of his book bag and headed back to the bedroom. At that very moment, I knew our relationship was over.

Looking back and jogging through my memory of China's movements, we had somehow managed to grow apart. I had been no angel and dealing with me had become more of a job to China. The fun loving and affectionate college boy I had fallen in love with had grown up. And though he still possessed those traits, his evolution into a man was no longer compatible with me. It had been one year since our engagement and nothing had been etched in stone. After 12 years of growing up together, encouraging each other, supporting each other's ideas, and loving each other, we parted ways. China has gone on to become a restaurant franchise owner and a men's accessories line designer. He is married with children and happy. Continued blessings.

With the breakup affecting my financial picture, I moved my business into the second bedroom, drew back on the daily ferry commute across the Hudson, committed to conference calls, and rocked out from there to maintain my lifestyle. I even hired a new assistant, Daina, who was based out of New Jersey as well.

Aside from that, I was emotionally disconnected from the world. After spending all of my 20s with China, it seemed as though it would take forever before I would get over the hurt of not having him around.

Chapter 13:
Baby D (2002)

Feeling the loneliness six months down the road after my breakup with China, I opted to hit the town with my client, On Air Personality Egypt and her manager Amber. The two had invited me on a radio promoted boat party in Weehawken, New Jersey where Egypt was the Host for the night's festivities. The night was hot. The sky was clear, the stars were bright, and as we sailed around the Statue of Liberty, a pleasantly plump guy walked out onto the deck and introduced himself as I was gazing at the moon.

His smile was magnetic and his eyelashes were hypnotizing. "Hi. It's a beautiful night and so are you," he smiled. Holding out his hand for me to shake it, he said, "My name is Mark."

"Hello." I smiled. "My name is Lynn." We had only been on the boat for 30 minutes and already, someone was approaching me. Don't get it twisted. I am good looking, but the men on the boat looked like they were shopping at a meat market. As Mark and I talked, Egypt worked all night entertaining guests on the mic while Amber networked for additional gigs for her client. Sailing up and down the Hudson, Mark and I talked and laughed non-stop. He was a real estate investor and a single father with three sons. It didn't dawn on us that four hours had come and gone until the boat docked back in Weehawken.

"I enjoyed our brief time together," Mark stated and I just laughed because of the time that had flown by.

"It was nice meeting you as well." I blushed.

"May I have your number? I'd love to take you out before the weekend is over if it's ok with you," he smiled. I gave him my number. Our chemistry was undeniable.

"Dang, Lynn!" Amber yelled over to me. You were missing in action all night, but from the looks of it, you may have met a nice catch," she smirked as Mark walked off. Mark was handsomely dressed in a nice tailored suit and open collared shirt. His coordination was on point and he smelled good.

"Yes. I think I did get a nice catch," I said and the two of us high-fived each other.

Our first date would be the very next morning. The two of us stayed up all night and talked on the phone. Our first stop was the Diner in Edgewater where we ate breakfast and walked up and down the river's walkway on the Hudson. We walked and talked and sat down on benches for breaks until it was almost dinnertime. Checking my phone, which had been placed on "silent," I noticed a few missed calls from my mom. "Excuse me for one second. I need to speak with my mom."

Dialing her number, she answered immediately, "Hey, Ma. What's up?"

"Papa Joe died. He died in his sleep this afternoon," she didn't hesitate to get the words out of her mouth. While I gasped for air, tears started to form in my eyes. "Lynn. Are you there?" my mom asked.

"Yes Mommy. I'm here." My grandfather had been ill for quite some time. My grandmother, Mommy Ethel had passed five years prior and the two had been up in age. Though I knew his time to meet God face to face was near, the reality of it happening still hurt. "When do you want me to come home?" I asked.

"Well, your cousin Ima-Eyen is going to take the bus down from Boston and meet up with you. So coordinate with her, but get down here as soon as possible." I let her know that I'd do what she requested, let her know that I loved her, and hung up. Mark had been standing closer to me than I had noticed so he knew I had received some bad news.

"Do you need anything?" he asked.

"No. I'm good. Just upset." I weakly responded. The two of us then sat down on a bench while I placed a call to my cousin to coordinate the travel. After working out the logistics with her, I dialed my mom back to inform her we'd be home within 24 hours and she was happy to hear that.

"I know you don't need anything, but it may be a bit much for you to drive. I'd love to offer you and your cousin round trip tickets to DC. That way you can take a load off and not have to concentrate on the road." I loved his suggestion and took him up on his offer. He was right. Driving would be too much on the two of us. Ima-Eyen and I were both extremely close to Papa Joe and I was appreciative of Mark's gesture.

Following my grandfather's funeral, it had been four months and Mark and I were still going strong, very strong. As I began to unpack my things, butterflies filled my stomach as Mark lifted up my long wavy black hair to kiss my neck. "I'm so happy that you've moved in with me," he whispered between the soft wet pecks on my neck. Putting my things down to turn around and face him, he kissed my lips. I hugged him tightly and then I... exhaled.

As one of the top hip-hop publicists in New York City, I

finally took a moment from my hectic schedule to focus on my personal life. Handling rap artists and planning huge events for award shows, my personal life had suffered tremendously over the past year as President of my own public relations and artist booking company.

Perched up on a cliff in West Orange, New Jersey our view of New York City was spectacular. With floor to ceiling windows there was no need for curtains or window treatments. The house sat so high up on Undercliff Terrace that neighbors could only look up to the house.

Hopping into my CLS 500, I headed to the store for some wine and trinkets to celebrate the move. Hearing the phone ring, I answered while simultaneously rolling my eyes. It was my mother. "Hi, Mommy," I answered in an annoyed tone since she had disrupted the mental notes I was taking of tonight's romantic plans.

"Hi, sweetheart. I just wanted to call and tell you that I love you, but I do not agree with this move." she hissed.

"Ok, Ma!" I responded abruptly. "This is like the 50th time you've mentioned this to me. I hear you. Ok?" I was sooo annoyed.

"Well, I just wanted to say it again. It's not too late to move back into your apartment. I will even foot the bill for the movers," she gestured.

"Mom. I will be fine. I will speak with you later. Ok? Mark and I have plans for the night so I need to get off of the phone. I love you. Goodbye." And I hung up the phone before even hearing her response.

Born and raised in Washington, DC to a divorced pair of socially elite parents, it was taboo to shack up with a man before marriage. Obviously my parents didn't recognize that times had changed and marriage was not regarded in the manner or fashion that my parents had grown accustomed to.

Getting settled into my new digs with my new sweetie, the two of us spent the majority of our days in and out of furniture stores and consulting with interior decorators on the overall style of our home.

When the house was up to par and presentable enough to start having guests over, Mark suggested, "Why don't we have a get together? You invite a few of your girlfriends over and I will invite a few of my friends over."

"Oh. That sounds nice. What do you have in mind?" I asked.

"We can just freestyle it. I can fix a few things for

everyone to nibble on and we can either order the fight, play board games, cards, or whatever happens to come up."

Walking over to Mark, I hugged him, kissed him on the lips and smiled. With a soft grip of my butt, I could tell he was excited, so I ran up the steps to grab my phone and called my friends.

Party day arrived and our friends started pouring in. It was a Sunday—Columbus Weekend in October to be exact. My girlfriends Ashaunna, Aisha, Katrina, Trina, and Joy stopped by. The night sky was clear and perfect. We could see the city's skyline from our windows and the view was amazing. We entertained well together.

Six months into living together, reality started to kick in. Everything wasn't all roses. My mom was right, but I wasn't about to admit that to her. Mark and I were not the couple.

Waking up feeling really low and drained, I went straight to the bathroom to relieve myself and brush my teeth. While hitting the corners of my mouth, I leaned into the mirror to check out my skin. My Vitaligo was getting worse. I was now looking like a raccoon. The pigmentation around my eyes was all white. I looked crazy. To add insult to injury, I was out of makeup and my money was also low. And I was too determined not to ask Mark for another thing.

As my cell phone rang, I skipped out of the bathroom to see who was calling. It was Daina. "Hey, Lynnie Pooh. How are you?" she asked.

"I'm good Baby D. What's up?" I asked.

"Awww... nothing. I was just seeing what you were up to. I didn't know if you had any plans for today cause I was going to stop by." She answered.

"Oh. Ok. Cool. I could use the company. What time you coming'?"

"I should be there in about two hours." She confirmed.

"Ok. See ya then." I said with a smile on my face.

Hanging up with a light smile on my face, the frown was fading. I had not seen Daina in months and though we had been speaking on the phone more frequently, I was really excited to see her. Looking at the clock, I clicked on BET to watch Pastor Creflo Dollar. Over the past two weeks, I had begun to make it a habit to watch him on TV. My spirits had been hitting an all time low so I figured a spiritual regiment might work.

As soon as the remote reached BET, I heard the announcer say, "We now bring you Dr. Dollar. The message is already in progress."

"Trouble don't last ALWAYS! Your mouth can burn off in one day, everything you've been dreaming of. Prosperity comes into your house by talking. Until you talk it, you can't take it. The Bible says, life and death are in the power of the tongue. Some can't say it with their mouth, cause it's not in their heart. If you speak negatively, you are creating negative thoughts and things. Proverbs 12:14 From the fruit of his lips with good things as surely as the work of his hands rewards him." Dr. Dollar was really preaching this morning. I mean... can I get an Amen? My spirits were starting to lift from his sermon.

Folding up the last bit of clean laundry, I tucked the towels into the linen closet and jumped in the shower. Washing quickly in case Daina arrived earlier than the projected time, I dried off and dressed in 15 minutes. I needed time to figure out my face. I was down to my last lil bit of makeup and I at least wanted to look presentable for her visit. I had makeup left in the corners of its container so I grabbed a clean Q-tip and dug into it. Gently placing my MAC studio fix onto my eyelids and around my eyes, I was impressed with the way the makeup always seemed to bring my skin back together. But who wanted to do this every day? Not me. Oh GOD. There's got to be a better way. I need a miracle for my skin now. And just as I threw the soiled Q-tips into the garbage, the doorbell rang.

"Heeeeyyyyyy, Baby D!" I opened the door and yelled.

"Hey, hey, hey! How are you?" Daina asked as we embraced each other.

"For _moi_?" I asked, noticing a slender gift bag.

"Oh yeah. I brought you some wine cause we need to celebrate." She cheered.

"What are we celebrating?" I asked.

"The re-launch of your company. Lynn you need to get back out there and make something happen. This whole fake house thing you got going' on ain't working for you or me." She hissed.

Taking the wine out of her hand, the two of us headed to the kitchen while I began to pull out some wine glasses, grapes, and potato chips.

"And where is Mark anyway?" Daina asked with an inquisitive look on her face.

"Who the hell knows. He probably went to go rob a bank cause bill collectors are calling left and right about the mortgage, the car notes, and everything else. I just don't understand how he can live like this. He has money here in the house to take care of everything. But he says that is his savings. So... go figure."

"Ok. Well guess what? You can let his ass drown in debt alone. It's not your debt. And you don't owe him anything," Daina hissed.

"So what's up? What's on your mind? 'Cause you look like you on a mission of some kind." I asked.

Grinning from ear to ear, she responded, "The VMAs are coming up next week in LA, Lynn! Let's go to LA. Seriously! You haven't been out there in a year and you look like you could use some sun. You've been trapped up here in west bo bo for months now. Enough is enough. Even if you aren't ready to get out there, then I am, so let's go. If you don't want to do PR anymore, then you can at least co-sign me. Besides, Dante' still needs a deal, so let's take him as well. This would be a great way to get him out there as well." Dante' was an R&B artist I had been grooming for quite some time. Though he had a lot of talent as a writer, labels weren't buying him as an artist. While the momentum to get him signed was dying down, we still pushed forward, but not with as much aggression.

Daina was his #1 fan.

"Alright fine. Say no more. I'm in." Now, the hard part was breaking the news to Mark who seemed to want to have a heart attack every time I wanted to go somewhere without him.

"Grrreat! I can't wait. I'm so excited! Lynn. This is what you need. And shooooot. This is what I need." Lifting her glass to toast, we then began to put together the itinerary while Daina ran down the list of events going on in LA that particular week.

After making plans for our trip, I walked Daina to our carport and saw her off. "Don't flake, Lynn." She turned back to say.

"I won't. I promise." I replied.

Later that night, Mark called to check in. "Wassup?" he asked.

"Nothing much. Daina set up a few A&R meetings for Dante' next week in LA, so I'ma fly out with them to make sure everything goes smoothly." I answered.

"Oh... aight. Cool. How much you need?" He asked.

"Oh. One of the labels is paying for it, so I'm good." I

lied. I just didn't want anything else from him for now. He was in too much control of the purse strings so I wanted to throw him a bone to let him know that I still had something more valuable than money—contacts.

"Oh. Good. I'll be home late tonight. Don't stay up and wait for me though. It will be really late." He said.

Hanging up the phone, I couldn't believe the conversation went that quick and smoothly. I was broke, but I wasn't busted and disgusted. I had a few dollars— and I do mean a few dollars left to my name so I went into that stash in order to make the trip happen.

The night before our trip, Daina called to check, confirm, and double check that we were still "on" for the trip. Reassuring her that I was still going, the two of us reminisced about our last trip together. We had gone to Florida with Rockwilder for a music convention and we had had a ball. Hanging up the phone, Mark walked into the room.

"What the fuck were you laughing about?" he asked.

"I wasn't laughing," I answered just to defuse any possible arguments.

Snatching the cell phone out of my hand, Mark started

scrolling through the phone.

"Give me my phone!" I screamed as my privacy was being violated.

"Who were you on the phone with? And why are you acting so guilty? It better not have been anotha nigga!" But not finding anything wrong on my screen, he tossed it back to me, grabbed what he was looking for out of his dresser drawer, and left back out again. This was becoming his normal routine—to scream, go to the dresser drawer, and leave. I had soon narrowed it down to the "Scream & Leave" tactic.

Arriving in LA, I breathed in the Los Angeles air (mostly known as smog), we stood outside waiting for our ride to scoop us up. Kitty, a college buddy and a now extremely good friend of Dante's was picking us up to take us to the hotel.

Honking the horn like a maniac everyone looked into the direction of the blue Maxima. Leaning on the horn and waving hard, we noticed Kitty burst out laughing and lugged our stuff over to her vehicle. "Hey Y'all!" Kitty screamed while hugging us simultaneously. We were overjoyed to see her. "And who is this thang with y'all?" It was sooo apparent that Kitty was a country girl from Washington, DC.

"Oh. This is Daina," I replied. "But you can call her Baby D cause that's what we all call her." Hugging her as to accept her as family, we all piled into the car and headed to the W Hotel in Westwood. Located in a residential neighborhood between Bel Air and Hollywood, the hotel was in a great location and not too far from Rodeo Drive.

"Kitty. After we check in, we have some time to kill. Will you take us to Roscoe's?" I asked.

"Oooh Yeah," Dante' butted in.

"No problem," Kitty responded.

Pulling up to the hotel, we checked in quickly, dropped our bags off in our rooms, and headed right back down to the car where Kitty patiently waited for us. Hurrying down the steps, we noticed the hotel's security guard leaning into Kitty's car, "Uuuuhhhh Ma'am. You've been sitting here for too long. You are going to have to move your car now." the security guard yelled out.

Looking at him, she politely responded, "Ok, sir. No problem. My friends are actually standing behind you, so we are leaving now." she replied.

"No. I need you to pull off now," he responded.

We all looked at him like he was crazy. "You mean you want me to pull off before they get into the car?" Kitty asked.

"Yes. Now!" he raised his voice as if he were a real police officer.

"Oh paleeease! Excuse me," and we all got into the car. "No need to take your job that seriously. I said we were moving," Kitty hissed. The security guard was looking as if he were getting ready to arrest us. "Ok extra sensitive security guy. We are leaving now." We all burst out in laughter and sped off. We couldn't believe this guy. What is it with security guards? Their egos are through the roof! From mall cops to club bouncers, there is a trait about these men that has to exude authority.

Arriving in front of Roscoe's, we pulled up, got out to get in line, and allowed Kitty to find a parking space. The line moved along quickly and before we knew it, we were in our seats and placing our orders. I ordered a sunset (lemonade and iced tea) along with three wings and a waffle. Roscoe's to me was like crack to a crack head. I can eat Roscoe's for breakfast, lunch, and dinner whenever I'm in LA. Following brunch, the four of us hit all of the shops and boutiques we can't normally find in NYC.

When Kitty dropped us back off at the hotel, the security guard was nowhere in sight. "Oh. I guess we scared him off!" Kitty yelled out. We all burst out in laughter looking around to see if he was in front.

Grabbing our shopping bags out of her trunk, we exchanged hugs and kisses and waved her off until her car disappeared into the distance. The three of us were exhausted. Leaning up against the wall, we waited for the elevator in the hotel lobby for what seemed like forever. Dante', Daina, myself and four other guys crammed into the sleek elevator. Clearly over capacity, no one was budging. The wait was so long that no one wanted to risk another ten minutes before getting to our rooms. On the ride up, my assistant notices one of the guys and she immediately introduced herself, Dante' and me to him. Kanye introduced himself and his three comrades.

"We are about to chill till the Reebok Party later tonight. The three of you are more than welcome to come up to my room and kick it," he mentioned as the elevator doors opened up for us to exit. I was the first one out of the elevator. "Ok. What's your room number?" Daina asked. Dang she bold. I just want to get to the room to pee. I ain't thinking' bout them nappy head negroes... fo real though.

As the doors were closing, one of the guys yelled out their room number. "Okaaayyyy..." Daina yelled back. "Giirrrrllll... do you know who that was?" Daina asked me. "Uuuuhhhh... no and I really don't care, Daina. I'm so tired and all I really want to do right now is pee," I whined.

"Oh Lynn paleeease! We don't have much time here. We only have two more day left here so we might as well make the most of our time." she begged.

"Oh... alright," I responded. I was just already over the whole LA thing. Mark had not called me. While we did speak, it was only when I picked up the phone to call him—only to be rushed off the phone. My sixth sense was kicked into full gear. I knew something was wrong. Daina was right. I did need to make a NEW move— and fast, but I just didn't have the energy.

Making a few minor adjustments to my gear and face to head upstairs with Daina and Dante', the two were already waiting for me at the door. "Y'all look like puppies waiting to go out for a walk." It was if the roles had been reversed. On the norm, I was the motivational one, the one who pushed everyone out of the door, the one making everyone else brush their problems off of their shoulders. But today, I was the one being motivated and I actually liked it.

Walking down the long corridor, Daina playfully placed an ice cube inside of Dante's shirt. It took him a second to figure out what was happening, but when he did, all hell broke loose. Daina was violently chased down the hallway. I was cracking up—as I had just passed Dante' my bottle of water. Threatening to douse her with the bottle, Daina called a truce and we got onto the elevator. Arriving to Kanye's room, the door was opened before we could knock. "Oh. Y'all made it," one of the guy's said. "Come on in. I was just heading out to get some ice."

His friends literally put on a show for us. As Kanye' laid down his entire Marketing strategy for his soon to be released album, "College Dropout," he then got up and performed "Jesus Walks" for us! He and his friend, Poet Malik Yusef, had a dance down packed and everything. They explained to us how the music video would be and how, "Jesus Walks," would soon break down stereotypical barriers in radio— and we believed every bit of it. Overall, I could really relate to his vision—as I had yet to obtain my Bachelor's Degree like him and have opted to take a path less chosen, the path of "Do What You Love and The Money Will Come."

In taking the time to exchange dialogue, we all hung out at Nelly's Reebok event. We were all laughing, joking, and vibing well. Loving our energy, Kanye' extended our stay and offered Dante' the opportunity to write and record with the Nappy Roots. Though that particular song did not come out, Kanye's kindness to pay it forward motivated the three of us to move forward in our future endeavors.

Arriving back in New Jersey, I was now excited to get things going again. However, when I walked into Mark's house, the negative energy started to smother me. Mark was not at home when I arrived, but the thought of his return made me cringe. So as I dragged my suitcase up the four stairs to our bedroom, I began to take notice of how junky the room looked. Taking notice of the bed, the sheets were strewn all over the place. It was as if there was a rush to leave or it appeared as if a fight had broken out. Walking closer to the bed I gasped. A pair of pink laced panties peered out of the pillow case. And guess what? You got that right. They were NOT mine. I started to hyperventilate before my phone started to ring. It was Ashaunna. "Lynn. Is that you? Are you ok?" my long time colleague asked me. I had not spoken to Ashaunna since my last get together at Mark's.

"No. I'm not ok Ashaunna. Can I call you back?"

"Yeah. Ok." And she hung up.

Wiping the tears from my face, I began to clean up the

wrecked bedroom. A huge hole was in the wall with my heels from Aldo sticking out of it. It was time to go. But I had isolated myself so much from the world that I didn't know who or what to turn to.

The doorbell rang. Not knowing who it could be, I threw all of the rubbage into our bedroom and closed the door. Ding dong ding dong ding dong, the bell kept ringing. Hurrying to see where the fire was, I looked through the stained glass door to see Ashaunna's face peering back at me. "I'm sorry Lynn. This isn't like me to just show up at your door but I was worried about you. You sounded like you were in trouble, and from the looks of things, you are in trouble."

Just as I gestured for her to come into the house, Mark entered from the back door with a frazzled look on his face. He had an evil look in his eye. Heading up to the bedroom, I followed him. "Hello. How are you? Is everything ok? 'Cause by the looks of things, you had a busy week while I was gone. He didn't look at me or answer me. He just walked over to his dresser drawer and flung it open in a rage. This startled me, but I didn't say another word. He looked me in the eye and said, "Yeah. I was busy, but so were you," and he left the house. What the hell did he mean by that? Slamming the door behind him, I went down to finish speaking to Ashaunna.

"I'm sorry, Ashaunna. I just got back from LA and you just walked into the middle of some drama."

"Oh it's ok, Lynn," she replied. I went on to tell Ashaunna from beginning to end about my life with Mark and how it had gradually become verbally and emotionally abusive over the past year. "Lynn, you are more than welcome to stay with me until you can get on your own two feet. *Mi casa* is *su casa*," she said smilingly.

Though I didn't take her up on her offer, I did thank her, asked her to communicate with me more often, and began to pick up the pieces of my life. It was during this time I began to really listen to the words Dr. Creflo A. Dollar was speaking on the TV screen. Over the years, I would often listen to his sermons, attend church, and gain some inspiration and motivation, but I didn't know how to apply the word to the things I needed in this world. I yearned for more from God. "To obtain the things you need in this world, you must find the scripture in the Bible that applies to your need. You must locate the words, read the words; meditate on the words; and then speak the words that apply to your situation," he said during the sermon entitled, "Receiving the Manifestations From God." "For example, if you have been diagnosed with Cancer, then you search the scriptures for healing. You still do your due diligence of going to the doctor and seek medical attention, but you also lean on God's word and his promises. So the scripture, by the stripes of Jesus ye are healed would apply to a situation such as this." Dollar taught.

At that very moment, a light bulb lit up inside of me and I was on fire for God. I listed all of the things I needed, such as my own apartment, my own car, a better business, and peace. I then went to the back of the bible where a concordance was located to find those key words. From there, I flipped to the pages where those scriptures were printed and jotted them down in a notebook. I read those scriptures, meditated on those scriptures, and repeated those scriptures day and night until all of the things I wanted in life had manifested. To this day, I still do the same thing. My list is continuously changing and being updated but the practice is still the same. Every day presents new challenges and I stick to the word every time. It's the only thing that works for me. At the end of the day, when the Student is ready, the Teacher (God) appears.

Chapter 14:
Wu-Tang Clan (2004)

The first step to getting back on my feet was to get out of the house. Ashaunna had scheduled an interview for me at the Rza's recording studio in the city where I was to become the Director of Operations.

"Hey, Lynn. So I set the interview up for tomorrow at 2pm," Ashaunna mentioned over the phone.

"Oh. Ok. What should I wear? I mean I know it's a studio, but should I dress corporate? And is there anything in particular I should be mindful of?" My questions started rambling. I was full of nervous energy.

"Girrrl, no. Lynn. Just be yourself. Sell yourself and you will be all good," she replied.

Arriving the next day to the plush studio located on Thirty-Fourth Street in midtown, I was a few minutes late. As the doorman asked me to sign in, he then instructed me to the correct floor.

When I arrived to the studio's door, I rang the doorbell and a light skinned slender brother with a Caesar haircut let me in. "Hi Lynn. I'm Divine. Nice to meet you." Divine had no smile on his face and he looked soooo serious. This made me nervous, but still in all I shook his hand, walked into the studio and cracked a light smile.

To my surprise, Divine turned out to be extremely nice; modest; and down to earth. His no nonsense facade was just a front. "This is our private lounge area," he said as I was being taken on a guided tour. "We have two bathrooms and one bedroom. The Studio's main feature is this updated open area kitchen and exposed brick loft style space that goes perfectly with our antique pool table."

"This is nice," I responded. And that was real 'cause the studio was extremely nice. Divine took pride in his brother Rza's studio and I didn't blame him.

"So basically, the job is yours if you want it. I'm not paying much; however, Ashaunna did tell me you are trying to get your business back up so I can let you rock and I'll pay you five hundred dollars per week plus any commission off of any bookings." Divine said.

"Bet," I smiled and we shook hands. The interview went smoothly with Divine. My job was to book studio time for upscale clients in need of "private" recording sessions. The studio was off the chain. It was very modern and a bit ahead of its time. Located on Thirty-Fourth Street between Tenth and Eleventh Avenues, the twenty-five hundred square foot condo had been converted into a state of the art recording studio equipped with a one bedroom suite; two plush lounges; a pool table; access to the roof top patio; and a magnificent view of the city. The main attraction to the space was not just the equipment. It was the ambiance that made the space special. Granite counter tops; a juke box; plush pool table; and a wide open space with a loft style feel was what often captured visitors. I had more success booking the space out for events than studio time.

Clients such as Grammy Award winning music producers Rockwilder and Chucky Thompson often booked out the space for their recording needs when Rza was not locking out the studio time to record music for soundtracks. Working out of the studio was a great jumpstart to getting my business back to basics; however, it wasn't easy.

The commute to the studio from New Jersey wasn't easy either. I had to get up extremely early in the morning to have Mark drop me off at the bus stop. Even though our relationship wasn't on the best of terms, he was very supportive of my new-found energy, but he didn't know that I was using and storing my energy to get away from him.

Three months into the new position at the studio, I was really starting to catch a stride.

"Hey, Lynn." Divine said.

"Hey, Divine. What's up? How are ya?" I asked.

"I'm doing well. Listen. Rza and I are thinking about selling the studio. He's rarely ever here now. He's been getting so much work on the west coast from working on soundtracks that it no longer makes since for us to hold on to the studio." he replied.

"Right. I understand where you are coming from and I kinda figured that," I responded. When they brought me in to start renting out the studio, I could tell that it was once Rza's home away from home. The idea of renting out the studio had come about since he was no longer occupying the space as much as he used to.

"Yep. So if you know of anyone interested in purchasing a space such as this, let me know. We are looking for $1.2 million and of course we are willing to pay you a commission on the sale." Divine was Rza's older brother and Manager. He often ran his brother's day to day business and any lingering business from the infamous Wu-Tang Clan. Talks of a reunion were in the works and Divine was one of the persons spear heading the reunion.

"Ok. Cool," and I immediately started to look for someone who would be interested in purchasing the space. Picking up the phone to call Ashaunna, she provided me with a few suggestions on who may be interested. Around this time, Ashaunna was the General Manger for Full Surface Records, the record label owned and operated by music producer Swizz Beatz. "You know what? Swizz may be interested in purchasing a studio space. I will ask him." said Ashaunna.

"Ok. Just let me know. As you know, we can go half on this commission thingy," I offered.

"Oh, but of course," Ashaunna replied and we hung up from each other.

The days were starting to get longer and the summer was now in full affect. The commute to the city was not as brutal and standing at the bus stop early in the AM was no longer a bummer. Business was picking up at the studio and with HobbieCom, and as my business started to pick up, Mark started to tighten the purse strings even more. For every dollar I made, I had to make it stretch further. He went from paying my commuting costs to not paying for anything and that was almost three hundred fifty dollars a month. Already, I had signed on Chucky Thompson's DC based record label and internationally known, DJ L for public relations services. The retainers were low, but I was determined to make it. The commute, my cell phone bill, food, and day to day upkeep of myself was all I was able to do. I was making things work and Mark was noticing.

He was noticing so much that he even got back into me again, but I wasn't interested. I was on a mission and I was almost out of there. "Hey, wanna go out to a comedy club tonight?" he asked. "The cast from the Dave Chappelle Show will be there tonight." I hated comedy clubs but for the sake of keeping some type of peace in the house, I agreed to go.

Leaving the office a little earlier than normal, I took an early bus home so that I could shower and get dressed for our night out. I was not looking forward to the night, but I deemed it necessary to put on a good face since I was still living under his roof. "Hey," Mark said as I stepped into the house. "Hey. How are you? How was your day?" I asked—not that I even really cared. It was becoming more and more unclear every day as to what Mark actually did for a living but since I no longer cared to know, I just kept the conversation and questions very basic and general.

"Oh. My day was good," he smiled back at me. There was something soft and reminiscent about his smile. It was the very same smile I had fallen in love with. Was Mark changing and coming around? I had no idea, but all I knew was that I needed to stay the course.

"Ok. Great. I'ma shower and change up a bit."

"Cool. I'ma run out real quick. I'll be back in one hour to pick you up. Is that cool?"

"Yep. Sounds good to me," I yelled back at him—as I was already in our bedroom. Turning on the shower to get the water warmed up, I walked into our huge walk-in closet to select something to wear. Pulling out some sleek black slacks and a simple blouse (my trademark), I then pulled out some thin Gucci sling backs and laid them out onto the bed. I was starting to get excited a bit about going out. Since I was never a night person, it often took a bit more energy for me to gear up and hit the streets. That was definitely a downside to my position. A publicist is supposed to be versatile with timing; however, my body and I didn't often agree with that pre-requisite. After Ten, I was often a zombie—I mean I was always found fast asleep somewhere. I was never of any use to anyone after 10pm.

Jumping in the shower, it was now 7:30pm and I was already starting to get a little tired, but I was determined to kick up the energy. By the time 8:45pm rolled around, I was dressed and napping lightly on top of our still made up bed when Mark walked in. "Oh Boy. You still want to go?" he asked me. With a sound of disappointment in his voice I jumped up and said, "Yep! I'm ready. I was just taking a quick cat nap until you came back." I was beat and I hoped to continue the front till we made it back home.

"Ok then. Let's get going. It starts at 9pm." Grabbing my purse, I double checked myself in the mirror and headed out to the car port. The night was nice and brisk. As we pulled out of the driveway, Mike slipped on R. Kelly's CHOCOLATE FACTORY album and "You Made Me Love You" started blaring through the speakers. Despite all of the drama surrounding this man, his music was undeniably addictive. R. Kelly has a song for just about every mood. Followed by that was another song entitled, "Forever" and when that song came on, Mark grabbed my hand—as if to extend an olive branch for the night. "Oh no he didn't? I muffled to myself. It'll be a cold day in hell before he is ever going to get any of this again, but I just squeezed his hand back and went along with the "pretend game."

When we arrived at Rascals Comedy club in Montclair, we noticed that the parking lot was packed. The valet attendant flagged us towards his direction and Mark steered over to him. As one attendant opened my door, another opened Mark's door and handed him a ticket. We proceeded to the club's entrance hand in hand. Getting seated quickly to our table, we placed our food and drink orders—as waitresses often rushed orders at clubs such as these because there was always a food/drink minimum for purchase. The first act arrived onto the stage and he was hilarious. Contrary to what I wanted to do, my body was not responding to any of the jokes or the atmosphere, the Amaretto Sour I was drinking became more of a muscle relaxer than a stimulator and the booth we were sitting in shortly turned into a sofa where I proceeded to lean more and more into it. Relationships, sex, children, and family members are often the topics of discussion for comics, and as the night moved on slowly, I started to nod, though Mark seemed to really be enjoying himself.

By the end of the night, Mark was nudging me to wake up. With a disgusted look on his face, I could tell that he was heated I had fallen asleep. I was upset with myself as well because I really wanted to make a conscious effort to stay awake. Reaching for his hand, he snatched it away and handed me the keys. "You drive since you've had time to take a nap," he snapped. And I didn't even bother to argue with him. I took the keys, placed them into the ignition and headed home. The night chill and Mark's coldness woke me up enough to drive. It wasn't five minutes into

the drive before he started to go "in" on me. "I mean....
You couldn't stay awake for one more hour—sixty more
minutes? Damn Lynn".

"I'm so sorry. I don't know what came over me. I guess
I was extremely tired. I apologize for being rude," I
responded.

"Whatever. That shit was embarrassing. The waitress
asked me if you were alright cause with the way you
were slumped over, she thought you were drunk," and
he kept on and on until we pulled into the driveway.
Turning off the engine, he grabbed my face so that I
could turn towards him. He was enraged. "Don't you
ever disrespect me like that again." Mark yelled.

"Ok. I said I was sorry. What more do you want me to
do?" I asked.

At that moment, Mark pulled a gun out on me and
cocked it to my face. "Bitch! I will blow your brains out!
Don't you ever disrespect me again! You got that?" he
asked.

I didn't even respond to him. I didn't even nod. I was
horrified to say the least and my heart had just about
jumped out of my chest. So when he withdrew the gun
from my face, I jumped out of the car and ran down the
street. I don't know how I managed to get to the

Dunkin Donuts on Northfield Avenue in West Orange. It was easily a mile and a half away from the house, but I made it. And once I got there, I pulled out my cell phone.

Just then... my phone rang. It was Ashaunna. I was sobbing and she could barely understand anything I was saying. A Dunkin Donuts employee walked over to me and took the phone from my ear. "Hello. This young lady is here at the Dunkin Donuts on Northfield. Oh. Ok. Ok." And he hung up from her.

Fifteen minutes later, Ashaunna pulled up in her truck and I climbed in. Not even asking me what happened, she drove off, she just lead me up to her apartment in Hackensack, handed me some pajamas, and I climbed into bed.

The next morning I woke up in a daze. My head was pounding and the thought of last night's drama started coming back to me. Sitting up in the bed, I reached for my phone, which was laid neatly onto the nightstand. I had thirty missed calls. Twenty-five of them were from Mark, a few from Joy, and the others were from the Studio. Joy and I had managed to maintain a close friendship after running into each other during my move to Edgewater.

Reaching out and re-connecting with my mother, I told her everything that had transpired over the time I was with Mark. During my time with him, I had alienated myself from my close friends and family—even Kim. Never the less, I was welcomed back with open arms. When Ashaunna returned home from work, I took her up on her original offer. For four months, I shared a queen-sized bed in a well decorated one bedroom apartment with her in Hackensack, New Jersey.

"Girl, guess what?! There is a building behind my complex in Edgewater, right? And they have a one bedroom apartment for rent," Joy blurted out anxiously over the telephone. It had been six months and I was still staying with Ashaunna.

"Oh... ok," I replied as if Joy had totally disregarded our previous conversation about my bad credit and my inability to apply and get approval for a decent apartment. My ego was shot and my spirit was bruised but I had the faith of a mustard seed at this point.

"Anyway! I called the number on the building, met with the Landlord, and I saw the apartment," she exclaimed. Wondering just where Joy was headed with that mouthful of information, Joy went on to say, "Girl! I got you an apartment!! I just kept it funky with the Landlord. I just told him about you and your situation and he says that if he gets a good vibe from you then you can have it!!! The only catch is that you'd have to give him three months rent in advance. But we can cross that bridge when we get to it." Joy assured.

"What!!!!?"I asked in excitement. I jumped out of my seat and dropped the phone in excitement. Picking the phone up from off of the floor, I quickly checked to see if Joy was still on the line.

"Lynn? Lynn! Lynn? Are you there?"

"Yes! Now repeat what you just said. 'Cause I had dropped the phone"

"Girl! I basically got you an apartment right across the street from me! All you have to do is meet up with me tomorrow at 1pm and I will take you to see it and introduce you to the Landlord. It's all good girl!" Joy proclaimed.

"Ok! Thank you," I said in shock. "I will see you tomorrow. Goodnight." Hanging up the phone I was in disbelief. My phone rang again.

"Girl! I'm NOT playing. I am for real. So I better see you tomorrow." Joy repeated.

Laughing out loud, I responded, "I will be there!"

Curled up on my couch in my new place, I started to look at the annual VMA Show on MTV. Daina had become a prime example that with sheer determination, you can make it. It had been a full year that she had been working as Kanye's independent publicist.

So it came as no surprise when two years later, as I ritually watched all of the Award Shows in 2004, Kanye was the talk of them all. My point is that Kanye had a vision. Long before my assistant, artist, and I knew him, he had a vision. He talked about his vision when he met us. He made us see his vision and touch his vision. Having him share his vision with us was inspiring and to this day it is more so motivating because I saw his dreams come true first hand. He spoke his dream into a reality.

Chapter 15:
Cam'Ron

Getting my regular weekly car wash at the Celebrity Car Wash in Edgewater sans Armorall on the tires, someone nudged me while I was intensely watching the workers wipe down the car windows. Looking up to focus on the nudge, I noticed Big Joe staring down at me. The car wash was the "who's who" of celebrities and their cars on River Road.

"Hey! What's up Big Joe?" I had not seen Big Joe since the two of us worked together at Don Pooh Entertainment. Big Joe, whose real name is Joseph Sherman, stood at six feet five inches and weighed damn near three hundred pounds. Similar in build to actor, Michael Clarke Duncan from the movie *The Green Mile*, Joe's physique was no joke. Nobody messed with him—I mean nobody.

"Nothing. What's up baby girl? What you been up to?" he asked while leaning in to give me a hug. Joe had worked for Don Pooh as Foxy Brown's bodyguard.

Hugging him back I sighed, "I'm still doing PR."

"Really?" he asked.

"Yep. Why what's up?" I asked 'cause I was in need of additional clients.

"I'm now managing The Diplomats, you know, DipSet." Joe replied.

"Oh really? Wow! From bodyguard to manager. I hear that!" I congratulated.

"Yeah. Matter of fact, I'ma give you this address. I don't know what you are doing tomorrow, but stop by and meet the newest member, Juelz Santana. He's really hot and I need you to help me get him off the ground. Plus you are already familiar with Cam, so you good." Taking down the address on a napkin, I also jotted down Joe's number.

The next day, I hit Joe up early to confirm our meeting at the studio. "Hey, Joe. This is Lynn. We still good for today?"

"Hell yeah. Matter of fact, some of the staff members from Def Jam will be there as well. So this would be a great introduction with the marketing rep, who will be in charge of Juelz's project." Joe replied.

"Ok. Cool. I'll see you later." I waved.

As the day moved on closer to our meeting time, I

reminisced on my days of working with Pooh, Joe, and Cam'ron. I had grown up and matured professionally so much since then, and I was looking forward to working with my peers again to share my growth as a Publicist.

Driving to the studio, I spotted the Pizza Hut and Nail Salon Joe told me to look out for. Then I pulled into the back of the nail salon where several guys were standing outside laughing and joking. Noticing Joe, he guided me into a parking space. I parked, took a deep breath, and exited my vehicle. "Hey! I'm here! Hello everyone!" I said with enthusiasm and a smiley face.

"Hi. Hello. Hey," were all of the responses I received back from the guys.

"Lynn. This is Juelz and this is his Road Manager and Brother, Twin." Looking up at them, I couldn't initially tell the difference between the two.

Extending my hand to shake Juelz's hand, I then asked, "Are you guys twins?"

Shaking Twin's hand, he smiled back and said, "Nah. We just look a lot alike." The two were nice. Their energy was good and though I was already comfortable, their smiles welcomed me into their lives. Twin and Juelz were the same exact height; however, over time, I eventually got the hang of their differences. Juelz was slimmer. Twin's face was rounder and he was slightly heavier than his little brother; however they both rocked the same goofy smile and dimple.

"Let's get started," Joe said. We entered Juelz's recording studio, located at the borderline between Teaneck and Bergenfield, New Jersey. It was nice and it smelled of new paint. The walls were painted red while the couches were black. Surprisingly, for a studio, it was neat and clean. Photos of Juelz along with the other DipSet members flanked his walls. Roc-A-Wear posters of Juelz posing with his son stood out most. It was apparent in the photo that he was in love with his son, and as I stopped to stare at it, Twin proudly said, "That's my Brother and my Nephew Juju. He was a newborn in that photo, but now he's almost two." As they continued to escort me to a sitting area, Joe doubled back to the door. "I'll be right back. I think some of the staff members from Def Jam have arrived." Joe said.

As I sat quietly with Twin and Juelz, Joe was back at the door within a minute with two of Def Jam's finest, Amber Noble and Shari Bryant. The two stood in the doorway and I immediately stood up to greet them. I had known Amber a few years already. She managed on air personality, Egypt. The two were my neighbors in Edgewater and clients when Egypt was a radio personality for WBLS. So I was happy to see her and to know that we could possibly be working together again. "Oh. Wow. Lynn is the publicist you are referring!?" Amber mentioned. "Done deal. I already know her work ethic so I'm cool with it." she confirmed.

Joe, Twin, and Juelz were all smiles. The meeting was off to a great start, and as the seven of us sat down to meet, Shari whipped out her note pad while Amber started to fire away at questions for Juelz. "Basically, we want to get the concept of the album down on paper so we can come up with a Marketing Plan," stated Amber. Shari was quiet. Even though the guys seemed to be more familiar with Shari, she still sat back in the cut and took notes. It was obvious that she was playing her position and I admired that.

"Basically, I want to call the album 'WHAT THE GAME'S BEEN MISSIN'" stated Juelz. "Because I am what the game's been missing."

I thought to myself, "Alrighty then." Juelz wasn't cocky, but he was confident, and if he didn't believe it, then nobody else would. So he had my attention. He had the entire concept of his album along with the sequence of the songs laid out in his head. It was obvious that he had been waiting for this moment to get it all out—and he did.

By the time the two-hour meeting ended, we were all clear and on the same page with the concept, marketing strategy, and release date of his album. Amber, Joe, and I even worked out my retainer agreement and start date. Today was a good day— nah... make that a great day! And as I headed to my car with Joe, I thanked everyone and acknowledged that it was nice meeting them. "Thanks so much Joe. I really appreciate this and I can't wait to work on Juelz's project." I beamed.

"No problem, but listen, even though I worked out the retainer through Def Jam, I need you to handle the PR with that fee for all of the DipSet members. I'm out here trying to get my hustle on and I need you to look out for the brand with that budget. That's got to get done." said Joe.

"Say no more. I'll do it." The budget Def Jam was paying was definitely enough for me to handle the group. Besides, their projects were not even coming out simultaneously. So that was no problem.

"And since their projects are spread apart, I will need your assistance with their performance contracts. I'm on the road every weekend with the guys and I'm too busy to get the documents out in a timely manner. I have the template. You just need to fill in the information I provide you and then send it off to the promoter. Ok?" he asked.

"Gotcha. I got it. You are really milking this cow, Joe. But it's all good. There's a lot of positive energy going on so I'm with it." I replied.

"I know it may seem like a lot, but I got you. I just need you to have my back," he said back to me in the most serious of tones. Big Joe was known to be an intimidator, but I was nowhere near threatened. To me, he was like a monster on the outside with the heart of a puppy, loveable. His mob type stare didn't intimidate me. Besides, I knew what I was signing up for and I was all for it.

As the days turned into weeks and weeks turned into months, I was already four months into the swing of things with Joe and DipSet. Everything was going smoothly. I had met with each member on several occasions, but hands down, Juelz had become my favorite. His energy and drive forced everyone around him to be the best they could be. He would never take "no" for an answer and I couldn't fault him for it. His single, "Mic Check" was blasting all over the radio and his follow up single, "The Whistle Song" was starting to take off. His musical momentum was right on target for his album's release date.

In addition to working with Juelz, I had gotten the hang

of handling the performance contracts and occasionally, I would even fly out and/or drive to the shows if Joe needed extra help with the guys. Often times, DipSet members would be booked separately all over the country.

With one particular upcoming performance in DC during Howard's Homecoming weekend, I was definitely down. It was my hometown and my alma mater. I was too psyched. Diamond, Twin's girlfriend and I had become good friends in a few short months, so she was down to keep me company on the drive to DC.

Diamond was a thick light skinned Puerto Rican from Harlem. She and Twin met months prior at a club in Manhattan and the two had been connected at the hip ever since. So in our day to day dealings, she was always a female I could chat with between Juelz's media interviews at the studio.

Arriving in my hometown of DC, I was excited about being home and being able to floss at my alma mater's homecoming with the hottest rappers on the planet.

Shoot... this is a great look for me.

As my phone started to ring off the hook, I only responded to calls I recognized and/or cared to answer. Everyone wanted the opportunity to walk into the club with me, but I knew it would be hectic so I didn't entertain that thought except for my girl, Alecia who'd more than likely have to work anyway. She was my DC club buddy. If I was at home and wanting to party, she was the connect. Her family owned various nightclubs throughout the Adams Morgan area of DC for years—particularly Kilimanjaro's, a world-renowned Caribbean nightclub.

Traffic in DC was bumper to bumper. Georgia Avenue, the main strip capturing the entire length of the city was one huge block party with students and locals jumping in and out of cars while smoking and drinking.

Frustrated with the traffic, we dipped off to a side street to catch the drive-thru of Wendy's. The line was outrageous. Inching up slowly to the order window, almost an hour had gone by before the two of us got back to the hotel and started to get dressed. Dragging slowly to make it to the lobby for Juelz's performance at Kili's Kafe we were both too tired to do anything.

With a knock on the door, Twin came in to check on us. "Yo, I don't know if y'all still wanna roll with us tonight. Niggaz are in these streets acting crazy. There are just too many people out tonight. So if y'all roll, throw on some sneakers or something so you can keep up. I don't have time for y'all to be looking' cute cause if something pops off, I need to know that y'all are good" Twin barked.

"Yeah... ok," Diamond responded. "I'm tired anyway." she said.

"I'm beat myself. Y'all should be good though. My cousin Alecia will be there. You got her number, right? And if anything, call my phone," I yawned.

"Aight. Bet." he said.

Undressing and grabbing the remote, I scrolled down the TV Guide Channel while Diamond wrapped her hair to go to bed. Turning to watch Bishop T.D. Jakes, he began to preach on "Yielding to the Holy Spirit."

"Sometimes you gotta pay attention to what the Holy Spirit is telling you. Slow down. And before you make any moves, just ask Him what he wants you to do." Nodding my head to agree with what the Bishop was saying, I listened intensely to his entire message. I was starting to get increasingly intrigued with messages about the Holy Spirit and wanted to learn more about this third part of the Trinity (Father, Son, and the Holy Spirit). Clicking off the TV and scooting down in the bed to really get some sleep, the hotel phone rang. It was Twin. "Yo! It's all good here. Come over here. They are taking care of us and the drinks are flowwwwwing. Ya dig?"

"Oh, Please. We are in the bed sleep", I replied.

"Oh! You gotta get up and come. Matter of fact, pack your stuff up cause we are going to get right on the road from here. I mean we can stay til tomorrow, but the club is closer to the highway than the hotel. You feel me?", I asked.

"Awww man. I'm so beat. But okay. We're coming." Waking Diamond up to inform her of the night's re-mix, she was game. Throwing back on the clothes we originally intended to wear, the two of us zipped up our bags, completed a quick hotel check-out, and headed to the car.

It was 1am and the streets were still packed in Northwest, DC It looked more like Mardi Gras than Howard Homecoming and yet the energy about Homecoming was different. What used to be a school event was now a National Event. Not just students, but people from all walks of the party life flocked to DC for the weekend. Hotels were oversold and lines at clubs were wrapped around corners. And Georgia Avenue? Forget about it! It was a parking lot that spanned at least three miles. The night was dreary, damp, and cold.

By the time we arrived near the club, it was emptying out. As Diamond and I maneuvered through the back streets of DC, we hit New York Avenue and we were outta there! And just like Monopoly, we passed GO and did NOT collect the money. There was something eerie about the night. I would later come to learn that it was the Holy Spirit telling me to get out of town because as soon as we hit the city limits of Edgewater, New Jersey, our phones started ringing off the hook. Diamond's call was from Twin. He wanted to check in on us to get our whereabouts. My call was from Big Joe, "Yo! Where are you, Yo?"

"Uummmm.... I'm at home in my bed." I answered.

It then dawned on me that I had not even communicated to Big Joe to let him know I was leaving town. "What bed? Are you at your mother's house?" , Joe asked.

"Why all the questions though?" I asked. "I'm back in Jersey."

"Cam got shot last night." Joe yelled.

"Whaaaatttt!!???? Are you serious? Joe! Don't play with me! Y'all play too damn much." And I hung up the phone. Some things were just not to be played with and I had it up to my neck in practical jokes. So when my the cell phone rang again, I was ready to blast Joe. "Hello?"

"Lynn. Listen. I'm NOT playing!!!" Joe screamed to the top of his lungs.

"What!!!!!???" It was true. I had never seen Joe scream and or yell like this in my life. And he was always yelling or fussing about everything.

As the details started to unfold, Cam'ron had been shot after leaving H2O Nightclub within the city's limits by an unknown assailant. While Cam and his entourage in top-notch vehicles locked into New York Avenue's strip, filled with homecoming traffic, they had no choice but to chill out and move with the flow. As Cam approached a red light, a man holding a gun jumped out of an SUV and immediately started to fire off at him while he was sitting in his bright blue Lamborghini. Pointing the gun at the driver's window, the gunman let off a round of bullets that riddled the car's glass. With Cam'ron in the driver's seat and his best friend, Huddy, on the passenger side, the two escaped death by a narrow margin. With injuries to his wrist and hand, the two were able to duck into the car's compartment to shield themselves from further harm. Summed up as a car jacking gone completely wrong, only God could have stepped in to intervene with this robbery.

Checking immediately into Howard University's Hospital, the media started to swarm the building—wanting a statement.

"Hurry up and write the press release so that a statement can be issued," called Big Joe again. "The media is really starting to crowd the lobby of the hospital." As rumors started to quickly spread about Cam'ron's condition, I had to collect the facts, Cam and Huddy's side of the story, and then throw it all together. Just as I was putting the finishing touches on the paper and before he could call for yet the tenth time, I finished it. Servicing the press release immediately to all New York City and DC media outlets, it took no time for the "real" word to spread about the incident. Often artists are unable to tell their side of the story before the newspapers and other media outlets start to tell their own version of the story. So it was truly a blessing to get his point of view documented on paper before the word was created.

As the days went by, the story popped up in several publications, including the *Washington Post*. Though there was even a quote in there from me, I still didn't like the way my artist had been portrayed. I didn't even like the quote from Cam, which read, "I got shot and my album drops on November 22nd. We love Howard." I couldn't believe his quick statement. It was a shameless plug for his upcoming album, but at least he gave props to Howard University for having such an amazing weekend.

As the years rolled on, DC Police never found the shooter, but one thing was for sure, Cam continued to put out music with or without the Dips, and Huddy was his right hand.

Chapter 16:
Big Cat Records/ Gucci Mane

It was a hot spring day in late May of 2005. While holding the phone for a Sprint representative to come on the line, my other line chimed in. Looking at the caller ID, I didn't recognize the number, but I noticed it was from Atlanta. Clicking over, I answered in a rushed tone, "Hi. Lynn speaking. How may I help you?"

"Lynn? Girrlll... what's up? It's me, Vickie."

"Oh! Hey Girl. How are you?" I asked.

"Fine. Do you have a minute?" Vickie asked.

"I'm on the phone with Sprint. So can I call you back in few?" I replied.

"Girl. Can I hold? Cause I really need to speak with you." Vickie gestured.

"Ok. Cool. Hold on."

Clicking back over, I could hear the Sprint rep saying, "Hello. Hello. Hello."

"I'm here!" I yelled.

So after I blasted Sprint for partially disconnecting my cell for seventy-nine cents, I clicked back over to speak with Vickie, an old colleague from the Untertainment days.

"Sorry about that Vickie. Sprint was tryna disconnect my phone for seventy-nine cents. Can you believe that bull crap?" I asked.

Laughing out loud, "Girl... all these cell phone companies have lost their damn minds. Okay? Well girl, let me tell you why I'm calling." she chimed.

As Vickie went into her spill about how she was the General Manager for Big Cat Records, an indie record label based out of Atlanta, she went on to explain that they were in need of my services. She went on to explain how the label had started from humble beginnings by putting out compilation mix tapes and that they had signed their first artist, Gucci Mane. Going on and on about Gucci Mane, Vickie then went on to explain the DRAMA. "We have a major problem with this project. Though the single, "So Icy" featuring Young Jeezy is taking off, there is so much drama behind the record, it's unbelievable.

"Oh. That's great. The more drama, the more story angles, the more sales," I exclaimed.

"Well... if you want the drama, then the buck stops here."

Vickie went on to explain how the record originally belonged to Gucci Mane and how Young Jeezy was guaranteed a record deal provided that he could deliver the very same record as his own to Def Jam. Sitting down pretzel-style on my brown leather sofa, my eyes popped open when Vickie said, "And girl, don't you know dudes tried to rob Gucci while he was at his girlfriend's house over this damn song?"

"Reeeeaally? I asked.

"Well... tomorrow, Jacob is going to call you." Vickie said.

"Jacob? Jacob York?" I asked.

"Yeah girl. He's running the label." she said.

"Oh Lord! Now I really don't know Vickie. Jacob is too overbearing and besides, he may not even want me to do it once he realizes that you are recommending me. I mean. Did you forget that he and Leota fired me from Untertainment?" I had her recall.

"Girl hush yo mouf! Jacob is the one who told me to

give you a call!" she shouted.

Raising an eyebrow at the words that Vickie just spoke, I leaped up off of the couch and said, "Shut up! Are you serious?" I asked.

"Yep. They knew you were dope when they fired you. They just couldn't afford to keep you on payroll." Smiling at Vickie's comments, I did a quick flashback of the time when I was fired. Reflecting and questioning whether or not I was a good publicist at that time, it now all came together.

"Ok. So I will draft a plan and contract for you guys to look over. Once you've had a chance to go over everything, give me a call. I'm free anytime between twelve and four." I replied.

"Ok. Cool. And don't worry. This account will be easy. The song is hot and Gucci has a lot of charisma." Vickie assured.

"Ok. Thanks Vickie. And thanks for thinking of me." I said.

When I rolled over to shut off the alarm sounding from my phone, I hopped up sleepishly and headed to the bathroom. Switching on the light, I saw a centipede scurrying to a hidden shelter. Screaming to the top of my lungs, there wasn't much more I could take of my apartment. Every spring and fall, an average of three would be discovered daily. Shaking my head, I made a mad dash to the kitchen to get the bug spray. Why me? And not now, I have to get out of here. I always set my alarm to the exact number of minutes needed in order to shower, get dressed, and head out to the airport. But now that the centipede had impeded upon my time, I was way behind schedule. So opting to just brush my teeth and throw on my clothes, I left my hair doobie pinned up, grabbed the trash, my LV duffle bag, and headed out the door. As I hurried down the hallway to the steps that lead to the building's garage, I completed a mental check of all of the things needed for the business trip.

So many mixed thoughts ran through my mind as I headed to the airport. For one, what am I getting myself involved in? Gucci Mane had a single heating up the charts down in the A; however, there was drama. Pulling up to terminal C at Newark Airport, I parked in Short Term Parking. As I entered into the airport and headed towards a self-service kiosk, checking in was a breeze and so was the walk through security.

Arriving to the gate, I had a few minutes to spare before boarding the Delta flight to Atlanta. "Good morning ladies and gentlemen. We will be boarding flight 1322 in just a few minutes. The plane is currently pulling up at the gate now."

Reaching into my over stuffed carry-on, I grabbed all of the googled information my assistant Daina had pulled off of the net about the rapper. As I browsed the headlines of each page, the word MURDER stood out. As I began to read, the flight attendant made the announcement, "Good morning. We will now begin boarding passengers with small children and/or passengers needing extra assistance. First Class Passengers are also welcome at this time." As I stood up to board the plane, an African-American flight attendant stepped towards me as if to block me from walking any further, so I handed her my boarding pass. "Sweetheart. Have a seat until your row is called. We are only boarding First Class passengers and passengers needing assistance." she stated.

Looking at the lady with the biggest grin on my face, I cleared my throat, "Maybe you didn't notice, but I am in First Class ma'am." I smiled.

Tugging the ticket aggressively out of my hand, the lady didn't even bother to apologize. I didn't even wanna put out the energy to "go in" on her; however, as I started to head down the walkway to the plane, I turned and exclaimed, "And you have a blessed day!" Shaking my head, I sat down into my oversized seat and commenced to reading up on Gucci.

The flight was smooth. I slept the last hour there and was only awakened by the landing of the plane. As I exited the plane, I powered on my phone to call Vickie and let her know that I had arrived. Nerves started to hit me a little. Negative thinking started to cloud my mind, but I just rebuked that energy and kept it moving. Casting down negative images was an ongoing process for me and I was determined not to let the enemy have my mind.

Walking out into the Arrival Area, I stepped out into the ATL sun. It was early and already, it was scorching hot. I spotted Vickie immediately. Time had not changed her a bit. She was bling'd out and fabulous as usual. "OMG! Lynn. Look at you! You look great!" Vickie smiled.

"So do you!" I exclaimed. We then hugged and hopped quickly into her vehicle. It was too hot to chitchat in the heat. The ride to Big Cat Records was fast. Vickie and I talked nonstop on the way to the label. We had so much to catch up on. When I had last seen Vickie, she had gotten married and had a daughter. Now, she was single and separated, but still in all, she seemed to be happy.

When we pulled up into the record label's parking lot, I noticed other familiar company names that were strategically placed on the right side of each company's doorway.

As Vickie pulled her Mercedes into a reserved space, I got jittery. The thought of seeing Jacob after all these years brought back an old feeling of anxiety. I could hear Un saying, "You ain't shit." Again I knew I was the truth and that is why I was called. I casted down those negative thoughts. Walking around to Vickie's side of the car, she placed her arm onto my shoulder and said, "You will be fine. Girl, they need you!" And I was happy to receive the reassurance. Following her up a small ramp and into their office, Vickie opened the door and we stepped into a nicely decorated foyer. As she waited for the receptionist to come back to the desk and buzz us in, I walked around the small area to check out the life-size photos of each artist. Gucci Mane, Rasheeda, Buju Banton, and a few others I had never heard of aligned the wall.

Bzzzzzzzz...the door sounded and Vickie and I walked in. "Have a seat here in the conference room Lynn. I'ma go get Jacob and Cat. Help yourself to the snacks on the table and/or any of the sodas." she suggested.

"Ok. Thanks Vickie," I replied.

Reaching out to grab a Poland Spring water bottle, Jacob peered into the doorway. I immediately stood up to shake his hand, but he embraced me instead— like a brother would hug a sister. "Ms. Hobson! You look great. And I don't need to know how you've been because I've seen your movement. So let's just cut to the chase. Cat's not here. He had to meet with his attorney so I will just brief you a little later at dinner. For now, I will have Vickie give you a tour of the office and introduce you to our staff."

"Ok. It's great to see you as well." Jacob's energy was great. He pretty much looked the same though, just a few pounds heavier.

When Vickie and I pulled up to the restaurant, it looked more like a huge rustic, refurbished warehouse. Equipped with a circular driveway, the valet grabbed our doors before she could even put the Benz in Park. The doors to the restaurant were huge mahogany. The hostess quickly asked for our names and Vickie responded, "York." "Oh yes," the hostess exclaimed. "Mr. York is running a little late so please have a seat over in the bar area and he told me to let you know to help yourself to whatever you'd like." she said.

Nudging me with an impressive smirk we headed to the bar. The feminine-like waiter switched on over to us and took our orders. After placing our drink orders,

Vickie and I were able to catch up on more personal talk. Her daughter was now six years of age and she was separated from her husband who was still living in Brooklyn. She then went on to tell me how she was living in a cute complex in Lawrenceville, Georgia— right outside of Atlanta.

"So what's up with you, Lynn. You're looking fabulous. Are you and China still together?" Vickie asked.

"Girl no. We broke up three years ago. Long story. And I actually just got out of an abusive relationship." Looking in disbelief at me while sipping on her Apple Martini, I just nodded back to her as a confirmation to my words.

"Wow. Well congratulations for getting out of that. Are you okay?" she asked. "Girl. You know we've all been in some crazy situations before."

"Yeah. I'm fine. I've just chosen to be single for now. And I've just been concentrating on my career. HobbieCom is my boyfriend. It's going on one year and I am grateful for everything" I humbly replied.

The restaurant was very nice and chic. It looked as though we were dining in a tropical rain forest. Plants were structurally and architecturally hung from the ceiling and exotic flowers lined the tops of the booths to allow for privacy at each table. Slender light fixtures hung down and looked as if they were suspended in mid air. A wine wall gave it a cozy ambiance as well. In the center of the restaurant was a huge tropical flower arrangement that took up a quarter of the restaurant. It was clearly the focal point of the restaurant.

"This would be a great place to go on a date," I thought to myself.

Not even fifteen minutes into our conversation, Jacob walked in and towering over him was a six foot four, three hundred fifty pound wide bodyguard. Chocolate in complexion, I found it strange that he wore glasses. I mean, I have never seen security with four eyes before.

As Jacob hugged each of us, I nodded respectfully to security until, "Lynn. This is Big Cat. Cat, Lynn." Jacob introduced.

Oh Wow. He definitely is a Big Cat, more like Huge Cat. I mean... dang! He was big. Reaching out to extend his arm for a handshake, I did the same. His hands were super soft. I meant too soft, you know what I mean?

Signaling to the waitress that our party was complete, the four of us sat down. After ordering a quick round of drinks Jacob went into explaining to Cat the purpose of the meeting. "Well Cat, you know we need a publicist. So, I thought we'd call Lynn in. We've worked with her before and I think she's the best candidate for the job." pitched Jacob.

"Ok," Cat responded. "Tell me a little bit about yourself." I started to give my bio and the waitress came back to take our orders. Her timing was perfect— as I didn't want to be interrupted.

"Well I ..." and as I proceeded with my background, Cat listened tentatively. Jacob fumbled with his phone, and though Vickie was also listening, it was as if Cat and I were the only two at the table.

My business spiel was damn near memorized so this allotted me more mental room to analyze the "Big Man." Before meeting Cat, I was extremely nervous but when we sat down at our table, the jitters left me. His energy was calm, yet mysterious. Hiding behind his Cartier frames, I could see he was guarding his kind, gentle, lovable side. Though we were at a business meeting, I wanted to get to know him, personally.

Dinner breezed by and I landed the account before our main course arrived. The rest of our conversation was about current events and industry gossip. Big Cat didn't participate much in the table talk. However, the two of us sat directly across from each other so we had our own quiet conversation. He spoke to me with his eyes and his smile. His teeth were impeccable.

When the check came, Jacob immediately grabbed for it and said, "So Lynn. I know you are due to leave out in the AM but can you stay an extra day? We would like for you to meet Gucci and we'd also like to send you off with everything needed to successfully run the account. We can put you up at the Ritz in Buckhead." Gucci was due out on bail the next day so staying the extra day did make sense.

"Or you can stay with me," Vickie interjected. Vickie's memory was excellent. She remembered that I hated hotels.

"Ummmm... Yes. I can stay the extra day. Just let me make a few phone calls. And I'll opt to stay with Vickie," I replied. Yes. The Ritz Carlton was nice, but, I traveled so much that I was over all the hotel grandeur. I needed a home setting more often than none.

Towards the meeting's end, Vickie and I started on the drive out to Lawrenceville, a suburb of Atlanta where she and her daughter Kennedy lived. Located twenty minutes from Buckhead, the two of us caught up as Vickie began to ask about former employees from Untertainment who I still managed to keep in touch with.

Arriving at her apartment, I surveyed the complex and it was nice! It was a private gated community with a guard. The lawn was nicely manicured and the buildings were uniformly neat and new. I loved it already. "Oh Vickie! I like this already girl! You may have a hard time getting rid of me." The two of us laughed as she pulled into her designated parking space.

"You can stay as long as you'd like and visit as often as you like," she responded. Though Vickie and I were colleagues, we were also long lost friends. Vickie was instrumental in helping me to develop my spiritual life. She always encouraged me to have a personal relationship with God and I am ever thankful for her push.

When we got into her nicely decorated, summer themed apartment, I stepped out of the guest room and headed into the kitchen to continue talking to her. "Your apartment is lovely." It was cozy. From the furniture and the photo frames to the color of paint on the walls and the accessories, Vickie had her pad decked out. Her daughter, Kennedy's room was pinked out, just for a princess. She had already been tucked into bed and asleep by her babysitter when we got in.

As Vickie delved into her personal life, I came to find out that her fiancé' of two months had been missing for a little under thirty days—and from the sound of things, it was the norm. He had a substance abuse problem. So being engulfed in work and her daughter was the best way for her to cope. I understood. I couldn't necessarily relate to her situation, but I did understand.

"Soooo... Ms. Thang. Is it me or was Cat giving you the eye during our dinner meeting?" Vickie snickered.

I smiled wider than the Kool Aid Man. "Nah. It wasn't just you. I noticed it. He stared at me so much I was speechless, short of breath, and just damn near tongue tied."

"Oh Wow! That's crazy, Lynn. I do know that he is single and he has no kids." She smiled.

"Really? No baggage? That's rare. Normally some hoe would have trapped him by now. I mean, he's not the sexiest man alive, but there's something about that smile that just made me feel all warm inside."

"Are you serious? Well... you may have gotten yourself a package deal girl! A man and an account. Ha!" Vickie yelled out with laughter.

"I know. Right? I'm all for it. He seems to be different you know, not your typical executive. We'll see," I responded. As soon as I finished my sentence, Cat called my cell phone.

"Hi Ms. Hobson. Good evening. This is Cat. I was just calling to say that it was nice meeting you and that I hope you ladies made it in safely."

My eyes lit up and immediately Vickie knew who I was talking to. "Oh. Hey, Cat. Yes. It was nice meeting you as well. I'm super pumped about working with you and your artists. Thank you for the opportunity." I played it safe with my words, even though I really wanted to say something personal.

"You're more than welcome. There was so much positive energy coming from you and I look forward to working with you and getting to know you." Mmmhmmm. He was playing it safe as well, but I wasn't about to budge. What if my instincts were off? I wasn't about to play myself and lose the account before it started. Sheesh!

"Ok. Well thanks so much for calling. I guess I'll see you guys tomorrow." I was ending the call in a professional tone though I was growing disappointed at knowing that he had not said anything personal.

"No problem, but before I hang up. I just wanted to say that you are beautiful. I asked Jacob all about you. May I take you out tomorrow night for dinner after we are done with the day? I'd like to get to know you. I know we met under business circumstances, but there's something about you that I can't ignore." Cat said.

"Awwww... thanks so much for the nice complement. Dinner sounds good to me because the feelings are mutual." I just laid it all out on the line. Vickie was jumping and hopping quietly all over the kitchen. She was ecstatic about what she was hearing and so was I. While he was dishing it out, I was handing it right back to him on a silver platter and it felt good.

"Alright. Cool. Have a nice evening and I will see you tomorrow."

"Ok. Goodnight." and I hung up the phone. Lots of laughter came out of both of us. Vickie and I hopped around the kitchen like two elementary school girls playing 'ring around the rosy'. You would have thought one of us had won the lottery. Well at least I did feel that way. Heading to my room to go to bed early, I fell asleep with thoughts of Cat on my mind. He wasn't physically my type, but his smile and energy gave me a warmth like I had never felt before. I couldn't wait to see what the future had in store for us.

The next morning, Vickie woke me fairly early, "Good morning Sunshine," she said in a soft motherly tone. "It's 8am. I'm about to leave out and take Kennedy to school. I'm already dressed for the day. So you can go ahead and start getting washed up. When I return, I will just have some coffee and read my devotionals until you are ready to head out. Ok?"

"Morning Vickie. Ok. No Problem. I'll get up now. Can we stop at a McDonald's or Dunkin Donuts on the way into the city?"

"Of course. We will be in a bit of commuter's traffic so we can stop at either of your preferences before getting on the road." Vickie replied.

"Cool." I said. Vickie then closed my door and headed out. Showering and then dressing, I was antsy about the day. I was nervous about meeting this already infamous Gucci Mane and I was girlishly gitty at the thought of having dinner with Cat. Taking extra care with my hair and makeup, I prepped in a more detailed fashion for the day. When Vickie arrived, she approved the look and we were off to the city. "The Dunkin Donuts is off the beaten path, but we can stop at McDonald's. Is that Ok?" she asked.

"I'm fine with that." The day was hot and muggy. The expected temperature for the day was heading towards 95 degrees. Driving out of the McDonald's drive thru, I grabbed my bag and started grubbing right away. The traffic didn't bother me because I was starving. I ate very little the night before and the hunger pains had carried over.

As we pulled up to the Big Cat Records office, Cat and Jacob were sitting outside on the steps looking disgusted. Noticing the looks on their faces, Vickie asked, "What's up? What's wrong? Why the long faces?"

"It doesn't look like Gucci will be getting out today. The judge is backed up and though he made bail, it may be a day or two before he gets out," Jacob said. "So Lynn, let's just get started on our meeting. Unfortunately, you won't be able to meet Gucci today, but we will send you off with his music, bio, photos, your payment, and any promotional items you may need to get his PR push started."

"Ok. Cool. Let's just make the best of it," I replied. The two men stood up from the steps and we headed into the building where I was directed straight to the conference room. As Vickie invited me to sit, she darted out quickly to check her messages before things got underway. As the four of us strategized and came up with a plan of action, Gucci called into the label. The Receptionist announced over the intercom, "Gucci is on line one. Gucci is on line one."

Rushing to grab the phone, Jacob answered and immediately began to give Gucci the run down on me, his new publicist. With just minutes left to talk, I was able to speak briefly with my new client, "Hey Gucci. I've heard a lot of great things about you and I can't wait to meet you in person," I stated.

"Likewise. I'm excited about my debut album and I can't wait to put this all behind me," he replied, and before I could say anything else, the call dropped. Time was up and it wouldn't be until the next day that anyone would be able to speak with him again.

The rest of the meeting went smoothly. Jacob got up to shake my hand and welcomed me to the BC Team. Vickie hugged me and let me know that she needed to get to work. As Jacob and Vickie walked out of the narrow conference room simultaneously, I was left with Cat—staring at me across the table with that same smile that attracted me to him the night before. "Soooo Ms. Hobson. I guess it's just me and you," he said.

"Yep. I guess so." I smiled back.

"I figured we could grab some lunch instead of dinner

and then I'd take you to the airport around 6pm. If that's alright with you." Cat suggested.

"That sounds good to me," and the two of us got up and headed to the parking lot. My bag had already been transferred into his vehicle. As I headed to the passenger's side of his car, he reached to open the car door for me. He was a real gentleman. His old fashioned ways made me more attracted to him.

"So what do you have a taste for?", he asked. "I know of a great seafood spot, Italian spot, or a steak place."

"The steak place sounds tasty to me," I giggled. When Cat had asked me what I had a taste for, we were pulling out of the parking lot. When I replied, he grabbed my hand gently and drove off.

"The steak place it is!" The valet greeted us upon arrival. The waitstaff and the valet employees all seemed to be extremely familiar with Cat and this was a good thing to me. It meant that he enjoyed fine dining and he was an excellent tipper. Classy!

We both sat down hungry. I was already familiar with the menu—because the same restaurant has a location in the next town from me over in Weehawken, New Jersey. He started out with the spinach salad while I sipped on the lobster bisque. For the main course, I ordered the loin lamb chops while he ordered the eight and a half ounce filet mignon. We shared an order of steamed broccoli and corn pudding as side dishes. Eating was and always will be something that I don't shy from.

While we wined and dined, we each took turns to politely ask personal questions about one another and by the end of lunch, we both exited the restaurant more intrigued with each other. Driving me to the airport, we continued to talk and laugh. I didn't want the day to end, but I knew that if the personal side of our relationship was meant to be, then it would just be. As we arrived to the Delta Air Terminal, Cat retrieved my bag, opened my door and held my hand as I climbed out of his car. With his arms wide open, I fell into him. He gave me a huge hug and a peck on the cheek. His kind touch sent a chill through my body even though we stood outside in the smoldering heat. I said my goodbyes and promised to call once I arrived home safely. Today was a good day. I landed a man and some money. Whoop whoop!

It was a hot Sunday afternoon in mid August of 2005 and the account was well under way. When Cat pulled up on his new Hummer, I climbed in and gave him a huge hug and peck on the lips. Yes, things had progressed tremendously between us. We had been dating and seeing each other every other weekend for the past three months. During this particular stint, it had been almost thirteen days since we had seen each other and I missed his smile. For once, a guy's physical appearance didn't matter. I know, I know, you're probably thinking, "Oh, but he had deep pockets"— and he did. However, dating a nice looking guy with money was always me. Ya dig?! Don't get me wrong, Cat was generous. While visiting one weekend, my laptop blacked out. Now laptops in 2005 cost a pretty penny. But he spared no expense to make sure I had the best, equipped with all of the programs I needed in order to function. Trips to Neiman Marcus at Lenox Mall were a ritual. My weekend bag was almost non-existent (underwear and hair accessories) were all I ever really needed. Running to the mall to cop an outfit had become a "given."

"Honey, I'm hungry. Aren't you hungry," I yelled down to Cat. I had been on the computer all day trying to get familiarized with my new laptop while he was downstairs with his uncle and brother. The three of them were trying to figure out their next move with their investment property business. Cat was a jack of all trades—a true Hustla.

"Yeah. I can eat," he replied. So I placed my computer into sleep mode, grabbed my flip flops and headed down the steps to his great room.

"Hey. Do you mind if we grab something 'to go'? Cause Big Mama (his mother) is on her way over here and I just wanna finalize everything with my uncle and brother before she gets over here." Cat asked.

"Ok. That's cool. No problem." I replied.

"I just wanna make our plan air tight before we present it to my mom 'cause she will pick through the whole think with a fine tooth comb and that's nerve wracking. Besides, she's bringing some ackee and salt fish and I don't know if you'd like that. It's a Jamaican dish that I love. Maybe one day you can have her teach you how to fix it for me." Cat smiled, knowing good and well I was not the domestic type.

"That sounds promising," I replied with a girlish grin on my face.

As we pulled into the mini mall that housed the Rotisserie Chicken Spot, Cat located a space quickly. We parked and then went into the restaurant. Looking behind him in somewhat of a paranoid manner, I asked, "Is everything alright?"

"I'm tryna see right now. Did you happen to see anybody following us?" he asked.

"Uuuuuhhhhh.... No." I didn't see anyone. But I wasn't

looking either." I replied in a curious manner.

"Ok. Well, I want a half chicken white meat with mash potatoes and string beans. And make sure they give you a few extra biscuits to go with it." Handing me forty dollars, he then stated, "I'ma go pull the car around so that when you come out, I will already be in the front." Cat directed.

"Ok." I was wondering what all of the nervousness was about. While waiting in line, I could see Cat reach for his car keys as he headed to the truck. I almost didn't even want to order anything to eat after noticing his movements and his confirmed disposition. I was like, Shooot. I ain't even that hungry if there's drama. Food ain't even all that important. And in that instant, I lost my appetite. Before I could turn to make a mad dash to the door behind Cat, the server asked, "May I take your order?" So I proceeded as originally planned. For a southern spot, the server gathered the food together fairly quickly. I paid the twenty-four dollars for our food and dashed toward the front door. I noticed how Cat's truck was positioned strategically close to the restaurant's entrance so I hopped in and he locked the doors before I could even reach for the automatic lock on my side.

Placing the food behind the driver's seat, I positioned the food, and then reached for my seat belt. Before I could even situate myself comfortably, there was a loud knock on the glass. It startled me and I jumped up. There was a tall black man knocking hard on Cat's window on the driver's side.

Cat rolled the window down slightly. There was just enough space for Cat to hear what the guy wanted. "I'm lost. Can you tell me how to get to Toys R' Us?" the man asked.

"Oh. Naah. I'm not from around here," Cat replied. Out of my peripheral vision, I could see another guy approaching my side of the car. He looked rough and rugged, like he was out to get a dollar any way and any how. I also spotted a white hoopty pushing up towards us—as if to block us in, Cat sped off. He sped off so fast, we may have driven over the guy's feet. Screeching out of the lot and onto the main street, Cat put the pedal to the metal and we were out!

Before pulling completely out of the mall, I could see three guys from the side view mirror scurrying to get back into their vehicle to follow us. I was horrified and that is mild to say. My heart raced as we dipped into traffic and began a high-speed getaway from people who obviously meant to cause us some harm. "I'm scared," I managed to say between gulps of air. And then a still small voice said to me, "Pray."

Even at that instance, I was too frantic to think of a scripture. The only thing I was able to get out of my mouth was "feathers." I repeated "feathers" over and over again at a fast repetitive rate. "Hold on, Lynn," Cat said as we sped into the alley behind yet another mini mall. Peering out from the alley's end, Cat had lost them. We then proceeded to take a much longer route home.

"Hey. Are you ok?" Cat turned to ask me as we waived at the guard to let us into his complex.

"I'm good. I just thank God that you can drive," I nervously replied. My heart had not stopped beating fast even though the coast was clear.

"Thank God for security. And thank God for gates," Cat replied.

Tucked away behind beautifully manicured spruce trees, the Buckingham Complex where Cat lived was located in the heart of Buckhead, a suburb of Atlanta. His gated community looked like money. Each townhouse was identical to the next. The landscaping was groomed to perfection, and the clubhouse looked extremely exclusive.

Turning onto his street, he immediately reached for his garage opener. We drove right into the garage while simultaneously peering into our mirrors for followers. And neither one of us got out of the truck until the garage door was completely closed.

The next morning as we lay in bed, Cat turned to ask me, "What the heck were you saying feathers for when we were tryna get away," he asked inquisitively. I smirked, turned to him and then replied, "I was trying to remember a particular scripture in the bible but in all of my fear, I totally forgot the scripture. It was actually Psalms 91 and all I could remember was the part where it says, He will cover me with his feathers," and we both just burst out in laughter. I had messed that one up royally, but I know God knew what I was saying.

I loved Atlanta and the cost of living there was extremely affordable with a milder pace. For the money an average person would spend on a nice one acre home, a one bedroom condo in the best parts of New York was hardly obtainable. The weekend was over. Cat and I had an incident that brought us closer together. That night would never be forgotten and from that day forward, there was always closeness between the two of us.

Not long after my account with Big Cat Records and my personal relationship with Cat got underway, a major roadblock had been reached. As I lay in bed one night waiting for Cat's "goodnight" call, I checked the time on my cable box and noticed that he was twenty minutes late with his call. Like clockwork, he always called at 10pm. Milling around in the room an additional twenty minutes, I couldn't take it anymore so I picked up my cell to call him. I got no answer. Worry and insecurities came over me. I then called Vickie. "Hey Vickie. Sorry to call you so late," I immediately said.

"Oh. Lynn. Girl. You know it's ok. What's up? Is everything ok?" she asked.

"Actually, I know this may sound crazy, but it's 11pm and I have not heard from Cat in well over five hours, and he normally calls me every night at 10pm. It's kinda like our date," I chuckled to her. Vickie and everyone with the exception of Jacob were very supportive of our relationship. Both of us had just gotten out of bad relationships so everyone always thought that we were well-deserving of each other.

"I haven't seen or heard from Cat today. You know he went down to Miami with Gucci earlier this morning to support him for his promotional tour so I didn't even bother to go into the office today. Now that I think of it, it is kinda strange that I haven't heard from him," she said.

And just as I was about to give some feedback to what

she was saying, my other lined clicked. It was Cat. "Oh! Vickie. That's Cat calling on the other line now, so I'ma call you back."

"Ok. Don't forget! I just wanna know that everything is alright as well."

"Ok. No problem" and then I clicked over.

"Heeeyyyy," I answered in a questionable tone.
 "Hey," he replied in a very sullen tone.

"What's up? Are you ok? You sound drained." I was anxious and my feelings were hard to conceal.

"I am more than drained Lynn. I can't talk long. We will have to talk extensively in the morning. Ok? Long story short, I, Acesta, and Gucci were arrested tonight. My mom is on the line with me 'cause I was only allowed to make one phone call so I asked her to patch me into you after I spoke to my attorney. Ok?"

"Oh. Ok. Hi Big Mama." I said.

"Hi Leeen," she replied in a tired and worried sounding Jamaican accent.

"But is everything going to be ok?" I asked.

"Yes. Everything is going to be fine. I will call you tomorrow once I've posted bail. Ok?" and before I could even reply, the phone went dead. I assumed his time was up. I didn't bother to call Big Mama back. My relationship with her was too new so I waited patiently overnight for his call and explanation to his arrest. As day break came, I woke up on top of my comforter. I felt as if I had been out drinking all night. The hangover feeling loomed over me and that's when I knew I had some serious feelings for Cat.

As I sat on the toilet, in mid-stream, I heard the phone ring. Dang! Why can't I stop using the bathroom so I can get the phone?

Flushing the toilet, I ran to the phone thinking it was Cat, but it was a missed call from an unknown number— more than likely a bill collector. Checking my messages, it turned out to be someone from the media wishing to get a statement for Big Cat's gun charge and Gucci Mane's arrest. What!? I was shocked. What the hell was going on? Opting to not return the call until I had gotten a chance to speak with him, I just collected all of the incoming messages throughout the morning until he called. Finally, when 3pm rolled around, Cat called.

"Hey," he said as his voice sounded even more drained than from the night before.

"Hey jail bird," I replied as a way to break the ice a little bit. Chuckling somewhat, he then began to tell me about the chain of events that occurred prior to his arrest.

As he started to tell me the story, all I could do was sink deeper into my plush leather sofa. Cat began to tell me the story from beginning to end of how some guys rolled up to them on the side of the road while they were trying to get their navigation together. From there, the unknown guys approached the vehicle. "So shiitttt. I thought niggaz was tryna rob us, so as two of the guys started to approach each side of my truck, I pulled out my gun and so did Acesta."

"Oh. Wow," I interjected while waiting for him to tell me more.

"Yep. And it turned out that they were undercover cops who had apparently been following us since we left Atlanta. They had been following us ever since Gucci's incident. They tried to say they were doing a drug bust or a random check." Cat stated.

"Oh wow," I was speechless.

"So now, since they were unable to bring us up on any kind of drug charges, they are attempting to bring me up on gun charges." Cat stated.

"Oh no!" I cried out.

"Yes, and Lynn it doesn't look good for me. I had a charge when I was 18. I did two years for a gun charge. I was young and dumb then. So this would actually be my second gun charge." And right as he mentioned all of this to me, my heart broke. I didn't know the law that well, but I knew enough to know that he was definitely facing some serious time— a minimum of four years is what popped into my head.

 As the months went on, Cat's days became consumed with spending time in court and with his attorney. He went harder with his label and the release of Gucci's album, TRAP HOUSE because he needed to keep up with all of the attorney fees he, Gucci Mane, and Acesta had started to accrue.

The only thing I could do to help was write a letter to his judge about his outstanding character and great business acumen.

We went from seeing each other every weekend to seeing one another twice a month. Our nightly calls diminished over time and we began to speak only during conference calls. Time had become stressful. I was really starting to miss him but in consideration for what he was going through, I fell back and just played my position as the publicist. That's all I could do. Gucci

Mane's TRAP HOUSE had been released and the big man was gearing up for jail time. One evening as the night started to wear down I looked at the clock. It was over. I lit my tuberose candle, turned off the lights throughout the apartment and got into bed. I was sad and before I could start to sulk, the phone rang. It was Cat.

"Hey," I answered.

"Hey, sweetie," he replied. "I know I haven't called you in a while for our nightly date."

"It's ok," I replied. "I understand."

"Well. It's all over with, Lynn. I got eighteen months and I have to report in eight weeks." I didn't say anything because I just didn't know what to say. I was speechless.

"Lynn? Are you there?" he asked as a result of my silence.

"I'm here and I'm sorry to hear this," I replied.

"Thanks. I could've gotten more time, but the judge received a lot of character letters on my behalf. I could've gotten up to eight years, but she was lenient." Cat said.

"Well, you know the word says in Proverbs 31:8 Speak up for those who cannot speak for themselves, for the rights of all who are destitute."

"Awww man. Thanks Pastor Lynn," Cat replied. The two of us always shared scriptures or spiritual advice with each other toward the end of our conversations.

"No problem. Cat. I will be here for you as a friend." I mentioned.

"Ok. That's exactly what I need from you. It would be selfish of me to ask you to do anything more." Cat replied.

"Ok," I replied in a solemn voice. I was hurting on the inside. I had met someone that I was falling in love with. So to have him snatched up from under my feet was truly upsetting, and I didn't know what the future held for us. I knew we had only been dating a few months, and we were still in the honeymoon phase of things, so sticking by someone during this part of the relationship wasn't realistic for me.

As time went by, Cat did his bid. And though Gucci's rap sheet got worse, his fame expanded. Released from Big Cat Records as the result of a nasty lawsuit between Big Cat Records and Warner Brother Records, they parted ways for a short period of time.

Once Cat was back up and running after completing his bid, I continued as the label's publicist, working with female rap artists, Rasheeda and KHIA who were signed to his label.

To date, Cat and I are still really good friends.

Chapter 17:
The Robinsons

It was a hot fall day. The temperature was scorching for October of 2005. The day's schedule called for me to go out with my client, Juelz Santana, and his family to look for a new home. They had outgrown their current condo and a much larger flat was needed.

While out house shopping, Juelz's friend Leland was escorting him around with realtor, Jiton Green, he referred to him. Leland was a tall handsome guy with smooth caramel colored skin, enticing dimples, and the most handsome smile I had ever seen on a man. From the outside, he was physically my type. When the introduction came, Juelz said, "Lynn. This is Leland. His mother is Sylvia Robinson of Sugar Hill Records. He has a son that wants to have a sweet fifteen party. So give him your number. I told him you would be the perfect person to pull something like this together." Juelz introduced.

"Ok. Hello," I said to this moving piece of caramel. I know that hit and then I burst out with the rap and started reciting the lyrics. "Hip-hop Hippy to the hippy ya don't stop a rockin' to the bang bang boogie…" Leland and Juelz began cracking up. I was dressed in a short-sleeved cotton button up polo top with jeans and sandals. Dressed conservatively, it was a shock to see me do such a thing. It broke the ice and a working relationship along with a friendship between Leland and I started to blossom.

Over the months to come, Leland's family, The Robinsons, had become my "go to" family for every type of hook up you could name. Nestled in the trees of Englewood, New Jersey, cars of every top name brand filled up the nicely paved circular driveway. A Bentley, an Escalade, a Mercedes Benz, an Audi, and even a Lambo made no room for my little Sebring Convertible.

I will never forget the Robinsons' reactions to my question upon entering the family's flat. "I'm sorry, but isn't it late March?" I asked.

Leland, his sons Antonio, Leland Jr., Darnell, Kasyn and Lea looked up at me. They smiled with their unmistakable Robinson hazel brown eyes. "Why the hell y'all got a holiday tree up in the middle of March?" I continued to ask. In the corner of the living room was a large white artificial tree adorned with white lights and decorations as if it weren't 70 degrees and sunny outside.

"Oh. You don't know Money, Lynn?" Lea asked me with a happy smirk on her face. Lea, the princess of the family stood watch as I waited patiently for her response.

"Tell her baby girl," Leland waved—as if he had prepared Lea over the years to answer the question in Robinson grandeur.

"There's a tree up in Mama Sylvia's house year round because every day is Christmas! Word! Aaaaooowwwww!" Lil Lea exclaimed. Reaching over to slap her a high five, her big brother Darnell repeated with the "Aaaaowwww" again. This family was and still is hilarious!

"I know that's right!" I replied while laughing out loud. "Every day really is Christmas." and from that day forward, I had a different perspective on life. It wasn't necessary to observe Christmas once a year, and from the looks of this family, every day was a celebration. Gifts were always being purchased and given.

It was this family that then gave me the moniker, "Money Lynn," because by the time I met the Robinson's I had been so over worked and under paid that I was no longer willing to lift a finger without a check. And besides, all of my ideas were always on the money. Aaaoooowww!

Upon starting the account with the family, my first

assignment was to plan Darnell Robinson's 15th birthday party. "I want my party to be a party to remember," he stated to me while I sat on a stool in their kitchen. Taking notes on everything Darnell wanted, I was floored. "My theme is Eddie Murphy's "Coming to America," he stated.

"Oh wow! Now that's HOT!" I yelled out with excitement.

Most kids who did a themed party very rarely selected a film. However, Darnell was all set with his idea. "Yeah. I'm sayin'. It can't be no other way. I'm a prince. Eddie played a prince in the movie and he was rich like me. So it's simple." With this family, money was never an object. However, getting them to pay up often was, but best believe once the money hit my account, it was always all good.

When MTV Producer, Wendy Plaut caught wind of what the Robinsons wanted for their Prince Darnell, they immediately signed the event up for the hit series, "My Super Sweet 16."

"I want to be Eddie Murphy from *Coming To America*, he stated to the producer during his preliminary interview. "I want everything from the film. I want the girls following me around with rose pedals and I want tigers there for my grand entrance. Whatever Eddie had in the movie, I want to recreate that." I was amazed by Darnell's insight into the hit movie, as it was way before his time.

Immediately, I started to think about the film from beginning to end. I started to gather visuals of the film's elements that I wanted to have highlighted within his party's theme. "Ok. So who would you want your Queen to be?" I asked.

"Money Lynn, that's the only thing I can't seem to figure out. I'm going to have to trust you on that one," Darnell stated. "Just make sure she is cute. She doesn't have to be famous, but she definitely needs to have that something special about her." Darnell insisted.

"Ok. No problem. I will look into it. I'm also going to go rent the movie just to get a little more refreshed on what your party should entail." I stated.

"Ok. Cool. Let me know when ya wanna start," said Darnell.

Hanging up the phone, I was too excited about his party and the challenge of pulling something of this magnitude off. At this point in my career, I needed to do something bigger and better and this party afforded me the opportunity to do so. I was up for the challenge.

While watching the film, I decided that the wedding choreography and the animals were a necessity. I immediately had my interns get to work on looking into the rental of animals such as elephants and lions. I pictured Darnell riding in on an elephant with his date and/or walking down the red carpet with two tamed lions on a leash. So as the quest to rent both got underway, we had no choice but to set up a trip to Florida where the world's best selection of safari animals were bred in captivity.

The next thing a prince needed was some jewels. Bling was definitely warranted in order to put his "look" together so we spared no expense when the two of us flew out to Chicago to pay homage to Debbie The Glass Lady. Ms. Debbie was the "go to girl" for all things bling. Celebrities such as Bishop Don Juan, Snoop, Lil Jon, and Paris Hilton have enlisted her services to have their prized possessions blinged out.

Boarding the plane in the wee hours of the morning for Chicago, I was tired, yet excited about the day's agenda. "Father God, I ask that you dispatch your angels around me, Darnell, and the camera crew. Keep us from any hurt, harm, or danger. I ask that the day is productive and fun. In Jesus name I thank you, Amen," I whispered to myself just before our American Airlines flight gained speed for takeoff on Newark Airport's runway.

Debbie turned it on for the cameras as we began to film her talking to Darnell about his blinged out party requirements. Greeting us as if we were her own children, the two of us entered the cozy apartment with MTV cameras on blast. When we arrived, she treated us like royalty. "Come on in Baby Boy and Money Lynn!" Ms. Debbie, her manager Tony, and I had been speaking extensively prior to our arrival about Darnell and MTV's requirements. As the cameras rolled, she began to ask Darnell what he wanted. "So tell me Prince, what request may I grant you today?" she asked.

I just chuckled in silence as the cameras recorded. The day was going extremely well—flawless as God would have it. "Well Ms. Debbie, I need a crown, a pimp cup, and a cane for my party. I want to be bling'd out for my special occasion," he smiled.

"A pimp cup?!" she exclaimed. "Child. What do you know about a pimp cup? For the sake of your age, we are going to say that you need a decorative chalice. Ok?," she answered with a motherly smirk on her face.

"That's cool." And then the two of them sat down to begin drafting what would become his accessories for the night.

When the four-hour taping had been completed, we

were hurried back to Chicago's O'Hare Airport where we boarded a return American Airlines flight back to Jersey. We were all exhausted. It was crunch time though. I was limited on time to produce all of the necessary elements for the party. Now that his accessories had been squared away, I had to tackle the idea of having Darnell ride in on an elephant and deciding on the usage of the tigers. Other details such as the entrance's choreography, ice sculptures, buses to transport students from the high school, his new whip, and a celebrity performance had already been secured.

Two days back in the crib and I was packing again to head out to Florida with Darnell and the rest of his family to take a look at tigers that I wanted to secure for his grand entrance.

"Money Lynn, I really want those tigers. I want tigers more than anything," he stated as the family's driver, Woodrow helped me climb into the vehicle. Darnell was making his demands before I could even greet him, his mother Vernetta, or his little sister Lea. He was excited, amped, and the pressure to have a banging bash was on.

"Well hello Robinson Family," I managed to get out before Darnell darted off the next question. We were three weeks into the taping and the invitations to

Darnell's party had already gone out. His entire Tenafly High School in New Jersey along with all of Harlem was abuzz about the prince's upcoming affair. Arriving to the airport, we met up with the MTV crew who got some quick shots of us getting out of the family's Benz.

Arriving to Florida, we went straight to the reserve where most of the lions in the country were kept. It was a large place where greatly endangered species in America were kept as well. This place was also home of the Liger (cross between a lion and a tiger). As the woman came out to greet us, she gave us a speech on the list of do's and don'ts while we were to be guests on the premises, but she didn't have anything to worry about. She obviously didn't get the memo that us black folk weren't tryna touch nothing'! Now maybe those rules might have applied to the camera crew, but they damn sure didn't have to worry about us.

As we started the tour, we visited various parts of the reserve. Our first stop was the chimpanzees. They were adorable! "Oooh Mommy. Can I have one?!" Lea asked as the tour guide handed her one to hold. The baby chimp was too cute, dressed in a pink dress and diaper.

"Girl, you must've bumped your head," Vernetta replied to her daughter. "I don't even want you to keep the two puppies you've got at home now," she hissed as Lea began to feed the monkey a piece of fruit. Pouting harshly, but still enjoying the moment, Lea sucked it up and moved on. While the crew was surrounding Darnell to get his reaction to the chimps, he became adamant about his tigers.

"Listen. I came here for one thing only and that's for my tigers. Two of them. I want two of them for my grand entrance. Let's stay focused people," Darnell stated in a stern teenager's tone. I adored Darnell. He was a humble kid with a swag like no other. Though he sometimes attempted to be obnoxious, it never panned out. He was a sweetheart.

As the day continued, we visited the tigers last as a way to build up the camera momentum for Darnell's suspense on screen. When we arrived at the tigers, he perked up. Pointing through the cage at the two he particularly wanted, they were brought over to us as close as possible for a better view. "Mommy. I really want those two tigers for my party. Can we just wrap them up and take them with us?" Darnell knew damn well that wasn't happening. We all knew the rental of the two beautiful Bengal Tigers would be a process— and a complicated one. So there was no need for his mother to even respond.

"What we can do is come over to this picnic table to discuss the logistics of your party. As you may already know, the tigers would be driven up North," is what the Guide told us. "Now, what part of New York will the party be held?" she asked as the application process began.

"My party will be held in New Jersey," Darnell stated.

"Oh my! When MTV called to get clearance, we thought the party was going to be held in New York City." The lady turned beet red. At that moment, I knew something was terribly wrong. "I'm so sorry to tell you, but tigers and any other wildlife such as this are not allowed in the state of New Jersey for rental." I was furious. But as the state of New Jersey would have it, animals of this nature were not allowed for this type of use. It was in fact, illegal. We had hopped on a plane and driven miles to the reserve to be told that we could not have tigers at Darnell's party. It was hot as hell. I was hungry, annoyed, and ready to go! Darnell's face was blank. His mother was pissed and lil Lea just looked confused. As the cameras rolled, I tried to keep my cool and we all made it out of there in one piece before exploding. This party was costing the Robinsons money and we didn't have time for any mistakes. However, the shock value for television was awesome.

Needless to say, the ride back to the airport and the flight were in complete silence. No one had anything to say. We wouldn't even allow for the cameras to roll. Pissed was an understatement to how we felt. Yet and still, I needed to find something different for Darnell's party entrance.

Arriving back to my Edgewater apartment, I checked my messages. I perked up at one particular call. It was a lady from upstate New York. "Hello Ms. Hobson. I'm calling you back regarding your inquiry to a camel rental for an upcoming party in New Jersey. Based on the date you specified in your email, we do have Daisy available." I jumped for joy out of my seat as I continued to listen to the message. "New Jersey laws are extremely strict on animal rights, so you would only be able to have her for no more than four hours." That was fine with me. Shooot, I only needed Daisy for ten minutes! I called her back the very next morning and locked it in. Other than Darnell's parents, he had no idea until the day of his affair how he would be making his entrance. We kept it a surprise.

In no time, party day arrived and the night was already being delayed. Time was ticking and Rihanna, Darnell's date was late! I selected the young aspiring platinum artist from a recommendation of a Def Jam Records executive. In fact, she was two hours late to be exact. Time is money and I was a witness to that on this particular night. The animal rights people were watching their clocks and time was ticking on the venue and food preparation. The food stations had already been prepared. The ice sculptures were starting to melt. And the camera crew along with the producer, were growing frantic. All I remember doing was spazzing out. I picked up the phone and called Rihanna's manager. "Where the hell are y'all at!? Time is money. We are all out here with these cameras and this damn camel looking crazy. This is not only a bad look for you and us, but it's costing us money!" In all honesty, I wouldn't have felt as bad for Darnell's date being late to the party if I wasn't the one who selected her.

"Calm down, Lynn," Yves said on the other line. She was the marketing rep from Def Jam Records who was speaking on behalf of Rihanna. We are five minutes away. We apologize for the delay.

Before I could get another word out, they were actually pulling into the venue's driveway. Darnell sighed a loud sound of relief. He was dressed to the nines with his cane, crown and chalice. The two of us ran down to the animal's portable stable to alert the care taker of Rihanna's arrival and then we got the show on the road. Darnell's eyes beamed when he finally got a chance to take a look at his ride to the party. "Oh Wow! Now that's what I'm talking about!" He was too amped. We all were.

As the two mounted the camel, Rihanna apologized profusely. Seeing the cameras and the crowd, it hit her that this was not just an average Sweet 15, this was a production. As the two headed up the hill, the red carpet was rolled out. Kids were screaming at the top of their lungs when the two rolled up on a camel and the choreography started. Our rendition of "Coming To America's" wedding scene started, and we didn't skip a beat. The grand entrance was perfect and so was the rest of the party! Darnell and his friends rocked out to a performance by Juelz Santana, a birthday serenade by Lil Mo, and music by Fatman Scoop. I love making my clients happy, and to this very day, Darnell had the best MTV "My Super Sweet 15" there was.

Two years down the road, I received a phone call from Darnell. "Money Lynn. Hold on. Someone wants to speak with you."

"Hello," a faint frail voice said to me. "Money Lynn? This is Lea. I know you are busy, but will you please do my Super Sweet 16 for me?" Lea sounded so sweet and innocent over the phone.

"Hey Lea. You know I gotchu girl. What you want your theme to be?" I asked.

"I want a gothic glam theme," she stated.

"Oh. Ok. That's different," I responded and right away my wheels started spinning. I knew the exact spot where I wanted to have her party. "Lea. I know the perfect place in the city where we can have your party. It's called Blood Manor and it's in the 20's on the Westside of the city. It's one of the city's most infamous haunted houses. I can get Bryce to choreograph a thriller type of entrance for you and we can get this party crunk real quick baby girl." I remarked.

"Oh! See. That's why I love you so much Money Lynn!" When we hung up, I immediately started to plan.

It was a warm October Wednesday when I got the most thought provoking call from Kim. I was standing in the Post Office line to collect a few packages filled with decorations for Lea's upcoming party when the call came in. "Hey girl. What's up?" I asked. I was already expecting a call from her because she was pregnant—due to have her second child. Today was the day she'd find out the sex of the baby.

Kim was trying her best to communicate, but I wasn't understanding one word she was saying. The phone reception was horrible. "I can't hear what you are saying." I told her.

"Girl! I'm having not one girl, but two. I am having twins!", Kim exclaimed.

"What!!?? Wow. That's amazing!!! Twins!? Oh My!" I jumped for joy. Everyone in the post office was looking at me like I was crazy.

"This is all so overwhelming. I am excited and overwhelmed at the same damn time, Lynn." Kim stated.

"Everything will be alright. God won't give you what you can't handle.", I assured her.

While listening to Kim tell me about the news, I briefly I drifted off in thought. I realized that I needed to make a doctor's appointment for a checkup.

Congratulating her once again before gettign off the phone, I had to switch back into party mode. Lea's party was around the corner and I was behind schedule with the timeline MTV had created for me. While standing in line, the thoughts of my conversation with Kim took over my mind. She definitely gave me some food for thought. Here I was, 38 years old and I had no husband or child. My biological clock was ticking. I was dating a booking agent who was nine years younger, but the relationship wasn't serious. It was just something to do. You feel me? My career was my husband, but I wanted it all—the career, husband, and the kids.

The post office was packed. I stood in line, sandwiched behind between the ropes and chattering Korean customers who were also rushing to meet the cut off time to send their packages off to their country. Over the years, Edgewater had become a town where Koreans migrated. A Japanese Market by the name of Mitsuwa drew Asians from all over Bergen County.

The invites were mailed and I picked up boxes of decorations that had been undelivered to my home. Carrying the packages to my car, I set them on the roof, popped the trunk open, and placed the three boxes into the vehicle. I was drained and as I drove the short block back to my crib, I opted to leave the packages in the car. I was too pooped to be bothered with boxes.

I had two hours before I would go on a Halloween house scouting hunt with Lea. On Clinton Place in Hackensack, New Jersey, a residential neighborhood was notoriously known for pulling out all of the stops with Halloween décor. From graveyards and mummies to fog, blood and whatever else you could imagine, annually, this block drew thousands of local residents out to take part in the scary sites.

When I arrived onto Clinton Place, there was a homeowner already starting to decorate his house. Cobwebs, large spiders, and coffins already ordained his front yard. My mouth dropped open. It was just a few weeks before Halloween and his house was already looking spooky. MTV wanted us to select a location where Lea would give out the invites to her Gothic Glam Affair and this house was already looking perfect to me. I was the first to arrive, Lea pulled up with the MTV crew and they unanimously decided that this house would be perfect as well. From there, we introduced ourselves to the homeowner and begged him to allow us to film Lea's "Invite Give Away" segment on his front lawn. With very little hesitation, he agreed. We were all set to come back in a few days to tape and Lea was super excited about it. Her party was definitely going to be different than any other kid's—and I was going to make sure of it.

As party day arrived, words such as hectic and crazed were an understatement. It was party day and the intensity of having a flawless sweet sixteen was way above level ten. Lea's Gothic Graveyard cake created by Aliyyah Baylor of Make My Cake in Harlem was perfect. The baker managed to make a number one and a number six like a coffin with bugs, cobwebs, spiders, and blood oozing off of it. Though it was scary to the eye, the red velvet cakes with cream cheese icing were a dream come true in my mouth.

The grand entrance was under way as Lea pulled up with her date, Skull Gang Member John Depp, in a bright orange Challenger, the Grand Entrance was under way. Lea performed "Disturbia" with her crew and danced her way right up into Blood Manor while teens and on lookers screamed with excitement. DJ L spun the night away and DipSet Member, Jim Jones performed his hit "Ballin" for the Teen Queen, Lea. The night ended with a huge surprise that I wasn't even expecting. I knew that Lea was going to be getting a vehicle for her birthday; however, I had no idea that it would be two. A Range Rover and an Audi were covered in huge Red Bows. The party was pure pandemonium. Teens came out in droves dressed in their best costumes and renditions of their idols. At the night's end, I pat myself on the back and kept it moving, looking forward to the next HobbieCom Signature Event with my check tucked into the back pocket of my pants. To date, Lea and Darnell's episodes are two of the hottest parties to be aired on MTV.

Don't get me wrong. I worked hard for the money; however, there's nothing more rewarding than seeing huge smiles on the faces of my clients. I lived for that. Smiles and happiness at awesome outcomes is what continues to motivate me to be the Publicist that I am today.

Chapter 18:
Chris Brown's MTV Birthday

As I pulled into the parking lot of my gynecologist's office, I cringed. I absolutely hated going for my annual GYN checkup. "Oh wow," I mumbled to myself. I had forgotten to put lotion on my legs. In the summer time, I never put lotion on under my clothes because the summer heat always moistened my skin as the day moved on. Oh well... I will just look like a ghost today.

Heading into the overcrowded waiting area, I signed my name onto the clipboard and found one seat in the far corner of the room. As I pulled out my blackberry to run through all of the morning's emails, I simultaneously scanned the room and wondered what each patient was there for. She must be here for an STD because she looks like she stinks. She looks like she is about to burst any moment now and she looks like she's hoping that she's NOT pregnant.

After one hour of watching "People's Court," reading emails, and scanning magazines, my name was called by the receptionist. Jumping up as if I had just won the lottery, I headed over to the door where I was buzzed in to be escorted to the Examination Room.

"Soooo... Lynn. What can we do for you today?" the

nurse asked. "I'm just here to get a checkup," I answered. "Ok. So take everything off from the waist down and the doctor will be in shortly.

"Ok," I replied as I hopped down from off of the examination table to start undressing. While tucking my underwear inside the pocket of my jeans, I found $20. "Oh wow. I guess I will have a nice lunch today," I said to myself.

With a knock on the door, Dr. Bruschia came into the room. "Hello. How are you?" Dr. Bruschia mumbled. He barely looked at me. It was clear that he had something else on his mind, and before I could reply, in walked the nurse. As the doctor motioned for me to scoot to the edge of the table for my annual pap smear, he made a weird noise. Finishing up the pap smear, he motioned for me to sit up. Removing his gloves and throwing them into the trash, he sighed, "I, I felt a few fibroids." he said.

"Oh really? Is that bad? Is that cancerous? Will I be able to have children?" I asked.

"No. They can be removed with surgery. They are not cancerous. However, the likelihood of you being able to have children is highly unlikely." He reported.

I looked at him with heartbreak in my eyes, he seemed

to me unmoved by his findings. He handed me a slip for a sonogram for the masses found and excused himself from the room so that I could get dressed. Getting dressed slowly with tears in my eyes, I managed to make it to the car before breaking down.

Picking up the phone to dial my mother's number, I was wailing by the time my mother answered. "What's wrong sweetheart? Calm down. I can't understand a word you are saying. Calm down and speak to me slowly." She whispered.

"The doctor said that I have fibroids and I will not be able to have kids." I cried.

Gasping at the words that came out of my mouth, my mom hung up from me, made a phone call and called me back quickly.

"Lynn. Where are you?" She asked.

Crying... still, "I'm still in the doctor's parking lot in the car."

"Ok. Well calm down. I just called Dr. George. He's my GYN and I'd like for you to come down for another opinion next week." Mommy said.

"Ok, Mommy."

"Now you call me when you get home and everything will be fine. Ok?"

"Ok," I sobbed.

I hit an all time low. It was my life's dream to have children. I was devastated.
As the week rolled by, the doctor's appointment in Washington, DC could not have come soon enough. Bad dreams equipped with sleepless nights took over the five days leading up to my second opinion. Getting any work done was next to impossible, and I was blessed to not have to report to an office job.

When Dr. George finished my exam, he motioned for me to sit up. Speaking with his West Indian accent, he said, "Wow. You are a strong young woman. I felt at least three fibroids that would put you at the weight and size of a 36-week pregnancy. And that's full term."

"Wow," I replied.

"The bad news is that if you don't remove them, they will continue to grow. The good news is that we can remove them so you can have some babies." He smiled.

That was music to my ears.

"When would you like to do the surgery? And keep in mind that it will take you six to eight weeks to recover." He asked and mentioned.

"Ok. So anytime between Thanksgiving and Christmas would be great." I answered.

"Sounds good. Get dressed. I will brief Martha, my receptionist and she will schedule something for you."

"Ok. Thank you Dr. George." I said.

"No problem," he replied.

Making my way back out into the reception area, Martha motioned for me. The two of us scheduled a preliminary sonogram and the surgery simultaneously with the Washington Hospital Center and the ball was in motion.

Heading out to the car where my mom waited patiently. I climbed into the car and gave my mom the play by play of what happened. "Oh great! Now does that make you feel a little better?" she asked me.

"Yes. I feel much better. Besides, the date of the surgery is right before the holidays. There won't be much activity work wise anyway." I replied.

As the holidays quickly approached, the surgery went off without a hitch. It was a success and in four short weeks, I was back in the big apple and back at work.

By the middle of March I was swamped. My colleagues from LA called me to step in and help them with a few of their heavy hitting hip-hop clients. They were publicists known as Powerhouse PR. They were a collective of four females who owned their own companies. The four often came together collectively to support each other with huge events and projects they were working on, and each one helped for free. The exchange always ended up being fair. Kita, Monique, Arian, Katarah, and Jocelyn. Arian landed Chris Brown as a client and he was soon turning 18.

"Lynn, girl, I need your help," Arian mentioned over the phone.

"Ok. What's up?" I asked.

"Do you still have your contact over at MTV? Cause I want to do a huge celebrity birthday bash for Chris in New York and I really want MTV to cover it," she went on.

"Oh. Really? That would be cool. Lemmee reach out to Wendy and see if they are filming and I'll hit ya back." I replied.

One successful event ALWAYS produces an opportunity for bigger and better things.

Arian and I had met one year earlier in the 8th floor lobby of the Marriott Marquis in Times Square. I was having a media day there for my then-client, Trick Trick, an indie rapper based out of Detroit, and Arian was in town to meet with a few potential clients. Arian had walked over to where my media day was held because she too was from Detroit and she recognized the Detroit rapper from afar. The chemistry when we met was great and we often kept in touch via email. If there were ever a time when she needed red carpet coverage for any of her clients who were New York bound, I was always happy to assist and vice versa.

I went on to meet Kita and Monique (publicists on the "TO Show") and then JC (Jocelyn Coleman). We all hit it off. We were all on our grind and no one ever seemed to have an ego.

Sending emails back and forth to Wendy, it was a no brainer that they wanted to have a "My Super 18th Birthday Bash" for him on MTV. So once the episode was green lighted, we went on to select a theme and timeline for Chris Brown. The theme would be "Off The Wall," a Michael Jackson theme and the timing was perfect—as Chris had just performed for MJ at the

World Music Awards in London.

"Hi Ladies. We really want this party and Chris'
birthday to be way over the top," Tina Davis specified
over the conference calls and on all of the emails from
that day forward.

"We gotchu, Tina," Arian replied.

After that, conference calls with the team went from
weekly to daily to damn near every minute. There just
didn't seem to be enough time in the day to get all of
the tapings fit into Chris' hectic schedule. On the
itinerary was an invitation selection segment, a home
lifestyle segment, a venue scouting segment, and
several other major components that went along with
filming the special. We had a lot to accomplish in a
small amount of time.

As the sun peered into my bedroom blinds, I tossed
and turned. I so didn't want my sleep to end, but I had
a long day ahead and my "to do" list was endless.
Managing to roll out of bed and into the bathroom, I
felt nauseas with each movement. Hold up! Where is
my period? I wondered. Yeah. I wanted to have
children but not at that moment and definitely not that
day. I had way too much to do! Besides, the guy (Joe) I
was dating at the time was nine years younger than me
and the chance of a serious yet long-term relationship

just wasn't happening. Don't get me wrong, he was a good guy— a newly laid off single parent with an eight-year-old daughter. I called a gynecologist in Bergen County and made an appointment for the very next day.

When I got up from the toilet, I went back into the bedroom to grab my phone. Scrolling to the calendar, I gasped. My period was one week late. I didn't know whether to shoot myself or jump for joy. To make things more specific for me, I threw on my flip flops, grabbed my purse, and headed to the car. The pharmacy wasn't on my original "to do" list, but it was definitely the main event of the day. Ya dig? Racing back up the hill to my apartment, I parked my car, ran up the steps, and tore open the test. In less than three minutes the word PREGNANT appeared clearly onto the stick's window.

Calling Kim who was pregnant with twin girls and due in eight more weeks, she answered in a sleepy tone. "Kim! Wake up!" I yelled.

"I'm up now since you yellin' in my damn ear. What's up?" she asked.

"Girl. Are you ready for this?" I asked.

"Oh Lord. What? What is it? Lemmee sit up in the bed

first cause you know I damn sure can't take anything standing up," she chuckled.

"Girl. I am pregnant!" I yelled.

"What! You lyin'!" Kim yelled back.

"Seriously! I'm pregnant! I reported.

"Yaaaaay! OMG our kids will be besties like us," she shouted with excitement.

I was soooo happy. Doctors said that I wouldn't be able to have kids, but here I was PREGNANT! At this point, I didn't even care about what the baby daddy was thinking. I was having my baby finally and that's all I really wanted.

During our very first taping with Chris Brown, I remember sitting nauseously at the table inside of Justin's Restaurant in Atlanta, trying to hold down my lunch while discussing the need for Theme Consistency throughout the party. I was sick as a dog, but as the cameras rolled, I sucked it up. Wherever or whatever it took to tape the episodes despite Chris' hectic schedule, Arian and I were there.

In addition to a traditional MTV Birthday Bash, Chris had three more components added onto his Special.

One was a celebrity charity basketball game that was held in Harlem at the Riverbank State Park the day before his scheduled party. The second component was a separate party that was created by the record label specifically for his fans. The third and final component was his private Michael Jackson "BAD" themed bash to be held at Jay-Z's 40/40 Sports Club located in the heart of midtown Manhattan. We had our work cut out for us.

Chris was extremely specific with Arian and me about what he wanted for his party. "I want the MJ theme to flow throughout the entire night," Chris stated while we just nodded at each of his requests. His invitations were made of a soft metal with the embedded "Off The Wall" album as the backdrop for the invite. A red velvet sheet covered the invite once it was removed from the envelope to help maintain the invitation's gloss. The invitation to say the least was BAD!

The entire filming process for Chris' birthday was long and grueling. It became extremely strenuous for Arian, the Staff, MTV's Production Crew, and me to keep up with Chris' schedule. Segment tapings took place in Atlanta and Virginia in addition to New York.

On the actual day of the party, the late great Michael Jackson took what was an eternity to come to the phone, and it took all I had inside of me to hold onto the snack I had had earlier in the day. All I wanted to do was barf all over my phone, Arian, Chris, and myself.

As the cameras rolled, MJ's Assistant kept continuously saying, "Please hold for Mr. Jackson." Another five minutes went by and he came back to the phone, "Please hold for Mr. Jackson." So when it was collectively decided by Management, MTV Producers, and myself that Mr. Jackson was taking entirely too long to come to the phone, we hung up and kept the party going. The combination of my pregnancy, the pressure of needing to please the birthday boy along with the annoyance of the crowd and cameras was just too much to handle, but at the end of the day, I didn't let them see me sweat. I held onto my snack for the night and kept the party moving.

Rihanna, music producer Bryan Michael Cox, Teyana Taylor, and several other celebs showed up to congratulate Chris on becoming a young man. Jennifer Hudson sang a soulful version of "Happy Birthday" and gifts were presented to Chris as well. The night was a success. Chris Brown and Michael Jackson did eventually have a conversation which resulted in talks of a collaboration before his passing.

The day after the party, my Goddaughter Kiara and I slept until 6pm the next evening. We were beat and my apartment was a mess. It looked like World War III had taken place. My colleague and now good friend, Jocelyn was fast asleep on my living room sofa as well. Events such as this always took a lot out of me and I was more than happy that it was over. Kim had also given birth that morning to her beautiful twin daughters. Jourdan and Janae had arrived. Whew!

Three days later, I had my apartment back and I was almost back to some type of normalcy—but not quite. I was pregnant and I had NOT had an opportunity to wrap my head around it, nor had I had a chance to have a serious conversation with the sperm provider.

It was a spring Sunday afternoon and I had chosen to spend the day indoors. Being a couch potato was something I needed to work on. I was always working. Relaxing was something foreign to me, but as I flipped channels to see what was on TV, nothing was on.

Opting to watch some arena football, I thought of my dad and our football watching episodes with him. My dad would sit down in his plush chair from noon til nine and watch nonstop football. Every Sunday, my dad would ONLY get up out of his chair to either poop, piss, grab a Coca Cola, peanuts, some Candy Corns, or his bag of Utz chips. That was it. "Don't walk in front of the TV!" he would often yell out to me and my sister, but we would never listen to him. Faye and I would find every reason under the sun to walk past my dad and his TV. If we walked past the set three times, we'd notice how he'd begin to get agitated—especially if his Redskins were losing.

"I'ma tell you one more time!" he would yell out to us. "Walk pass this TV again and you will get in trouble!" As the game often intensified, daddy's threats became more serious. The thing about football was my sister Faye and I only knew how to keep score. We were not knowledgeable of plays, moves, or the time that needed to be made in order for a win. The two of us would often convene in the kitchen up under my stepmother with uncontrollable giggles. "Y'all are asking for it. Leave your father alone," she would warn. Diane spent her Sundays in the kitchen fixing or prepping for a week's worth of meals. She was very organized. Nevertheless, havoc was wreaked with a failed attempt to walk pass the TV. My dad would reach his breaking point by tackling us to the carpet with big hands that were like huge bear paws and administer the sloppiest wet kisses to our cheeks. Like a drooling English Bull Dog, Dad would deliver the tickles and kisses until we gave up. The living room and TV from that point on were all his.

Reminiscing about my childhood, I fell asleep before halftime. When I awoke, I ordered a chicken parmesan sandwich from Pizza Club in Edgewater along with a side salad, and a Snapple. It was getting late, and since I was now single, there was really no need to cook for one person.

Formulating what my week was shaping up to look like, I tidied up, jumped in the shower, and climbed into bed. However, my sleep was short lived when I woke up with sharp pains in my abdomen. The pain was excruciating. I felt so bad that I could not even sit up. It was as if I was paralyzed. "Oh God! Help me!" I yelled out while holding my stomach. "Please. Somebody. Help me!" I was screaming at the top of my lungs, but I was in my apartment alone and no one could hear me. Not even five minutes had gone by and Joe walked in the door. To this day, it was a miracle. The two of us were on the outs and I had not spoken to him in days. Seeing him enter into the room, I yelled to him. He turned on the light and saw the horror on my face. Reaching in his pocket to grab his phone, he dialed 911. As tears rolled down my face, I knew it was my baby. Holding my hand to lend support, he seemed to have been too shocked. "Calm down, Lynn. It's going to be alright. The ambulance is on the way." he comforted.

Whaling like a coyote, I cried out, "I'm scared. Please tell them to hurry up! Something is wrong with me! Something is wrong with the baby," and before I could finish my sentence, my apartment doorbell rang. As my baby's daddy ran to the door, he buzzed the EMS Worker into my home. Asking me a few questions, they lifted me onto a cot and carried me down to the ambulance. "Babe, I'm going to meet you at the hospital. Ok? That way we'll have a ride home." He didn't even wait for my response, but I did agree with him. The ambulance ride was pure hell. The driver hit every bump and pothole on River Road, and that road on a normal day was pretty smooth.

Arriving to the hospital, I could hear the EMS Team relaying my vitals to the Emergency Room staff. "She's pregnant. She has a fever and her blood pressure is sky high."the femaile EMS worker announced.

"Ok. Thanks," said the head nurse. "We got it from here. Ms. Hobson, hello. We are going to give you a sonogram. We think your baby may be in trouble." Moaning the entire time, I was in too much pain to even respond so I just nodded my head. My baby daddy was nowhere in sight. I wanted my mommy. I had not told anyone about the pregnancy except my mom, Kim, and Diamond. Rushing me into an x-ray room, a sonogram was given to me. "Wow!" I could hear the technician exclaim. "I'll be right back. I need to go and get the nurse or doctor." Leaving me in suspense, I was left alone for less than five minutes, but it seemed like an eternity. The room was cold and the walls were white and bland. The equipment looked serious and I wanted nothing more than for the pain to go away.

"Ms. Hobson. We need to talk to you," said a nurse. "The doctor who is on call for the night is less than 20 minutes away. It looks as though you have an ectopic pregnancy. This means that the baby was not planted correctly during conception. The baby is growing inside of one of your fallopian tubes and it looks like it's about to erupt. We will need to perform emergency surgery. This is a life threatening situation." While gently talking to me, the nurse was steadily preparing me for surgery. "Unfortunately your baby will not make it and it doesn't look like we will be able to save your fallopian tube either. Our main objective is to get you stabilized. Alright?" she asked. I just nodded. My heart was broken.

Administering some pain medication to me and taking some blood, I began to rest easier. My baby daddy walked into my Emergency Room cubicle just minutes before I was rolled off to surgery. "I'm sorry it took so long for me to come back here. There's no phone reception back here and I needed to get in touch with your mom." I just nodded and at this point, that is all I could do. It was "ok" to let a few tears lose. I knew the ER staff would not be bothering me for a few more minutes.

Thirty minutes was the amount of time it took for the doctor to arrive. Entering my cubicle, he introduced himself to me. My baby daddy had stepped out to relay a play by play to my mom who was worried to the tenth degree. "Hello, Ms. Hobson. I'm the on-call surgeon for the night. I won't ask how you are doing. I just know that you are a strong woman and that you are enduring a lot of pain at this time." As he talked, I just looked at him. My nonverbal communication let him know that I was listening to his every word and that I was also understanding of what he was saying. "You are ten weeks pregnant and the baby is growing inside of your fallopian tubes. I'm sure the nurse explained this to you, but it's my job to explain this again." So as he went over everything again, he said, "So we are going to have to remove her. Ok?" and I just nodded. I was in too much pain to even care, yet my heart continued to break more after he said the word, 'her'. How did he know? Did the tests tell him the specific sex of my baby?

When I awoke, the sun was beaming on my face. A heavy-set nurse was leaning over me, calling my name. "Ms. Hobson, take this. This is pain medication." Tapping a switch to have me sit up in the bed, it felt as though my abdomen was ripping apart. "The doctor gave you staples. You will be in the hospital for the remainder of the week." Dang, it was Monday!

Looking up to check out my surroundings, I could see the New York City skyline from my hospital room window. "Take this medication and try to eat some of this breakfast because you should not be taking this medication on an empty stomach. You're also hooked up to a catheter, so don't worry about getting up to go to the restroom. We will help you get out of bed tomorrow. Ok?" She had rambled so much off to me at once. I didn't remember anything she said. I just went back to sleep. Awaking the next morning, I noticed two cards, a Pooh bear, and a balloon. Diamond and my baby daddy had been by, but I was too knocked out to notice. Turning my head towards the window, I saw my mom curled up neatly in a reclining hospital chair. Draped in a comforter from my house, she was sleeping also. As I tried to turn more towards her, I could tell that she had been in that position for quite some time. She looked uncomfortable, but I knew she wasn't going anywhere. I was happy to see her.

Taking a moment to reflect on what had transpired over the previous 48 hours, I was heartbroken, hurt, drained, and angry. How come this happened? How did this happen? I had so many questions. Recalling my initial visit to the OB/GYN, I remembered the doctor telling me that the fetus was too small to notice on the sonogram. "Come back in four more weeks," he said. Not even considering that I may have had an ectopic pregnancy, he let me go on about my merry way.

Waking up out of her sleep, my mom sat up, looked over at me, and noticed the tears in my eyes. "Hi, baby." I looked over at her and started to cry even more. I was devastated. Handing me a tissue, she said, "I'm here 'til you get better. Don't worry about anything else. Just focus on yourself for once, Lynn."

My mom still reminded me of the black version of Erica Kane from *All My Children*. Dressed in a casual bejeweled outfit with sunglasses, I chuckled at how she managed to keep them on her face while sleeping in the chair. Her wig was always intact and I took a few minutes to just focus on her. "How did you get here?"

"I took the train up. Richard drove me to the train station in DC and your boo picked me up in your car from Penn Station in the city." My mom was now onto her fourth marriage. My stepdad Eugene was caught cheating in St. Thomas with a flight attendant so my mom kept it moving. "Your boo said he had some errands to run so he dropped me off and said he'd be back before visiting hours were over." she said.

"Ok," I responded. I was so unenthused about his whereabouts. Our relationship was basically over and I had already determined that I was not going to force the relationship because of my pregnancy. Though God had sent his angels to administer to me through him, deep down I knew he had come back to get the rest of his things. Since that was the case, there was no need to badger him about anything. He showed up right on time and for that, I was grateful.

During the course of the week, I had become physically stronger. I was able to make it to the restroom on my own and I was ready to get out of there and into my own bed. "Lynn, while you were sleeping, the doctor came by. They are discharging you today."my mom smiled.

"Yes!" I yelled out.

"Don't get too excited. The doctor wants you on bed rest for the next four to six weeks, Ms. Thang. So don't go making' no plans." Mom said.

"I'm not. I'm just ready to go home." I said.

My mom was a real trooper. Over the course of the week, my mom would come to the hospital at the start of visiting hours and leave one hour after visiting hours ended. Leave it to black mothers to break the hospital rules. After my discharge, she went back home for a day to grab some things and tie up some loose ends. She was back with me for another entire week. I needed her, but as I started to heal, mommy started to wear on my nerves. When it was time for her to leave, I was sad to see her go though.

Three weeks into my recovery, I was starting to get bored. I awoke at 2am to use the restroom. I had become completely thrown off with time because I was wide-awake. The blinds in my bedroom were cracked open and I just stared up to the moon. Its glow always held my attention, and as it shined I would often notice and sometimes even take pictures of the two rays that came from it. The rays would often look like the shape of a cross and I would be so mesmerized by this—to the point where no one could ever tell me that God does not exist. The moon's cross shaped rays have always been my own personal confirmation of the blood that Jesus shed for me. As I lay in bed and reflected on the year, I began to tear up. I had been through so much. I was exhausted. I knew I couldn't continue on this path for much longer. A new plan had to be put in place.

Chapter 19:
Adventures with Arian (Lil Wayne)

It was now July of 2007 and I was just starting to get back into the swing of things. It had been almost twelve weeks since the loss of my baby and I needed some air. "Lynn. What's up girl? It's me, Arian. I'm in New York this weekend for Wayne and Juelz's show. I know you have been healing from your loss, but I would love to see you. Call me," Arian said on the voicemail message I had just checked. After erasing the message, I went to take a look at Juelz Santana's calendar. He was indeed scheduled to perform on the same bill as Lil Wayne at the Beacon Theatre in the city. So I called up Arian to say that I would meet her there. She was excited to hear from me. My workload was extremely light and I was only doing events at the time. I had been taking it easy since the loss of my baby.

As the day started to draw closer to an end, Twin called my phone. It was typical of him to call me whenever his brother had a show. "You know the show tonight is in New York. You should come. You never come to Juelz's shows anymore. Plus, we may go and get something to eat afterwards and I know you aren't going to turn down a meal," he said jokingly.

"You right about that!" I replied. "Plus Arian is in town to check on Lil Wayne. I haven't seen her since Chris Brown's party, so I'ma go."

"Ok. That's what's up. We meeting up at 6pm so don't be late." He responded.

"Aight" And when I hung up the phone, I hit the shower, dressed, and jumped into my car. It was 4:30pm when Twin and I had spoken so I was definitely in rush mode. When I arrived to our meeting place, I hugged the guys and cracked jokes with them. "We gotta get going," Juelz snapped to all of us. Wayne was in town and he was always excited to see him. The two seemed to have a good friendship and great working chemistry. Hopping into the phantom with Juelz, I cracked jokes with him and his driver Woodrow (regular driver for the Robinson family) and chatted it up with the two as we drove down to the Beacon.

It felt great to be back in the midst of things, and though I was with the guys that night, I wasn't really working and they knew it too. Upon our arrival, we pulled up behind Lil Wayne's tour bus and awaited the signal for us to enter. The back door was packed. Dialing Arian's number, I spotted her standing outside of Wayne's bus. "Arian!" I yelled out to her from inside of the Phantom. I could be so ghetto at times.

"Lynn! Girl! It's soo good to see you! Look at youuuu...all skinny and thangs!" I had managed to lose a lot of weight, but it wasn't a healthy weight loss process, so I just thanked her anyway. "It's soooooo hectic back here. Dudes are fighting over backstage passes and pushing and shoving to get in" said Arian.

"Oh wow. Well, I ain't with that. I can stay right here in Juelz's car with Woodrow until he's done." Walking over to the car, Twin handed backstage passes and tickets to me and Arian. "Yall good? Y'all can come in wheneva y'all ready. It's so hectic in there that I'ma just have Lz (Juelz) sit out here in the car til it's time for him to go on." Twin said.

"Oh. Ok," I responded.

"Well lemmee go and tell Cortez where I am," Arian mentioned. "I'll be right back." Cortez was Lil Wayne's Manager and Arian's point person for her client.

When Arian arrived back to the vehicle, Juelz was ready to start moving into the venue. Fans and groupies came from out of nowhere and by the time we hit the back door's entrance, over two hundred "friends and family" were in tow. "Awww man. Arian. Let's just get back into the car until that door calms down cause I'm not in the mood to be helping Twin regulate things today." Agreeing with me, we then climbed back into Juelz's plush white Phantom. The two of us talked it up so much that Juelz had performed and gotten back into the car within a matter of minutes.

"You done?!" I asked curiously.

"Yes! Where were y'all?" Juelz asked.

Laughing hysterically, the two of us said in unison, "We been sittin' in the car talkin'!"

"All this time?! Y'all missed everything!" he said looking disappointed, but we didn't acknowledge his disappointment. Instead, we just laughed, playing it off. At that moment, I felt like a mother or big sister who had missed her child's elementary school recital.

"What y'all bout to do?" Arian asked.

"I think we going to go get something' to eat. You know that's the only reason why Lynn is here," said Juelz, laughing with a goofy grin.

"Well, wait for me. I wanna say 'bye' to Wayne and Tez." Arian rushed.

"They are going to join us, but you are more than welcome to ride with us," Juelz stated.
When Arian got back to the car, we immediately

started to pull off.

"We are actually meeting up with everyone in about an hour, but I need to get something from uptown so we going to make a stop first." Juelz reported.

"Ok" we both responded. Pulling out of the congested back street of the Beacon, we headed to the West Side Highway with the entourage in tow, and as we began to approach the exit, Juelz noticed that we were being followed.

"Woodrow," Juelz said to his driver.

"Yeah. I notice.," he replied. Woodrow was on it! I dialed Twin's number and before I could say anything, he answered his phone by saying, "Yeah. I see the car following us."

"I think it's the Hip-hop Police," Juelz said. "'Cause they are following us way too close. A hood nigga wouldn't be rolling' up to us that close to the car. Arian call and check on Wayne. Let him know that the hip-hop Police out here are no joke." Juelz ordered.

Dialing Wayne's number, Arian got no answer. Then she dialed Cortez's number, E.I.'s number, and any and everybody else's number that could've been with them on the tour bus. She got no answer. "No one is picking up." Then Juelz picked up the phone to dial Wayne's phone, but he also got no answer.

"Woodrow. Pull over," Juelz said.

"Right here? Right now?" Woodrow asked.

"Yes. Pull the f*** ova. I wanna see who the f*** this is." My heart was racing. As we pulled over onto the side of Broadway and 153rd Street, Juelz jumped out of the vehicle to confront the navy blue Ford Taurus that was following us. As the tailgating vehicle pulled over, I immediately spotted it as a cop car. Juelz approached the car, four cops jumped out of the vehicle. "I'm saying. Do you have a reason as to why you are following us? What have we done wrong? Y'all been following us since we left the Beacon. This is some bullshit. Why can't yall just leave us the fuck alone?" Juelz yelled out. At this point we were all tired of the hip-hop police and to this day I still don't understand why there is a task force designed specifically for rappers in New York City. Within the past year, most rappers in NYC had become familiar with them and eventually, we all began to know them by name.

"We just wanna make sure you got home safe," one of them responded.

"That's bullshit!" Juelz yelled out. "I'm fine. I'm in my

hood and it's all good" By this time, the rest of the entourage was starting to pull up and a scene was starting to erupt. We were all asked to step away from our vehicles where searches had been started. Copying down our driver's licenses, running our records, and scoping out the vehicles we drove in had become the 'norm'.

Following an exchange of harsh words, our information checked out to be just fine and we were well on our way. We had been on the side of the street in Harlem for nearly an hour and a half and by the time we were done, no one had an appetite. Arian and Juelz were worried about Lil Wayne who had yet to answer his phone and it wasn't til the morning that we found out why.

Flipping on the TV in my bedroom, I saw a news clip flash at the bottom of the screen that read: Rapper Lil Wayne arrested last night on weapons charges. 'Oh snap!" I then called Arian who had already gotten the news. She and Lil Wayne's management team were already on it! It was crazy!

"He's good girl. They are posting his bail now and he will be out in time to keep it moving to the next city." Lil Wayne stayed on the road, but a gun charge in the city of New York was serious. "I'll call you once I get settled and it was sooo good to see you." said Arian.

Hanging up from Arian, I called Twin and Juelz. "See! I knew something was wrong!" Disgusted at the news, the two hung up and began to reach out to Cortez on their own.

During this point and time in hip-hop, rappers were quickly becoming targets for haters, robbers, stalkers, and cops who just wanted to get some notoriety under their belts. Artists were now under a more advanced microscope. As a publicist, I started to notice how rappers started to become misunderstood by the media, the public, and the police. From my experience of being around Artists, their weapons were not used to torment or rob others. Their weapons were used as a means of protection for not only themselves, but their family members as well. It was this very reason I had become a mouthpiece for my often misunderstood peers of prominence.

It would be three years before Lil Wayne would have to serve time for this offense.

I can't even count on my hands and toes the number of times I've heard about someone trying to extort celebrities. People have even called me on occasions to relay messages. The life of a rapper is not as glamorous as everyone thinks. Everything that glitters is truly not gold.

It was now September of 2007 and I had not seen Arian since our brief encounter from the Beacon Theatre. We had spoken, but very infrequently.

"Hey, Arian," I said when answering my cell phone.

"Hey girl! How are you? You've been on my mind," she stated.

"I'm doing good. I can't complain. I have another event I'd like to have you partner up with me on. You interested? I know you haven't been working much, but I could really use your help" she spoke.

"Well, what's up?" I asked.

"I'm putting together Wayne's Twenty-Fifth Birthday Party on a yacht in Miami and I have less than a month to put it together girl!"

"Oh really!? That sounds nice and different," I stated. I was already interested and not just because it was Lil Wayne. I was interested because it was in Miami AND on a yacht. I was tired of the typical celebrity birthday bash. "Count me in. I could use a change of pace." I said.
"Yaaaay! Well Jocelyn is on board as well. Can you get in on this conference call I'm doing later this

evening with me and the rest of the team?" she asked.

"Yep. Count me in. Have your Assistant email me the call's logistics and I'll dial in." I replied.

"Ok. Cool," Arian replied.

It had been a few weeks since I had spoken to her or Jocelyn and I had not seen her since Chris Brown's MTV parties. I missed Jocelyn. I was looking forward to their positive energy because that was exactly what I needed at this point in my life.

Hanging up from the conference call, we all agreed on the theme, guest list, attire, and designation of roles before and during the party. While Arian and her staff were to handle the overall logistics of the party, Jocelyn and I wrangled up the celebrities; invited the media to cover the Red Carpet; and followed up on mailed and emailed invites, while also enforcing the black and white themed Harlem Renaissance Party.

Less than three days to go with Lil Wayne's party, we all met up in Miami to put the finishing touches on décor; security; gift bags; the step & repeat; media confirmations; travel accommodations for VIP's; and more. The party was off to smooth sailing.

Landing into Fort Lauderdale, my client, Juelz Santana

started to ring my phone. "Lynn. I heard this is a 'black & white' party. I don't have anything black or white. I had packed a grey suit only. My shirt and shoes are black. So you gotta figure this out" In the midst of running around and calling to remind celebs of the attire, I had totally forgotten to enforce the dress code upon my own clients.

"Ok. I gotchu. You are staying at the Victor Hotel on Ocean Drive. I will have a suit to you in a few. I have some ideas. I gotchu." I assured.

"Ok. Cool. I want something from Gucci or Louis. Don't bring me no bullshit. Word up. It's your fault" Santana snapped.

I just hung up the phone. "What!? What is it? Things have been going so smoothly," Jocelyn looked over to me as we were heading to Denny's for a bite to eat.

"I forgot to tell Juelz about the dress code. I gotta go find him a suit and I mean like now" I huffed.

"Damn! I'm hungry. But let's do it! This can't be too bad," I said. But as we started to shop, locating a white suit was definitely difficult. It was now fall so white was not "in." Driving to the Bal Harbour Mall, an exclusive high-end fashion shopping center, the two of us split up. While I went to Gucci and Armani, Jocelyn went to Louis Vuitton and Ralph Lauren. We found nothing for Juelz to wear, and just as the two of us decided to try one more store back down on South Beach, I spotted a white suit on a mannequin posing in the Gap's window. "Girl look!" Jocelyn came to a screeching halt as the two of us salivated at the thought of finding Juelz a suit. Jumping out of the car before she could put it in park, I ran into the store and inquired about the suit. And before Jocelyn could walk into the store, I had the salesperson stripping the doll in the window and steaming the suit to perfection. Two hundred and fifty dollars! Whew. The suit was on me.

"Girl. Do you think Juelz will fall for a suit from the Gap," Jocelyn asked.

"Heck no!" I hissed.

"So what you going to do then?" she asked.

"I'm about to cut these tags out of the suit, for real, 'cause I'm not tryna hear it. I'll just tell him that we got it out of a suit place like Thomas Pink or something." I grinned.

"Hahahaaha! You are too funny! That would work"... and it did. Juelz loved the suit and handkerchief we purchased for him. To top it all off he didn't even have to pay for it. The two of us put out that little fire, headed to our hotel, got dressed, headed to the yacht, and began to stuff gift bags. We never got a chance to eat, but that often came with the territory.

Evening drew near and it was a beautiful warm breezy night. As the media started to line the carpet, celebs started pulling up. Tiny and T.I., Diddy, LaToya Luckett and Slim Thug, Juelz, DJ Khaled, Angie Martinez, Rick Ross, and more boarded the boat to show love to Lil Wayne for his 25th birthday party. Partygoers respected and adhered to the dress code. Boarding the Biscayne Lady yacht, females were dressed in their best Harlem Renaissance attire. Dressed conservatively, female guests wore dresses without a waistline, red rouged cheekbones, and pearls to fit the theme. Men wore suits and dressed conservatively.

The night was perfect and drama free! The only backlash from the bash was that my feet were sore for two days following the party.

Chapter 20:
Juelz Santana

Oklahoma City (Dec. 2007)

It was a typical travel day. Juelz and his crew were nowhere to be found three hours before departure and I was tired. Why can't they be mature and professional enough to be located so close to our flight time? Locking up my apartment with a trash bag in one hand and my trusty Hello Kitty backpack equipped with three pair of underwear, toiletries, a fresh hoodie, and my head scarf, I headed to the dumpster and then to the car.

Dialing Juelz's phone during the entire seven-minute ride to his studio, he still had not answered. Pulling up to the studio, I threw the gear to my Benz into Park and headed for the door. And just as I was about to bang the door out, it opened. It was Juelz grinning ear to ear. Looking too bothered by his smile I asked, "Why the hell were you not picking up the phone? Why can't you just be normal and answer the phone? I shouldn't have to drive all the way over here. I should just be able to meet you at the airport." I fussed.

"My bad, Lynn," Juelz said in a goofy manner. Just then a petite light skinned female peered from behind him with a painted on body suit and a platinum wig that clearly needed some adjustments.

"Well let's go! Tell Cobain to hurry it up as well. Big Boo is already at the airport" I yelled. Cobain was his DJ and Big Boo was the huge three-coach-seat sized security guy that regularly traveled with them. Juelz and Cobain scurried to get their shoes on and headed out the door.

Hoppin' into the back seat of my car Juelz asked, "Lynn, can I smoke in your car?" while he started to light up anyway. I couldn't wait until Juelz's brother and manager, Twin, was back in the saddle. I was covering for him on the road for a few shows because his girlfriend was expecting their third child. Juelz didn't normally trust anyone else to collect the money from promoters once the crew arrived to the performance city, except for his brother or me.

Arriving at the airport 30 minutes prior to departure, I handed the care of my car over to Steve, the recording engineer who also doubled as a driver when needed. "Only drive my car to the studio and back here tomorrow to pick us up. Ok?" I demanded.

"Ok," Steve responded sleepily.

Getting to the airport late was nothing new to me and

the crew and besides, we had become extremely popular at LaGuardia. Security had become used to our rowdy rush tactics and our mad dashes to the gate. I had the hurry hustle down packed. As long as one person in the group's travel party had a First Class seat, the entire travel party was allowed to skip the line. This burned a lot of Coach Class people up every time, but I didn't care. My job was to make sure we didn't miss the flight.

Catching the flight just short of having the doors closed on us, we got seated and buckled up as the plane headed for the runway, and just as I closed my eyes to say a silent prayer before take off, I felt someone's breath in my face. It was Juelz. "Boy! What are you doing out of your seat? You better go sit down!"

"You forgot to give me my sour patch kids". I reached in my pocket and handed the bag over to him.

"Sir! You need to have a seat. Sir!! Flight regulations say that you can't get up out of your seat during takeoff and landings!!" The flight attendant gawked over the intercom system.

Taking his hands away from me and Cobain, he yelled out, "Aight! Damn! I'm going. You ain't got to blow me up like dat!"

Heading back to his First Class seat at his own pace, passengers started their loud whispers, wondering who this rail thin rapper was with all of the bling.

Twenty minutes prior to landing, the flight attendant came onto the intercom. "Ladies and gentleman, make sure your seatbacks are up right and your tray tables are locked back in place. We will be arriving in minutes." As I gathered up my belongings and placed my iPod back into my bag, I started to daydream about the show. I hope this is a simple in and out type of show. I'm not in the mood for no bull crap from these shady promoters.

Twenty minutes went by and then 40 minutes went by. I did not notice the time because I had dozed off again. Waking up again to the smell of smoke in my face, I opened my eyes to Juelz. "Boy! You are going to get us thrown off this plane!" I whispered aggressively to him.

"Well let them throw me off. Scoot over." I unbuckled my seat belt and slid over to the middle seat as Juelz sat in my aisle seat. "Something is wrong Lynn. We was supposed to land like a hour ago and these niggaz are all up front acting all crazy and shit so please ask them what the deal is." he wispered.

Before Juelz could get his last word out of his mouth the

intercom came on. "Ladies and Gentleman, this is the Captain speaking" Oh Snap! "We are having some extreme difficulty with the landing gear. One of the gears seems to be stuck. This could be due to the cold temperatures outside. There is no need to panic. You have an excellent crew on board. Attendants roll the emergency landing infomercial and we will begin the steps to prepare for an emergency landing."

"See! Didn't I just say that something was wrong?" said Juelz.

Heart pounding heavily, I started looking intently at the infomercial. It was horrifying. I couldn't concentrate on the screen. All I kept seeing was my life flash before my eyes, while Juelz was bantering in my right ear about all of the things he needed to do and accomplish with his life. Besides that, the other plane passengers were in an uproar. No one was sitting still and all of the whispers had turned into loud open conversations. Ding Dong. "Sir! We need you to take your seat!" the attendant yelled over the intercom once again.

This time, it was Cobain standing over my aisle. "Move ova yo! Cause if this plane is going down, then I'm going down with my family. Word up!"

"Where are we supposed to move over to Cobain? Can't you see that there is someone sitting next to me?"

Seated next to me was a frail white lady who had already had her fill of my motherly scolding and Juelz's whining topped off with what was really going on.

"It's ok! I will get up!" Before Juelz and I could move into the aisle and out of her way to swap seats with Cobain, she had already climbed forward into an empty seat directly in front of us. We didn't know whether to burst out laughing or stay in the moment. Settling back down once more, the three of us peered into the aisle when we heard a commotion going on. It was the Captain himself heading towards the back of the plane with a tool box in his hand. Where the heck is he headed?

Stopping at our aisle, the Captain got down on his knees and pulled out a knife. With his neck beet red, he immediately started to cut the aisle's carpet to pieces in a wide square pattern. Locating a long square metal hatch, the Captain then unscrewed the hatch's hinges with his portable power drill and opened it up. With jaws dropped so low to the ground, the silence in the plane's cabin was deafening. Squeezing himself gently and calmly through the hatch, the Captain disappeared down into the baggage compartment for the longest fifteen minutes ever. The entire plane stared down at the hatch wondering how much longer it would take the Captain to reappear.

Emerging from the hatch with the tie missing from his shirt, he sealed the hatch back up with the power drill, grabbed his toolbox, and headed back to the cock pit with no sign of progress. Ding Dong. "This is your Captain speaking. I just manually cranked the landing gear. So let's just pray that it sticks. I am going to attempt to land this plane in a few minutes. I am just waiting for emergency crews to get in place and once they are in place, we will be all clear to attempt the landing."

"Get the fuck out of here," yelled Juelz. "This shit is crazy!!!"

Sitting shocked and in silence, I could feel the plane's elevation. They were going up further into the sky. Ok. I've seen this on TV before. They must be dumping fuel.

Not noticing how much I was shaking, Juelz grabbed my hand and Cobain put his hand on my knee. "Stop shaking yo. It's going to be alright."

"What are you talking about?" I asked. "I'm not shaking" But the fact was I was shaking so badly that my teeth chattered when I spoke to the guys.

"Ok, Ms. Prayer Warrior, pray". Cobain fussed.

"Thank you Lord for getting us to and from Oklahoma

City safely. In Jesus' name. Amen," Juelz yelled out so that I and everyone could hear.

"AMEN!" half the plane exclaimed.

As the captain started to descend the plane, there was no question as to which runway he was preparing to land on. There were fire trucks and just about every ambulance the city owned formed an aluminous runway of red and white lights while waiting for the plane's arrival. When the plane's wheels touched the runway, the gear locked in and landed, but as the captain started to apply the brakes, the wheels buckled and the plane slid to a complete stop... right in front of the gate... and just shy of crashing into the airport's vast windows.

"Thank you, Jesus!" I shouted as the plane came to a complete stop.

Upon landing into Cincinnati, we checked the board for the status of our connecting flight and it was no surprise that the flight had left us. The next flight to Oklahoma was not scheduled to leave for another five hours, so a nice flight attendant provided us with meal vouchers to eat at any restaurant within the airport and hotel vouchers for us to go and freshen up and/or take a quick nap.

Opting for the quick naps, hotel food, and an ordered movie, Juelz, the crew, and I headed out of the airport and to the Marriott to rest and regroup. Closing the door behind me, I threw my bags on the floor, made a call down to the front desk for a wakeup call, and then threw myself on the bed. Reaching for the pillow, I screamed into it at the top of my lungs. I needed to have a vocal release. I thanked GOD aloud numerous times. I was relieved and happy to be alive. I immediately started to count my blessings. I named each one aloud until I fell off to sleep.

Arriving back at the airport, we placed our belongings onto the rolling belt to be scanned and x-rayed by security. In front of us stood a pale white hippie woman with bags and a baby boy that she had warmly dressed in a Santa Claus outfit. I would never dress my child like that I thought while waiting my turn to go through the metal detector. Juelz stood in front of me, and instead of removing his fifty million chains, studded belt, rings, and anything else that could possibly beep, he was way more focused on the lady who decided to dress her baby up as the lil Santa clown he was. So of course he wasn't ready to immediately walk through the detector, and just as I was about to cut in front of him, he started to shove me for the opportunity to go ahead of me. When Juelz started to walk through the metal detector, I gasped and quickly snatched him back. "What the f*ck!" he yelled out to me.

Communicating to him with my big eyes and managing not to say one word, I motioned down to the floor inside of the metal detector. On the floor lay a huge bag of weed. When security motioned for one of us to walk through the detector, we both looked down in amazement onto the floor.

"Security!!!" the guard yelled. In no time, additional security was called over to us.

"Oh don't even try it. That shit ain't mine. You betta go get that white woman and baby Santa," Juelz yelled.

Looking back at the commotion, the entourage that had already made it through security by standing in line for other metal detectors watched him throw a fit. "Don't look at me because I'm black. White people smoke weed too," he went on.

"Sir. Calm down. You and that lady," meaning me, "can go." We quickly walked through, picked up our belongings on the other side and headed to the gate.

As we began to head to the gate, we began to give the details to the rest of the entourage. Security came running up behind us and passed us. Heading straight for the lady with the baby in the Santa suit, another bag of weed dropped out of her baby. "Wow! That is crrrazzzyyyy" we all seemed to say simultaneously as the lady was damn near tackled to the ground with baby in hand. The baby was immediately removed from her arms by an officer. She was then read her rights and arrested. This was just a typical day in the life of a hip-hop publicist.

Chapter 21:
Huddy (October 2010)

On one crisp October morning, I drove over to meet Twin to go over some paperwork and just as I was pulling out of his Fort Lee, New Jersey complex, he screamed over to me. "Lynn!"

I abruptly came to a halt as I watched his facial expression change. "Did you hear about Huddy?" he asked as I rolled down my window.

"No. What about him?" Huddy was one of Cam'ron's best friends. In fact, he was the passenger riding with Cam on the night he was shot during Howard's Homecoming Weekend in Washington, DC

"He died this AM on the George Washington Bridge."

"Oh my God! Are you serious? Are you sure? 'Cause you know how rumors get started. Maybe it was a fender bender and the rumor mill just got carried away."

"Nah. It's official. He's gone." And when he said that, I just buried my chin into my chest and exhaled. It had been almost five years to the exact date that he and Cam had been shot at in the Lamborghini during Howard's Homecoming in DC

"Lemmee call my man and ask." Picking up the phone to dial Kelly's number, I asked him if he had heard anything—and his response was, "I haven't heard anything. Lemmee call you back." And less than five minutes later, he called back to confirm the news. He had just spoken to his mother who was on her way to the hospital to identify his body.

Huddy died in the wee hours of the morning while traveling on the southbound upper level of the George Washington Bridge when his vehicle collided with a truck. This deadly accident stopped traffic for the entire morning rush hour with a traffic jam that spanned for well over six hours.

Pushed into companion mode, I was then hurled into being a helper—as my boyfriend Kelly was one of Huddy's really good colleagues. As the funeral arrangements got under way, I was blessed to written his bio within the "reflections" page of his funeral program. Several celebs such as Diddy; Ray Benzino; Dave Mays (*Hip-Hop Weekly*); and many more called in to give their condolences and to offer assistance to his mother.

Devastated from the loss of one of Harlem's finest, I wasn't the only one touched by Huddy's positive energy, and it showed on the day of his funeral. His funeral was not just a day of mourning, but a day of celebration. "I don't want a typical funeral," stated Mama EJ. "Huddy was always the life of the party and I want his home-going service to be just that—a party," and a party it was! As Phantoms, Bentleys, Benz's, and Beamers lined St. Nicholas Avenue, the motorcade turned into a parade. Harlem truly came out to honor one of their own. With well over five thousand people flooding the streets to catch a glimpse of his casket, his body was carried down several blocks from the wake to the funeral's location by a sleek black horse drawn carriage. As celebs joined in to party one last time for Huddy, it became a shoving match at the church's entrance for people to pay their last respects.

When the Preacher proceeded with his sermon, he stated, "Huddy was a blessing to so many people" and the over capacity church began to applaud and cheer. "And so that's what we all need to be, my young brothas and sistahs and especially the celebs sitting in the church pews. We need to all be a blessing to others until all of our people have been blessed." I didn't really expect to take too much from what I had already assumed would be a normal funeral; however, I received confirmation that it is extremely important to impact the lives of many in a positive way.

Rest in Peace Huddy!

Chapter 22:
Cuzo (Nov 2010)

It was a beautiful November day. Warmer than usual, there wasn't even a cloud in the sky. As Kelly (my man of two years) and I nestled into a booth at Houston's Restaurant in New Jersey, I ordered a glass of Riesling and he ordered a Ginger Ale. We ordered the traditional chips with spinach and artichoke dip and proceeded to gaze into each other's eyes. The two of us were celebrating his victory. He had won a court case today after the odds had been stacked up against him. When our drinks arrived, we toasted. "To victory!" We tapped our glasses, sipped and placed them back onto the table.

"So, Ms. Hobson, how was your day?" he asked. My phone started to ring, but I ignored it.

"Oh. My day has been good, uneventful. All is quiet for the most part. I'm about to enter a quiet period for my regular clients and a busy season for companies who may want to hire my company for holiday parties." I mentioned.

Nodding as if to be really intrigued with what I was saying, he reached over to grab my hand. For a guy, his hands were soooo soft. His smile was warm and his dimples were boyishly cute. And as I gazed into his eyes, my phone rang again. I ignored it.

"Your phone is ringing," he motioned. I cringed at the thought of an emergency—as Kelly often got irritated when my phone would ring off the hook like it was doing at the moment.

"I know. I was trying to enjoy the moment," but my phone kept ringing. When I answered, it was Ms. Debbie, Juelz's Mom. "Yes Ms. Debbie?"

"Lynn! Where are you?" She was yelling at the top of her lungs.

"Ummmm... I'm with Kelly at Houston's. What's up?" I asked like, what the hell is wrong with her?

"Leave Houston's right now and go to the studio!" Ms. Debbie insisted.

"Huh?" I was like Ms. Debbie done lost her mind.

"Lynn. Ok. Lemmee calm down. Go to the studio please."

"Ok, but why?"

"The guys are calling from the studio. Cuzo is passed

out at the studio. The guys are trying to administer CPR until the ambulance arrives."

"What!? Are you serious Ms. Debbie?" I asked.

"Yyyeeessss!!!" she yelled.

"Ok. I'm on the way." I just hung up from her and politely turned to Kelly, who was already in the middle of ordering his entrée.

"Ummm... I gotta go. There's an emergency at the studio and before I say something' I don't mean, it's just best for me to get there." I hurried.

"Ok. No problem," he responded in an understanding tone. Kelly was a music producer from the East Coast. He had produced music for several known Hip-hop Artists. He was a single Father with three kids. We had met years prior at a birthday party for Whitney Houston's father at Justin's in midtown.

"I can drive you if you'd like," he suggested. "That way you will be free to make any calls or texts message you'd like to make."

"Ok. That would be fine," I responded while heading out of the door. I didn't bother to motion for the waitress or anything. I was out of there. Trailing several feet behind me, I had no qualms about leaving him behind if he wasn't near our vehicles which were parked side by side. "Sorry for the delay. I wanted to let our waitress know the deal." Clicking the alarm off of his car and unlocking his door, I got into the passenger's side and we sped off. Lucky for me, he was already familiar with the studio's location.

Gripping my blackberry, I anxiously called Twin and as he answered my call, he responded, "I know. I'm on the way. I'm in the city so give me a minute. I'm almost on the Bridge."

"Ok. Cool." I replied.

"Just call me when you get there." Twin stated.

"Cool." I said.

"Aight." Twin hung up.

Just as I was about to dial Juelz's number, Ms. Debbie called. "Are you there yet?"

"I'm pulling up now. Lemmee call you back." We had arrived to the studio in no time. Turning into the studio's driveway, it was cluttered with paramedics and police cars and I literally jumped out of the car before Kelly could place the car in park.

"Hi. I'm Lynn, the publicist for the studio," I mentioned rapidly to one of the officers. "Where is he and what's going on?"

The officer started to respond immediately without any hesitation. "Hi. Well the paramedics just loaded him up into the ambulance. As of now, he has no pulse and no heartbeat." I gasped. Another officer walked over to me. "But the good thing is that we shocked him five times and his heart did respond. So that's not too bad."

Holding my hand up to my mouth, I looked to my left to see John Depp, Juelz's Artist, Two Step the Engineer, and Anthony, our handyman, coming out of the studio. Not wanting them to really see my facial expression, I straightened up. "Ok. Thanks officers. The ambulance is taking him to Holy Name Hospital, correct?" I asked.

"Yes." The officer replied.

"Ok. Thank you." I looked over at the guys and said, "Gimmee Cuzo's cell phone. NOW!" I was frantic. Running back inside, Depp ran out with his pearl white Blackberry. I then hopped back into Kelly's car and we sped off in an effort to stay close to the ambulance. My cell phone rang. It was Twin. "Just meet me at the hospital. I didn't get a chance to see him before they loaded him up into the ambulance. So just meet me."

"Ok. I'm already a few blocks from the hospital. See you in a minute," Twin responded.

Pulling up to the hospital, I turned to Kelly and said, "I'm good. You don't have to stay. Twin is going to meet me here so he will make sure I will get home."

"Oh no. I'm not going to leave you like this. I'ma wait right here for you," he responded. I just shrugged as if to concede and gave a half a grin. Twin immediately pulled up in his X6 and hopped out with the keys still in the car. I just looked at Kelly, who spontaneously ran over to the vehicle to park it. Thank GOD for people with common sense who say they wanna help and actually do so.

When Twin and I arrived to the Information Desk inside of the hospital's Emergency Room, I said to the desk clerk, "Hi. Our family member Michael Roberson was just brought in by ambulance. Can we go back?"

"Just one moment. What was his name again?" he asked politely.

"Michael Roberson," I repeated.

"Ok. Give me one second. Let me go back in the ER to see if they've placed him into a room. In the meantime, you can have a seat and I'll be right back." The receptionist stated.

The Emergency Room was empty so we had a wide selection of seats to choose from. Kelly and I sat in a section while Twin opted to stand. Not even five minutes went by before the desk clerk came over to us. "Ok. Follow me."

"I'll wait out here for you, Lynn." Kelly gestured.

"Ok. Cool." I replied.

Twin held the door for me as we went back to Cuzo's room. "Ok. Have a seat in this room," said the clerk. It was a small cozy little room inside the ER with a sign at the door's entrance that said, "Consultation Room."

"Awww, man. This can't be good," I mumbled. Why do they have us in this room? Just take me to him. I thought to myself. Opting to just stand outside of the room, neither one of us had a desire to go into that room. We were not going to further claim anything negative. A white male doctor and two African American staff members came peering around the corner.

The doctor looked the two of us in the eyes, and said, "I'm sorry, but your loved one didn't make it. The paramedics did everything they could do to revive him.

That team is actually the best, but we pronounced him dead on arrival as soon as we saw him." The doctore consoled.

Not quite digesting what he was saying, the two of us, just hung our heads as low as they could possibly go. I couldn't even shed a tear. I was in shock and numb to what was going on. The outcome just seemed to be so crazy. "Well, what was the cause of death?" I asked.

"Well I can't say for sure. You will have to wait until the Coroner comes back with the final autopsy, but it looks like cardiac arrest," he mentioned. Shaking my head in disgust, I mustered up the words to let the doctor and his team know that Cuzo's Mom was expected at any minute.

Opting to go outside for some fresh air, we walked outside of the ER and into the Visitor's Drop Off area where Juelz and the other Skull Gang Members waited patiently. Looking at the ghostly looks on our faces, everyone could immediately tell that something was wrong. "Yo!"Twin called out to everyone who seemed to be scattered throughout the parking lot. "Cuzo didn't make it. He died before arriving to the hospital."

Before he could finish saying those hurtful words, the guys started whaling and crying loudly. Our youngest member, John Depp, gagged so hard, he threw up on the hospital's sidewalk.

"Listen! Hush it up!" I said with apprehension. "Cuzo's mom is on the way and I don't know what she looks like, so that being said, you can't grieve right here. I don't want her walking up to the ER to find out this way." The guys tightened up. Some of them even left because the shock of it all was just too much to hold in or handle.

Thirty minutes had passed and there was still no word or sign from Cuzo's Mom. I had called her phone, but got no answer. "Twin. Let's go back inside. It's been a minute. Maybe she got in past us or something." Nodding our heads at each other, the two of us walked back in.

"Oh. The doctor was looking for the two of you," the desk clerk mentioned. Leading us back to the Emergency Room, we immediately spotted the doctor and staff that pronounced him dead. "His mom is here paying her last respects."

"Oh. Ok," we said in unison. Relieved that we did not have to break the news to her, the pain of Cuzo's death was unbearable.

Walking over to us was a heavy set white woman with glasses who managed to crack a pleasant smile. "Hi.

I'm Sue. I work with Michael's mom. I brought her here."

"Hello," I responded. Looking her up and down, I now realized why the two got by us. They were also in hospital scrubs and they looked like employees. Introducing ourselves, we exchanged numbers. She gave me her number and all of the numbers to Cuzo's Mom. As soon as the exchange of contact information had been completed, his mom came quietly out of the room, head hung low, with the look of severe heartbreak in her face. I immediately walked over to her. "Hello," I said.

"Oh. Hi. You must be Lynn and Twin," she responded. Darker in complexion, there was no mistake about it, she was definitely Cuzo's Mom. They looked exactly alike. We both hugged her and assured her that we would be there for her. We let her know that we had all of her information. Nodding her head, she and Sue walked off. Catching up to her quickly, I asked, "Can Twin and I go in and pay our last respects?"

"Why, yes. Go right in." Cuzo's mom permitted.

Turning back towards Twin, the two of us entered the room and there lay Cuzo, still hooked up to a mouth piece and a heart monitoring device. He looked normal—as if he were sleeping. Twin just stood in disgust and anger. He didn't say a word. I, in turn, touched his shoulder and rubbed it gently as I said, "Goodbye Cuzo. We will miss you." As we turned to exit, I looked back and walked over to him one more time. I just couldn't believe that he was dead. A part of me wanted to call on God with all of my might and exercise my God given right to speak to Cuzo's spirit and see if he wanted to stay on this Earth, but I was afraid. I didn't want anyone looking at me like I was crazy. Yeah... the hospital had pronounced him dead, but it ain't over til God says it's over. I guess I have some more growing to do in that area of my spiritual life.

When we got outside, I told Twin I'd check in with Cuzo's Mom tomorrow and give him an update after that. We hugged and parted ways. I then got into the car with Kelly and drove off. "Are you ok?" he asked me.

"No. I'm not ok, but I'm starving." Tears started racing down my face. I couldn't stop the tears. I wanted to keep it moving in order to mask the pain I was feeling.

"Ok. I gotchu," he replied and we drove right on back to Houston's to eat. I mean... what else was I supposed to do? I definitely didn't want to go back to the studio and I definitely didn't want to go home. I had the Hawaiian Rib Eye with a loaded baked potato and a glass of Riesling while he had the Rack of Ribs with

French Fries and a Ginger Ale. As we ate, there wasn't much dialogue between the two of us, but it wasn't awkward. It was cool. He understood my silence and I found comfort in that. When the bill came, I immediately grabbed for it. After all, this dinner was supposed to be a celebration for Kelly's win in court. "Oh. You got it?" he asked.

"Yeah. I got it. Despite what just happened, I didn't want the day to go by without acknowledging your victory. I paid the bill, left a twenty percent tip, and got up out of there. My cell phone had been on silent and I had well over fifteen missed calls. The Gang wanted answers and I didn't have too many to give. Scrolling down to browse at the missed calls, I did have a few from Twin and a few from Cuzo's mom. I returned those calls immediately. I drove all the way home on the phone—oblivious to Kelly driving in his car behind me.

Pulling up to my complex and next to me, Kelly had a sullen look on his face, and before I could ask him if he was ok, he said, "I'ma go by and check on my kids since you seem to have so much stuff to do." But I didn't understand. It was late and the kids had long gone to bed. It was a weekday and they definitely had school the next day. Making sure I arrived home safely, Kelly didn't even bother to say much. There was no conversation and the silence was awkward. So I got out of my car, closed my door, and headed to the building. I swiped my fob key for entry and before I could look back, he sped off. What was that all about? I had to check myself real quick to make sure I had not said or done the wrong thing. Kelly had been kind and considerate about the circumstances and though this was a victorious day for him, there was no way Cuzo's death could not become my priority of the day. Stepping into my apartment, I kicked off my shoes, removed my clothes, grabbed a throw blanket, and just sat in silence on my sofa. Hours must've passed by when I awoke because I had well over seventeen missed calls. It was now 10pm and as I took a quick scroll of the calls, I tossed the blackberry on my sofa, hopped into a hot shower, and went to bed.

The next morning, I was awakened by the sound of my cell phone. The battery was dying, but I could hear it downstairs on my sofa. My apartment was a modern one-bedroom loft. My bedroom was twenty feet high in a plush loft. It was carpeted with a modern bedroom set complete with a soft comforter. An over abundance of plush pillows decorated in chocolate and sea blue took over the bed. The downstairs was equipped with newly finished hardwood floors, modern light fixtures, granite counter tops, and top of the line kitchen appliances. My pad was niiiicccceee. With high ceilings, every loud or faint sound was magnified. The sunlight that peered into the cracks of my blinds were beckoning me. I opened all of the blinds and let God's light shine right on in to my place. Reaching for my phone, I hooked it up to my charger and headed to the bathroom. It was while I sat on the toilet that I remembered that Cuzo had passed less than twenty-four hours ago, and my normal morning mood started to fade as I recited my daily verse, "This is the day the Lord has made. I will rejoice and be glad in it." Slumping over in disbelief, I flushed the toilet, brushed my teeth, washed off my face, and headed to my office nook. I had 28 missed calls.

Scrolling through the calls, I noticed one missed call from Cuzo's mom and I immediately rang her back. "Hello. This is Lynn. Good Morning. I'm sorry I missed your call. I just woke up," I spit out all at once.

"No. It's ok. I just wanted to get an account of what happened at the studio because I just got off the phone with the Coroner and he says that at a glance, it looks like Michael suffered some sort of seizure." Her voice was soft and soothing. She spoke to me as if I was the one who had suffered the loss. As I gave her a brief account about what the guys had been up to, I let her know that Cuzo and the crew had been out dancing' it up and drinking the night before at a club in the city. She then said, "Well, the autopsy report will take about three weeks to come back. So we'll see what it says then. But in the meantime. Would you happen to

know anything about Funerals?" she asked me. "I have been fortunate enough to not have to put one together or go through the process before," she recited.
Since Huddy had just passed away, I knew exactly what needed to take place. "Well we just lost a close family friend a month ago so the process is pretty fresh in my head. A funeral home needs to be located. Do you have one in mind?" At that moment, I realized watching the entire funeral planning process for Huddy prepared me for this moment.

"Yes. I will give them a call, but the funeral home itself might be too small. So I didn't know if we needed to try another avenue." Kim recalled.

"Oh. By all means, call the funeral home. They may have some suggestions for you in terms of a location," I gestured.

"And you know Michael didn't have his insurance policy paid up. His policy lapsed in May. That was six months ago. I gave all of my children their policies along with their coupon booklets this past spring. I told them to pay their own policies since they are now grown and Michael never made one payment towards the policy." She sobbed.

Shaking my head in disgust, I said, "Oh my!" People

never think this life will ever end.

"So I will contact the funeral home and take things one step at a time. Michael did have fourteen hundred dollars in his pocket when he passed. So I will use that towards the expenses as well." She sounded tired, weak, and worn out.

"Ok. Just give me a call once you have contacted the funeral home and I will accompany you." I said.

After thanking me for my assistance, I called Twin without even looking to see if he had called when he answered on the first ring, I could tell that he had been trying to reach me. "Have you heard from Cuzo's mom?" he asked.

"Yeah. I just got off the phone with her. She's going to need money. Cuzo didn't keep a current life insurance policy" I mentioned.

"Ok. Whatever she needs, just let me know. Nothing else really matters right now." Hanging up from Twin, I called Kelly and then Trina to let her know what had happened. I didn't bother about any of the other calls. I just wanted to be on point in case Cuzo's mom called.

As the funeral process got underway, Cuzo's mom conveyed to me that she was in need of seven thousand five hundred dollars. "That will take care of everything, the death certificate, casket, embalming, and the venue." That was a breeze to obtain. Everyone loved Cuzo, so it came as no surprise when we were able to raise the money. As the funeral service was set to happen in five days, no one was admitted into Juelz's recording studio without coughing up a minimum of one hundred dollars towards the funeral. Some gave one hundred dollars. Some gave two hundred dollars and some gave five hundred dollars. However way the money needed to be accrued, we got it. It felt good to deliver the cash to Cuzo's mom. "Lynn, thanks so much. I don't know what I'd do without you." said Kim, Cuzo's mom.

"Awwww... no worries. I know for a fact that if I were in need, Michael would've done the same for me."

Smiling at what I had said, she went on to say, "We are not a very religious family so we are just going to have a Memorial Service. I don't want it to take place at a church so we will have it at the annex to a church in Hackensack. I don't want a Pastor to minister at the service and I don't want any religious music playing. I just want friends and family members to view his body and if they'd like to give remarks, then that will be allowed." Kim stated.

"Ok," I replied. Cuzo's mom, obviously had no idea

that people were not going to sit around for three hours and stare at him. And what if no one wanted to go up and say anything? What if there was too much silence between remarks? Sheesh! When we finished speaking, I immediately called Starr, one of Juelz's former Skull Gang Members and asked her to sing. She agreed. I had Nick, our in-house photographer and videographer, start to gather all of the footage and photos of Cuzo and he then began to put together a video montage of his life.

Instead of a program, our graphics girl, Marsha, created a flyer that basically invited everyone out to celebrate Cuzo' s life. One side of the flyer looked like an invite to a party, while the other side was his biography. Cuzo was the life of the party. His mood was energetic, fun and motivational. His mouth was reckless and whenever I pulled up to the studio, I had to always keep a few sharp words tucked up in my tongue in order to reply to the craziness he would throw my way. It was a "play of words" we all played with Cuzo and it was fun! He was reliable and whenever I couldn't get a pulse on Juelz's whereabouts, I could always depend on Cuzo to pull through for me on his location.

The night before the Memorial Service, I felt uneasy. I know I heard God correctly, telling me, "Help Kim send her son home and follow through on the entire process," and in my mind, I was like, "Ok. I gotchu." The process wasn't difficult; however, the fact that I heard from God when the service was in less than twenty-four hours bothered me. So I did what was natural to me. I picked up the phone and called Trina. "Hey Trina. So the Memorial Service is tomorrow. I'ma put some money into your account. I need you to come up here. You ain't got to do nothing. Just come. Ok?" I asked. For some reason, I felt I needed backup.

Not even hesitating, she sighed and replied, "Ok. We'll be there." "We" meant she and my godson. At just three years of age, Cash was clearly not a baby. He was a man trapped inside of a baby's body.

Hanging up and feeling a little more at ease, I said some positive confessions aloud until my spirit quieted down. "The Lord is my Helper. I shall not fear what man should do to me" and scriptures like, "It is God who arms me with strength and makes my way perfect." And then I began to praise God and thank Him for all of my blessings.

On the day of the Memorial Service, Trina and I arrived to the church early. We placed a flyer onto each of the chairs, placed various life-sized photos of Cuzo onto easels, and placed the Guest Book at the entrance of the church's annex. As people started to pour in quietly, I went into the hallway to call Cuzo's mom to check on the status of her arrival. Sounding upset on the phone, she stated, "Michael doesn't look the same. I had a chance to take a look at him after the funeral home had the clothes placed on him." Speechless at what she was saying, I did understand her, but it was the eleventh hour and there was nothing that could be done about his appearance "Do you want me to have the casket closed?" I asked.

"No. It will have to do. My family and I are getting into Juelz's car now. We should be there shortly." Cuzo's family lived two blocks from the church's annex. Juelz provided the family with his prized white phantom. It was a beauty. Though it was made to be driven by a chauffeur, Juelz often drove it around town as if it were a sports car.

And just as I was hanging up, Cuzo's Mom chimed again, "Lynn. When I was at the church's annex earlier today, there was a cross up. I told them to take it down. I don't want any religious symbols at my son's Memorial Service." I damn near dropped the phone. "Huh?" I replied.

"I want that cross down." I couldn't believe what I was hearing. With the phone to my ear, I located the church's Director and handed her the phone. It was not my battle. While the Director was on the phone with her, I went to grab Trina who was rocking Cash to sleep in the sanctuary. Motioning to her in an emergency state, she held up her finger as if to say "One second please." She placed Cash into his stroller, covered him so that no light came through to disrupt his sleep, and then she strolled on over to me. "Cuzo's mom is telling the church to take that cross down." Looking at me, Trina gasped and grabbed my arm tightly, "Are you serious????" she asked.

"Yes!" I replied in a loud whisper.

The two of us headed back in the direction of my cell phone which was being used by the church's director. We walked into her office without notice to anyone and got caught up in the middle of a heated argument between the Church's Director and six Deacons. "I will NOT remove that cross. That cross symbolizes the blood that Jesus shed for me. I will NEVER do such a thing!" the man yelled. He didn't quite care who heard him. Peering over his shoulder, the church Director then pointed over to us—as if to say, the customer is in the room. And as he quieted down, he looked over to us and stormed out of the office. "I'm sorry Sarah. I am saved, sanctified, and filled with the Holy Ghost and I had no idea that my friend's mom would have been that adamant about the cross." The whole situation didn't sit well with me. To me, the very root of who I am was on the line. Sarah saw my discomfort and so did the other members in the room.

"We have no choice, but to remove the cross," stated Sarah. "I have consulted with the Pastor. We should not have taken her money to rent the space. Normally the cross is not in the Annex, but since we are renovating the sanctuary, we've been holding our services in the Annex." She explained.

Bursting into the room, a few of the elderly women of the church entered the office, disturbed by what the Deacons had just relayed to them. "Had I known we'd be dealing with this today, I would not have volunteered," stated one woman who looked as if someone had just knocked the wind out of her. Upset that I was in the center of this madness, I left the office and leaned up against the wall in the hallway. How could I have ignored the signs. Didn't God tell me to help Kim? My head was spinning. As Trina exited the office, she walked over to me, grabbed my hand and led me to the church's kitchen. Some of the volunteers were in the kitchen in a circle holding hands. I knew what they were doing, so Trina and I joined in. "Now baby, your best friend has let us know your stance on this and we understand that your friend's mom doesn't want the cross up in the Annex. The Deacons have removed it and we will pray now to our Father for repentance. We will not have that blood on our hands. We know where we came from and who we are, so let us bow our heads in prayer. Father God we gather here this evening in this kitchen, and we ask that you forgive each and every one of us Father God for this error. Father God we plead the blood of Jesus over this situation and we thank you in advance for your forgiveness and answered prayer. In Jesus' name, Amen. It is well. It is well. It is well." We all said Amen again, opened our eyes, hugged each other and went about God's business.

When Trina and I entered back into the sanctuary, the big white cross which hung up in the Annex had been removed. The Annex had about twenty people or so who seemed to be oblivious about the cross being removed, but I wasn't. As more people trickled in, more flowers arrived to frame Cuzo's casket. As the Delivery guy began to uncover the most recent delivery, I began to praise God. It was a CROSS! A Cross made out of the most beautiful red roses you've ever laid eyes on. GOD not only replaced the cross, but he made sure it was RED to represent the blood that my Savior shed for me. Hallelujah! Does God have a sense of humor or what!? Trina and I just nudged one another and rejoiced. Tip-toeing back to the kitchen we asked the ladies to peek out and take notice of the new improved cross that graced the stage. The ladies were ecstatic.

Starting off the memorial service, Nick played the video montage of Cuzo which lasted fifteen minutes. There was footage of Cuzo cracking jokes, encouraging others, dancing with his daughter at her "Candy Land" themed Sweet 16 Party, and numerous photos of him and his family members from childhood to his death. Nick had done a wonderful job of putting it together. As I looked around, I spotted Kelly. He managed to show up after I had hardly spoken to him since Cuzo's death. Waving at me, I made a mental note to ask him what his problem was.

Next up was Starr. She was hoarse and shaky, recovering from a cold, but she made it happen. What did she sing? "I Love the Lord" of course, she sang it twice. Her angelic voice resounded throughout the Annex. Her angelic voice sent goose bumps up my arms. Thank you Jesus! When Starr finished singing, Skull Gang Members John Depp and Tobb Cobain took turns reading Cuzo's bio. They gave their own remarks and then several friends and family members got up to give comments. The Memorial Service was perfect!

When the night was over. Trina and I sat in my living room reflecting on the drama while Cash sucked on his nightly ritual—a popsicle. "Girrrl! I see why you needed me, 'cause that right there was CRAZY! Are you sure you heard God tell you to help his mom?" Trina asked while peering over at me. I was lying on my lounge chair, exhausted from the day.

"I think so Trina. I don't know what that was all about, but I'm just glad it's over with." I said.

Just then my phone chimed. I had a text message from Cuzo's mom. The text message read: "I will never forget you for all that you did. God put an angel in my path in my time of need and I thank you" That was my confirmation that what I had done was what God had asked me to do.

God often allows you to observe circumstances, so that when the situations comes to your very own doorstep, you will be prepared to handle it. Rest in Peace Cuzo.

Chapter 23:
Black and Blue (2011)

I met Slow and R. Bucks five years ago through Juelz.́
Slow was the hyper one, the big man with the big
vision, but no plan. R. Bucks was his sidekick who was
just down for whatever. The two were our motivators at
Skull Gang. They would come up with the craziest of
ideas.

Slow had these huge brown eyes that stuck out like a
lizard's whenever he would come up with a hot idea. R.
Bucks was the laid back Executioner who would often
take Slow's ideas and make them happen. Often times,
they have proven themselves to be very resourceful.
Whenever I was stuck in a bind, I would always call
Slow to see if he saw something that maybe I didn't
see—and often times, he would always work things out
for me. For example, we were on the phone one day
and he was like, "Juelz hasn't put out any music in a
minute, Lynn."

"I know, but he's just not motivated at the moment," I
mentioned to him. At the time, Juelz was being
targeted almost daily by local Bergen County Police
Officers on several different levels. Court dates
became a weekly routine aside from performance
dates on the weekend.

"I've got this hot record with Lloyd Banks called, Beamer Benz or Bentley. Lz would be hot on this record. I just need to get a verse from him." Thugging it out in the studio with Juelz for three days straight with no shower, no sleep, no nothing, I then started to encourage Slow and all of his Queens crew to throw in the towel. Juelz had been mentally drained as a result of all of the charges the DA was attempting to bring up on him, so music was definitely not his motivation at this moment in time.

Stepping out of my car after pulling up to the studio during day number three of the studio lockout, I then noticed Slow, Bucks, and their entire crew pile out of the studio as if it were on fire. Damn near running me over in the parking lot, Slow yelled out of the window, "We got the verse Lynn. We out!" As soon as Juelz had placed the finishing touches on the song, Slow was out and off to Queens. "Sis. I'm not playing. I know when I hear it. I'm not going to let Lz sleep on this one." Slow said.

Slow was right. His ears had been trained and honed by the best— 50 Cent. As his former Luggage Handler/Assistant/Road Runner, Slow had spent two crucial years grinding it out with G-Unit. From robber to roady, Slow was blossoming into a businessman. With the song mixed and mastered in less than three days, it was out on the airwaves, and not just on Hot 97, but nationwide within a week.

The video was organized and shot by NYU Film School Students for free within one a month of the song's release and had become the summer anthem for 2009. Selling well over seven hundred fifty thousand downloads to the single, the song, "Beamer Benz or Bentley" was soon certified Gold. And as the highly publicized song grew, so did the popularity for Slow & Bucks. They were already the "go to guys" for local industry needs, but now Slow & Bucks were evolving and it was refreshing to watch.

It was now the fall of 2010. Slow & Bucks launched their very own networking site called Slowbucks.tv. I was too flattered when the two called me up to work with them. "Lynn, we are in need of a publicist," said Slow. "So talk to my man Soop. Tell him what you need in order to get started and we are happy to have you on board." It was extremely close to the holidays and several accounts were starting to wind down for the year. So this new account was perfect timing. At the start of December, I had already completed their bios. I was hyped. This new business energy at the end of the year felt great.

Walking back to my car after closing the deal to do PR with Soop for Slow & Bucks, my Aunt Larna called. I knew that if she was calling then it was extremely important. "Hello," I answered.

"Hi Lynnie. This is your Auntie Larna. I know you are busy but this is extremely important," she rushed. My auntie could tell from my tone that I didn't have time for the bullcrap so she started off keeping it straight and to the point.

"I need you to talk to Sohnin. She's running with da wrong crowd. Her ass got locked up last night for disorderly conduct and I had to spend my last two hundred dollars to get her out of jail. I'm ready to strangle her. She's nineteen. She ain't got no job and she got kicked out of school." My mouth dropped to the floor while she was speaking to me. I hurried to the car to get out of the cold air, I started the car and listened to her babble on and on about Sohnin's mishaps. They were numerous and it was disappointing to hear. My aunt was definitely not the best mother, but she was the realest mother. My cousins, Sohnin and Osiah were damn near born crack babies. My grandparents practically raised them; however, when they passed away, my two cousins were thrown right back to my aunt who had straightened out her life as much as she possibly could in order to finish the job of raising her children.

Boop, my phone clicked. I had an incoming call. It was

Kelly. Boop. The phone clicked again. My auntie was so engulfed into what she had on her mind, I didn't want to click over and disrupt the conversation, so while she went on and on about my cousins, I sent Kelly a text message that read, "Baby. I'm on the phone with my auntie. She is in the middle of a crisis. My meeting is over and I'm on the way home." He didn't respond; however, I just wanted to communicate with him and not allow too much time to pass by without letting him know my whereabouts. By the time auntie had let out her last few words, I was pulling into my garage in New Jersey. I had been on the phone with her for damn near one hour while sitting in rush hour traffic from Harlem to Jersey.

The phone call ended when I said, "Auntie. I will call and have a long talk with Sohnin. Ok? I promise. I will make sure she gets on track."

"Ok Lynnie. I'm counting on you."said Auntie.

When I arrived home, I already knew that Kelly was not at my place. His car was not parked in my 'guest' space. So I just got in, kicked off my shoes, pre heated the oven for dinner, and poured myself a glass of wine. Today was a good day. I had decided to tackle Sohnin's issues in the morning. But in the meantime, I just wanted to get dinner started right away. I knew that Kelly would be a few minutes behind me. As I started the noodles for my infamous Turkey Spaghetti dish, I dialed Kelly's phone. He didn't answer. I then sent him a text. I was getting annoyed. Yeah, he called me. I couldn't answer, but I did send a text.

An hour later, Kelly was knocking at the front door and was soon facing me in the kitchen. I immediately apologized. "Baby. I'm sorry I didn't answer the phone. My aunt..." I started before he could cut me off.

"Yeah yeah yeah. Whatever. I don't know what you were doing or where you were at. I just know I was trying to reach you and you didn't answer. It could have been an emergency." Kelly just ripped right into me with his words.

And in my mind, I was like, "Damn. If it was an emergency, I woulda gotten more than one call." It was obvious that Kelly was stressed out about other things. His son was constantly getting into trouble at school, his six-year-old daughter was already a hot box, and his business wasn't taking off the way he desired.

"So... you don't believe what I was telling you?" I asked.

"Like I said, I don't know what the f*** you were doing. All I know is you weren't answering my calls," he responded in an aggressive manner.

Taking out the cash Soop paid me for the delivery of the bios for Slow & Bucks, I also pulled out the signed contract to show and prove my whereabouts. Brushing my money and the contract off of the table, one hundred dollar bills started flying all over the dining room. He was pissed and I couldn't understand where his anger was coming from. I was starting to get extremely upset. Today had been such a great day. I teared up, washed my face, finished dinner, and went to bed, leaving the prepared food covered on the stove top. Kelly didn't bother to eat. He grabbed his laptop and yelled up to me, "Tell that nigga to pay your rent also cause you ain't going to play me out," and before I could respond, the front door slammed. Who was paying the rent? Last time I checked, it was me.

I was too upset and too tired to even chase after him. I was growing increasingly tired of Kelly's mess. It's extremely difficult to function at work when there is chaos going on in the household. Kelly started spending more time at my place shortly after Cuzo's death and his insecurities from that point on started to increase daily.

"Hi Lynn. This is Danielle from Goom Radio in New Jersey," the voicemail message sounded off. "We loved having Slow & Bucks up at the station so much that we'd love to offer them their very own show. Their energy is amazing and we need this on our urban station," she went on. Calling her back right away, Danielle and I immediately went over the logistics for their very own Slow & Bucks radio show.

Two days after the start of Slow & Bucks' show, the station closed down, it was evident that the energy and drive that Slow & Bucks possessed was intoxicating and addicting. Everyone wanted to be a part of their movement.

My birthday was coming up and I really wanted to do something big, I started way too late on planning anything. The year before, Kelly had surprised me with a nice trip to Miami where he wined and dined me at the Fountain Bleu Hotel & Spa. It was fabulous. Chocolate covered strawberries, gourmet cupcakes from the hotel's bakery, and champagne awaited me upon check in.

That birthday was one to be remembered. Fast forward one year later, my birthday was quickly approaching and I was no longer feeling and/or wanting to be with Kelly. His insecurities had taken over our relationship and it had become a major problem.

"I don't want to be with you anymore. It hurts too much.

This relationship is no longer healthy," I texted him. Daily, Kelly would accuse me of stepping outside of the relationship, while the majority of my clients were male, it never even crossed my mind to cheat. Nothing good comes from cheating. Nothing.

"Yeah. Yeah. Yeah," he replied. I was so tired of him belittling my feelings and underestimating my threats of leaving him, but who could blame him. I was always taking him back after his bouts of insecurity, however, this time I was determined to put the nail in the coffin.

I texted back, "I'm done with you. I think you and Lil Kelly need to go to the Sears Tower and jump off of it." Wow. Did I really just send that message? I had gone way too far. I didn't mean it, but it felt so freeing. Kelly was in fact in Chicago with his son.

One hour later had passed by and he texted, "Wow. That's crazy. Is that how you really feel?"

"Huh? You mean y'all ain't dead yet?" I replied.

"SMH" was his only response for the rest of that day. I felt crazy. I was sooooo in love with Kelly. How did things get to this point? Where did everything go wrong? I didn't know and I was too exhausted to try and work it out. I was done.

The night had passed by and I heard nothing from Kelly. Day had come and I had gotten a text from him. It said, "I love you."

I texted him, "I love you more." I meant every last letter in that text. I really did love him, but I was still prepared to move on. I loved him so much that I was willing to walk away. As the evening drew near, Diamond and I took to the streets to shop for her upcoming wedding. We had a list of items that Trina had written out for us to purchase on that day. For Diamond's wedding, we were going to build a Candy Bar themed in colors of yellow, silver, and chocolate. When Diamond picked me up, we drove to our first stop, Pier 1 Imports without much conversation. She was babbling on the phone with her brother, Art while I was entrenched in my own thoughts. It was a nice summer evening. It was 7:30pm and the sun was still beaming. When we pulled up to the store, she ended her conversation with her brother and turned to me, "Oh Boy. You just need to let him go, Lynn. This relationship is causing you too much stress. If you could be happy and be with Kelly, then by all means do so. I ain't no hater, but this shit has got to stop." Diamond, Kim, and Trina had become extremely tired of talking to me about my situation, so I began to close up on them gradually over time.

As we entered into Pier 1, I immediately spotted the bowls and dishes Trina wanted to have the candy held in. "Girl! These are the exact type of containers Trina would want us to pick up." Before Diamond could respond, I immediately started to haul them two at a time to the counters.

"Yep. They look good to me," Diamond responded. She was so easy to work with. Since she had become one of my BFFs, Diamond was very familiar with our style. She loved our style and she was comfortable with the vision we had for her wedding. Event planning was a mjor component to being a Publicist.

"Ok. Cool," I responded. As we awaited the total, another Pier 1 employee started to bubble wrap all of the containers.

"Ma'am. Your total will be one thousand two hundred dollars." Whoa. That was pricier than we had expected, but we were still way under budget and ahead of our spending schedule. As Diamond handed the nice lady her credit card, she couldn't help but mention something to us as we walked out the door, "They have those same vases for half price across Route 4 at the Christmas Tree Shop. If they have them, you can buy them there and return these tomorrow. I know I work here at Pier 1, but if it's cheaper, then by all means, get the best price." Smiling at us with sincerity, we both agreed to head right on over there.

"Oh. Wow. If they have those vases, we going back to Pier 1 tonight," I mentioned to Diamond.

"I know that's right!" she replied. We loaded up her SUV and headed to the u-turn exit to get on over to the other side of the road. The sun was starting to set. The evening was beautiful. I had always thought that the Christmas Tree Shop was a seasonal store, but as we entered, we both came to realize that we were basking in a Summer Themed store equipped with vases, lemonade pitchers, wicker furniture, grilling equipment, and more.

As I went to reach for my cell phone, it sounded off. It was a text message from Kelly. I was just thinking about him. I had regretted what I had said to him over the text and I was missing him. I wanted to see him. "Lynn. I will be home round 8:30pm. Can you pick me up from the airport?" It was almost that time and there was no way I would make it from New Jersey to JFK. I was riding with Diamond for one and for two, we were nowhere near done. We had just gotten started. I couldn't ditch my client/friend for Kelly's last minute request. So I replied, "I'm not going to make it to you in time. I'm out with Diamond and we are heavy in the swing of wedding shopping."

"Lynn, stop looking at that damn phone. Twin wants to go bowling tonight. I want you to come out with us. It'll be fun. You need to get out and away from your desk and your drama and enjoy yourself," Diamond huffed. And without any hesitation, I agreed to go out with her, Twin, and his friends. I was forcing myself to do something different, something different from the expected.

Just then, I texted Kelly back and said, "We can meet tomorrow. I have a lot of things to do still."

"Ok. I love you. See you tomorrow," he replied and the conversation ended.

From there, I placed my cell back into its compartment. I was proud of myself for finally daring to be different. As I looked up, Diamond was staring at me and shaking her head. "We gone get you straight. It's going to be alright. Once that dude is out of your life, then you will start to live again," she said. I just nodded as if to agree. As the two of us walked up and down every cluttered aisle, we ran into the exact same vases on the last row of this big ass store. Marked in huge red stickers that read FINAL SALE, we snatched up all of them. For twelve ninety nine, we were definitely going to return the vases from Pier 1.

As the items were rang up, the two of us had become too tired to race back to Pier 1 for the returns. "Let's just do the returns tomorrow," Diamond suggested.

"Bet," I said. "Plus. I wanna stop at a store and pick up a cute little top to go with my leggings"

"Cool. I wanna get something as well," I said.

I knew I would see Reem tonight. Reem was cute. I had seen him a few times on his way to the gym with Twin, but I had not quite gotten the chance to really know him. I was curious. I was intrigued by my curiosity about him. This didn't necessarily mean that I wanted him, but, it was my indication that I was ready to move on from Kelly.

We pulled into our favorite store for all things trendy and cute. "Ok. We are going to be up in here for 15 minutes. We are already running late," Diamond hissed. As we walked up the ten steps to the store's entrance, I had already had an idea of my top's color and type. Within five minutes, I was standing on line at the register while Diamond still perused the store. "I can't find anything. Let me see your top," she asked. Lifting it up with both hands, she said, "Oh. That's too cute. Go girl." We both laughed. We both knew why I picked that top and it was because I am a founding member of the Itty Bitty Titty Committee. At least this particular top would provide the cleavage that I so desperately wanted. After handing me the two thumbs up, she then walked off to see if she'd have any last minute luck on copping a twenty dollar top. "No Luck," she announced when she came back. By this time, I was being handed my receipt. We walked to the car.

As the sun had completely set, the moon beamed down onto my arm. The sky was clear and the night was nice. A faint breeze blew a strand of hair from my tightly tucked bun into my face. I smiled. Though I was slightly worn out, the moon's glow gave me a surge of energy and I was looking forward to the night. Diamond pulled up to my complex to drop me off. "I'ma come back to get you round 10:30. Ok?" I agreed, jumped outta her whip, and headed into the house.

Trina and Cash were there to greet me. "What you doing rushing in the house like that? Girl, you were about to get cut up, 'cause normally you call before you come in the house." She was right, but I was rushing. I needed to shower, shave, and do something different to my hair. I often rocked a Chinese Bun that sat right on top of my head, but I wanted a different look. If time permitted, I was willing to try. Showering quickly, I threw on some black leggings and the black cleavage top I just purchased. I had opted to wear black because I had been noticing my weight gain. I had gained a good fifteen to twenty pounds of "relationship weight" and I was starting to be extremely aware of it. I had been back in the gym for only a few weeks and I had not noticed too much of a difference.

"Lynn, you look fine. You look like you've lost some weight. So stop primping in the mirror before Diamond leaves you. You know how she do," Trina complained.

"I'm going." I'm just not comfortable. I was starting to become very self-conscious about my looks. The weight wasn't dropping fast enough for me.

A text message came in and it was Diamond. It read, "Come down." So I grabbed my purse, checked the mirror one more time, and left. As I headed down on the elevator, I took a deep breath and became determined to enjoy the night. When I jumped into the car with Diamond, she said, "Oh. You look nice and relaxed."

"Thanks girl. You know I'm trippin off of my body right about now. I can't believe I gained all of this weight." I replied.

"Well, the good thing is that it will come off and you are doing what you need to do to take it off. You see, a girl like me woulda gone and gotten that fat sucked out a long time ago." She laughed.

"You crazy." Diamond had gotten lipo months after having her daughter. Her body was nicely proportioned. But for a girl like me, it would be just my luck that some wild crap would happen and then I'd be starring down at my body from heaven during my funeral. So I was cool off of all of that cosmetic crap. My motto: Work with what God gave you!

"We are going to go meet the guys at 4 West Diner first. They were hungry so they went to grab a bite while waiting for us. Cool?" she asked.

"That's cool." The diner was the new hangout spot. They had an outdoor patio that was super sexy with chairs and couches to lounge on. You wouldn't think that it was an actual diner cause it was so chill. Walking up to the table where Twin and Reem sat, I greeted them and then took a seat across from them. Reem was gorgeous. He was everything I was looking for in a man physically. I could immediately cross those requirements off of my list. The rest was to be determined.

As the guys were finishing up their Caesar Salads, the waitress approached the table to see if Diamond and I wanted to order anything. "Can I get you ladies anything?"

"No. We're good," I replied.

"Nah. May we please have four shots of Cafe' Patron?"

Twin asked. "We are going to start this off right, 'cause Lynn, can't come up in here acting all stiff and uptight." Stiff and uptight, I wondered. As far as I was concerned, I was chilling. But how other's perceive you is totally different from what you thing at times. The shots came and we all toasted and took it back to the head. Within twenty minutes, I was talking and interacting with the three of them more instead of being buried into my Blackberry. Whenever I was a little uncomfortable, I would use my phone to escape. This tactic always worked for me. Reem wasn't saying very much and his body language was hard to read. Sizing someone up in a second has always been my thang, but not tonight. I couldn't figure him out fast enough and that bothered me.

Reem and Twin reached for the bill at the same time. They split the bill. I liked that! Then we all agreed to head to our next stop, Bowler City in Hackensack, New Jersey. Upon our arrival, the four of us migrated to the counter where we all gave the bowling clerk our shoe sizes. Handing us our jacked up pair of bowling shoes, we turned our own shoes in and Twin paid for the games. I felt good. I wasn't drunk, but I felt NICE! "Can you bowl?" Reem asked me.

"Yes. I can bowl. I can do a lot of things, but I'm more about actions than words," I replied. Awww snap. Did I just say some fly stuff? I sure did.

"Oh. Ok. Actions, huh? We'll see." Reem smiled. As the game started to get underway, Reem could immediately tell that I was about my business. Twin, who was a semi pro was also amazed at my ability. I bowled with Twin on several occasions; however, I rarely was able to compete with his score. "We will be back. We are going to go place an order for us at the bar," said Reem. Twin followed.

While Reem walked off, I headed over to our table to check my cell phone, emails and text messages. I had twelve missed calls from Kelly and while I was just about to tuck the phones back into my purse, he was dialing my number again. My heart raced as I placed my phones back into my purse. I didn't want the drama so I just ignored the call. Turning to head back over to the group, someone tapped me on the left side of my shoulder. Looking into that direction, it was Kelly. "Hey. What's up?" I asked in a calm voice, though I was shocked and my heart was racing.

"Lemmeee talk to you for a minute," a calm voice said in my ear. I looked around and Diamond saw that Kelly was here. The guys had not gotten back from the bar. We walked together towards the bowling alley's entrance, but Kelly grabbed my waist as soon as we disappeared from the sight of my friends and shoved me into the wall in the vestibule. "Tell me right now that you love me and that you want to be with me," he said with a stern look on his face.

"Huh?" I asked him. I wasn't feeling that way at all. I was feeling what was going on in the bowling alley. Kelly was the furthest from my mind.

I looked him directly in the eyes and said, "No. This isn't love. I don't love you anymore. I don't want this anymore," and before I could finish saying whatever else I was feeling, he took my iPhone and smashed it onto the ground. He was clearly angry and I was growing scared. Fear started to take over my mind and body, but I showed no sign of emotion.

"You are coming with me. Now!" he yelled into my face like a Drill Sergeant.

"No, I'm not coming with you Kelly. We are over!" Falling onto deaf ears, he grabbed my wrist so hard that my silver bangle snapped into two pieces and fell to the ground. It was my favorite. As I motioned to grab the pieces, he got a hold of the back of my neck and shoved me completely outside of the bowling alley. I was terrified. I had never seen Kelly in such a rage before and I was not about to put up with whatever he was trying to dish out to me. Spotting a slim framed white guy outside of the bowling alley's door, I stated very calmly. "Please call the police. He's bothering me and I am in fear for my life." And I was! My friends were so far away from me—the lanes which seemed to be miles away were too much of a stretch for me to reach. I repeated again, "Sir! Call the police." He just stood there in shock while finishing up a cigarette. Kelly still held onto my wrist tightly and he was pulling me like a child who had just spilled all of the cans over in a grocery store.

Finally, I got one good jerk in and I yanked my arm free. I started to run back into the bowling alley to get help, but he caught me before I could reach the door. He over powered me.

"I know you aren't going back in there to your so called friends. Where are they now? You mean to tell me that you aren't going to come home with me so that we can talk?" Kelly asked.

Before I could answer Kelly, he struck me with a closed fist to my face. I felt my jaw snap. "I'ma ask you something. Are you seeing any of those guys in there?" I just held onto my face. He lowered my hand and struck me again. This time I fell to the ground. I screamed for my life, "Somebody help me!" While he started to stomp me out with the bottom of his sneaker, I covered my face with my arms while whaling at the same time.

The white guy came over to him and yelled out, "Hey! Stop! I'm going to call the police," but his words were no match for Kelly's rage. He kicked me repeatedly until he saw blood and as I lay on the ground, I could hear a familiar voice. It was Diamond yelling out and running over to him. "Leave Lynn alone!"

"Yeah. I'm done here anyway," Kelly responded as I lay curled up on the cement, crying out from the pain I was in. He went to kick me again, but opted to leave me be, oblivious to Diamond's request. Within seconds, he grabbed my smashed up iPhone and ran off into the darkness, like a thief in the night. Helping me off the ground, Twin and Reem came peeling out of the bowling alley, curious as to why we had been gone for so long. Twin took one look at my face and knew immediately what had happened.

"No that nigga didn't violate you like this!?" he yelled out. My hair was disheveled and my shirt was torn. My mouth was bloody and I didn't quite have my balance. My bowling shoes were off of my feet and I was being helped back into the venue with grey socks that were once white.

Sitting me down at the bar, Diamond started to dab cold water onto my swollen face. By the look in her eyes, I could tell that he had fucked me up badly. "We are going to have to get you to a hospital," she said with concern.

Handing Diamond another cup of water, it was the guy I had been pleading to for help during the attack. Rage overcame me. I then flicked the cup of water back up into his face and screamed like a lady in rage, "Why the f*** didn't you call the police when I asked you to? Huh?" I was furious at him. I looked for any and everything to throw at him until my friends restrained me.

"I didn't want to leave you. I thought it was more of a benefit for me to stay than to walk away and call the cops. If I wasn't there, he would've killed you," he stated. I wasn't trying to hear him. I wasn't buying it. "Besides, I didn't want to lose my job." I looked at him and tried my hardest to cough up some phlegm to spit at him, but my friends had me out of his face before I could follow through on my thought.

I had never felt so humiliated, violated, and disrespected in all of my life. With the craziest of clients who have cursed me out over the years and have called me everything but a child of God, this incident took the cake. As Diamond escorted me to the car, I was able to catch a quick glance at Reem who just stood there in shock, trying to wrap his mind around what had just transpired. I was embarrassed. There was no covering up the hurt, shame, and defeat at that moment. For all it was worth, I was exposed, naked, and vulnerable, and as I was whisked away by Diamond who started the process of getting me squared away, all I could do was cry. I didn't just cry, I was moaning. I was hurt, physically and emotionally.

"Lynn, you need to go to the hospital and get checked out. Do you plan to file a complaint or go to the police?" Diamond asked as we sat in her truck, waiting on my response. Pulling up next to Twin, Diamond said, "Y'all can go home. I'ma take care of Lynn. Keep your phone on and I will keep you posted," she said to her fiancé. They then drove off. None of the guys said anything to me. I mean, what could they say? They weren't there to protect me because they didn't know what was going on. It wasn't their fault. It was mine. I should've left his ass a long time ago. Picking up the phone to call Trina, Diamond ran down the chain of events to Trina. She was livid to say the least.

"I want to go to the police," I mumbled to Diamond while holding a tissue to my bleeding lip.

"Ok. You wanna do that before the hospital?" she asked. I just nodded my head and she then drove off. Pulling up to the Hackensack Police Department, I got out of the car while she parked closer to the curb. I waited for her to get out of the vehicle and we walked into the precinct together. The police officer on duty

could instantly tell that I had been assaulted. "Ma'am.
Were you assaulted?" he asked.

"Yes." I replied.

"Ok. Hang on. I'm going to call up an officer to take
down your statement and it looks as if you may need to
go to the hospital, so I will call the ambulance to have
you picked up and checked out while we begin your
statement." The officer stated.

"Ok." I replied.

The officer was on it.

As I regurgitated what had just happened to me, every
word I said had been dictated. The ambulance arrived
twenty minutes after I had gotten to the precinct and
they began to check my vitals while the officer finished
up the police report. "I'm going to need to take some
pictures of you, Ms. Hobson," the officer stated.

"Ok." I was numb to what was going on around me.
Diamond was sitting next to me and if there were any
questions she could answer, she answered them. I was
outraged. My mind and body had been violated and I
wanted Kelly dead.

When the paramedics arrived, they took one look at

me and immediately knew that I was the one in need of assistance. Two young white men came in carrying a gurney while a young Latina woman carried the medical bag. I was definitely not in need of a gurney, but I was in need of medical help. Besides, the two men looked big and out of shape. They probably woulda dropped my ass.

The officer who was assigned to me was a confused rookie. It was obvious because he kept asking for assistance with the paperwork from another officer and it was annoying. This is my life. I don't have time for no rookie to screw my paperwork up. "Ms. You aren't looking too well, so we are going to have you head over to the hospital to get checked out. I will type up the police report and when I'm done, I will come over to the hospital to have you review and sign it. This paperwork will take over an hour. Is that ok?" He asked.

"I'm fine with that." He was a rookie with a heart, who was personable. And I had a feeling that if he were not a rookie, my butt would've been sitting there, waiting and hurting.

"Ok, Ms. Hobson. Let's get you going. Will someone be accompanying you?" the female paramedic asked.

"Yes," Diamond answered. "I will follow the

ambulance in my car. What hospital are you taking her to?" she asked.

"What hospital would you like to go to Ms. Hobson?" The female paramedic asked.

"Holy Name Hospital," in Teaneck, New Jersey is best for me," I replied.

"Ok. That's fine," she replied.

As I started to raise up off of the iron folding chair in front of the officer's desk, I felt a little light headed. I stumbled for a hot second. My head had me feeling a little cloudy. "I will hold onto your arm while you walk down the steps and up into the ambulance," one of the male paramedics said. "You don't seem to quite have your balance Ms. Hobson." I lifted my right arm for the help and we stepped slowly down the six stairs that lead us out of the precinct and into the well-lit ambulance. After I was hoisted up into the vehicle and strapped in, Diamond peeped in to remind me that she was going to meet me at the hospital. I acknowledged her by giving the thumbs up.

When we began to pull off, the female paramedic said, "Ms. Hobson, I'm just going to take some vitals from you while we are en route." Reaching for my arm, she took my pulse. After jotting that down, she reached for my arm, wrapped a band around it and took my blood pressure. Shaking her head slightly, I could tell by her gesture that my pressure was through the roof. Jotting down those stats, she then said, "Ok. I just want you to relax a bit." Leaning back onto the side of the ambulance, she then reached for a light where she peered into my left eye. I could tell that she was concerned and that she was passionate about her job. From the looks of her face, she had definitely been around the block with this sort of thing before, but she treated each case as if it were a fresh finding and I liked that about her.

Pulling up onto the Hospital grounds, the two males jumped out of the front to check in while the female stayed with me. Not even five minutes went by before we started to climb out of the vehicle. "Ok. Ms. Hobson. We are going to take you into a room we have set up for you in the ER. A nurse will come to check you in and since it's not too crowded in there tonight, it should be no time before a doctor is able to see you. Take care and we wish you luck with everything." She said.

Turning to the three of them, I said "Thank you" as loud as my hoarse voice would allow. They smiled at me and turned to exit my room.

"Lynn. Everything is going to be ok," Diamond

reassured me. I was in a daze. In shock so to speak. I just nodded. I had no more tears left.

"So! What is going on with you Ms. Hobson?" a short African American nurse with a Caribbean accent asked me. "She was short and plump. Her bobbed wig looked more like a hat and she didn't bother to look me in the eyes when she spoke. I always had a problem with people like that. If you are speaking to me, then look at me. I just think it's unprofessional and it lets me know that you are just getting by.

"My ex-boyfriend beat me up." There. I said it. It was painful. But I got it out in as few words as possible. Her chubby ass looked up at me then though.

"Oh. Ok. Yeah. You are pretty bruised up." She then took my vitals again. My blood pressure, temperature, and my heart rate was jotted down onto a paper attached to her clip board. "Ms. Hobson. Can you please tell me what hurts most?"

"Yes. My ears, fingers, back, and head," I replied.

"Ok. Please take your clothes off and put the robe on that's in the plastic bag. The doctor will be in shortly," she said. "I hope you feel better." Not even looking back up into my face, she closed the door behind her. Rolling her eyes to the back of her head, I could tell that Diamond felt the same as me.

Taking off my clothes slowly, my body began to ache as I attempted to take my top and leggings off. Grabbing the air tight bag which housed my robe, I placed it on slowly and climbed onto the bed. Thirty minutes later, there was a knock at the door. It was the doctor. He was a medium built Jewish man with a lot of energy. It was apparent that he had just started the shift. The drain of the day was not in his voice. "Ms. Hobson, correct?" He asked.

"Yes." I replied.

"I've read over your chart and from the looks of it, you've sustained some pretty powerful blows." I nodded. I was just glad he didn't ask me to go over everything again. I was already tired of going over the chain of events. Taking a light out of his top pocket, he asked me to look directly into the light. "Wow. Ok. You do have a severely ruptured blood vessel in your eye. Taking a look at the side of my face, he then reached for his ophthalmoscope. "Turn to your left. I want to take a look into your ear." Looking at my outer ear first, he then touched my right ear lobe and eased the handheld device into my ear. After shifting it around my inner ear a few times, he pulled it out, discarded the protective covering and placed it back into his lab coat. Looking me over, he then examined my skin. " I see you have Vitaligo. How long have you had it?"he asked.

"Since 9/11." The doctor didn't even respond. He just looked at me as if he totally understood. We were on the same page. We had an unspoken dialogue going on as he continued to exam me. He could tell that I had been through a lot without saying many words. And he could also tell that I was strong. Yeah, that looser tried to throw a mountain at me, but God's angels made it as small as a pebble. Reaching for my shoulder, he tapped it lightly and said, "I'll be right back with your prescriptions and diagnosis. I am going to have a Technician come in to take a look at your fingers. Your left ring finger looks like it may be fractured." Looking down to check out my own finger, I saw it was all twisted up in the game and it hurt like hell.

"Ok. Thank you." I replied.

He turned to leave the room, leaving the door open and I didn't mind. I was feeling smothered in the small cubicle that the ER called a room. I wanted the air to circulate a little more. Hospitals are known for having the most germs.

Another knock came at the door came. A tiny white lady with glasses and a ponytail said "Hi, Ms. Hobson. I'm Janie and I will be x-raying your left hand this morning."

"What time is it?" I asked.

"Four in the morning Ma'am," she responded. It was late or rather early.

As Diamond yawned at the thought of the time, she waited patiently for my return back from x-ray. The x-ray room was freezing and the small glass plate where I had to rest my hand was even colder. "I just want to position your hand three various ways" And as she took each x-ray, she shifted my hand. It was throbbing. "Ok. That's it. We are all done."said the technician.

Putting up all of the equipment she used and wiping everything down, she opened the door so that the two of us could exit what felt like the North Pole. "It was freezing in there," I mentioned to her as we walked back into my room. She just looked up at me and smiled. The doctor was standing at the door awaiting the results so she didn't have a moment to respond, but I knew she agreed. Taking the film from her hand, he raised them to the light.

"Ok, Ms. Hobson. You can go in and get dressed. I'll be right in." Diamond was wrapping up a call with Twin who had called to get the play by play on where we were with everything.

Taking off my robe and reaching for my clothes, I got dressed just a painfully as I had gotten undressed.

Knocking on the door to make sure I was dressed, Diamond called out, "Come in."

The doctor was happy to see me dressed and ready to go. "Ok. Ms. Hobson. I have a few prescriptions for you. As he handed them to me, he stated, "You have a busted vessel in your left eye, a ruptured ear drum, a fractured finger, and a few scrapes and bruises on your back." So basically, he prescribed me some eardrops, compressors to go over my eye, a few braces for my finger, and something for the body aches that I would endure days after the attack. "Here is a doctor's note as well. I'm not sure if you are working, but I do want you to rest for one week. I don't want you to do anything strenuous." As he handed me the note, I snickered. The thought of me having to give a doctor's note to a supervisor at any job, made me cringe. I hadn't had a job in well over 15 years. It was cute because at the end of the day, clients don't really care if you got the crap beat out of you. They just want results. "Put some cold compresses on your eye as well. It looks like you'll have a nice shiner in the morning." With that he reached for my hand, shook it, wished me the best of luck and told me to await my discharge papers.

Another knock came and a lady walked immediately in before we could allow her entry into my hospital space. "Hello, Ms. Hobson. My name is Ms. Sally and I am an In House Counselor. I just wanted to speak with you a bit and ask a few questions concerning your attack." She was an older white woman with reddish hair. Her outfit was well put together and her accessories matched her outfit perfectly. Peering into my eyes, she asked, "Is the assailant your boyfriend?"

"He is my ex-boyfriend. He beat me up because I didn't want to get back together with him," I stated.

"Ok. Do you feel safe? Do you feel like your life is in further danger?" she asked. She was concerned. I could tell that she was really passionate about her job.

"I'm ok. He caught me off guard. He won't do that again. I'm not afraid of him. He's a punk. I have no intentions of getting back with him and I am ready to go," I said as nicely as I possibly could. I didn't mean to be rude; however, I just wanted to get home, take a shower, and get in the bed.

"Ok. I understand. Sign here and here's my card in case you'd like to follow up with me." She then passed her business card to me. I smiled and thanked her. Though it was summer, I was cold. The hospital was cold and I felt its temperature in my bones. I just wanted the night air to hit me to defrost my body.

After getting out of Diamond's truck she walked me to my apartment door and she handed me off to Trina. As Diamond knocked on the door, I held my breath in anticipation of her reaction.

"Oh, wow. I'm not even going to ask you if you are ok cause you are clearly not ok. You look crazy," Trina said in a soft tone. My godson, Cash was awake. He said, "Auntie Lynn. What happened to your eye?" He asked me five times before I could even make it to the living room sofa to have a seat. From the sound of his continuous question, I knew that the black eye was evolving.

"I got hurt," I replied.

"Well, what happened? Who hurt you?" he asked. I was like, really? Right now with all the damn questions?

"Cash. Leave Lynn alone. She will be fine." Trina insisted.

"Thanks so much Diamond for staying with me." I said.

"No problem. Call me when you get up." Diamond replied.

"Ok. Cool. Thanks again." She reached down to the sofa where I sat, and hugged me.

When Diamond left, Trina said, "I know you are tired, but you are going to have to tell me everything. I want to know what happened." Trina was all up in my area and I knew she wasn't going to back down until I provided her with every last detail, so I told her.

When I finished giving her the play by play, she began to speak. "You know, Kelly came by here around eleven o'clock. The intercom system rang and I knew it wasn't you so I didn't bother to get up from watching my movie to see who it was. I had just shrugged it off as if someone had the wrong apartment." Trina was a Lifetime channel movie buff. If the house wasn't on fire, then she wasn't going anywhere or doing anything. "Minutes had gone by and next thing I knew, he was knocking on the door. When I answered the door and saw it was him, I immediately told him you weren't home." I sat up and listened to her, taking in everything she said. At first I started to get angry on the inside because I just knew Trina knew better than to tell that low life where I was at and what I was doing. "So anyway, just as I was about to close the door, he asked me if I would call you from my phone because you were mad at him and wasn't answering his calls." Trina stated.

"Oh really?" I interjected.

"Yep, and when I told him no, he did seem to be agitated." He kept on with the questions, but I just cut him short. I let him know that you are a grown ass woman and if you didn't answer his call, then you were not trying to speak with him." That's my girl.

"I don't know how he knew where I was. We didn't even go straight to the bowling alley. We went to the diner first to meet up with Twin and his friend. Unless... he saw me at the diner and followed us. I mean, that's crazy. He's crazy." I was too tired to even tear up again. The sun was now up, so I couldn't sleep. I fixed myself some breakfast because I was starving. At eight am, I showered, dressed and drove myself to the Bergen County Courthouse located in Hackensack, New Jersey, which was two towns over from my home. Taking off my watch and placing my cell phone into a basket onto the medal detector's conveyor belt, the security guard looked at me like, damn, someone clocked you. I just looked back at him with the same intensity. I walked through the metal detector without needing a wand, grabbed my belongings out of the basket, and walked over to the Information Desk. "Good morning. Where is the Domestic Violence Department?" I asked the old white lady who sat up high in the booth. She gave me a polite smile and pointed to a door on my left where the letters read, DOMESTIC VIOLENCE UNIT. I then thanked her and headed into the door.

When I arrived into the office, a white female receptionist greeted me behind a glass petition. "Good morning. How may I help you?" She asked.

"My boyfriend beat me up last night and I am here to obtain an Order of Protection," I responded.

"Ok. I'm going to give you some papers to fill out." As she gathered four papers together, she placed them onto a clip board and handed it to me along with a pen.

"You live in Bergen County, correct?" she asked.

"Yes. I live in Bergen County and the incident was in Bergen County." I replied.

"Did you have any contact with the police?"the counselor asked.

"Yes. I have a copy of the complaint," I replied.

"Great. Do you have the complaint with you? If so, attach it as well. I will make a copy of it and give the original back to you."

"Ok. Thank you." I said.

"You're welcome."she answered.

I had a seat and began to fill out all of the papers, front and back. The questions were very detailed. Thank God I had all of Kelly's information stored in my phone. His mother's address which was the address on his driver's license, social security number, and date of birth were all handy within my handheld.

It took me 15 minutes to fill everything out. I handed the clip board back to the lady and she instructed me to have a seat until a counselor called my name. Five minutes passed by. I checked my watch. It was now nine o'clock in the morning. "Ms. Hobson." My name had been called. As I gathered my belongings, the door opened and an African American woman greeted me. "This way, Ms. Hobson," she said. Following her back to her well-lit cubicle, she instructed me to have a seat. "Ok. I have reviewed your paperwork. It looks very thorough. I have to now type up the formal complaint. I may have a few additional questions for your prior to you seeing the Judge," she stated.

"Oh. Ok. I get to see the Judge today?" I asked.

"Yes. He will determine if your complaint is warranted

to have a Temporary Restraining Order. From there, you will be provided with a court date. Your boyfriend will be served the Temporary Restraining Order until a court date has been set. Once a court date has been scheduled, the Judge will then determine if a Final Restraining Order will need to be put in place. Now, Ms. Hobson. Are you safe? Do you need a place to stay? Do you have any children with your boyfriend?" The woman was very informative. She was middle aged, older than me and her cubicle was a reflection of her spiritual life. Soft music blared from her computer's speakers and as she began to type up everything, I reached for my cell phone. Flipping through my blackberry, I noticed a text message from Kelly that stated "we needed to talk".

He had some nerve. Was he serious? What the f*** did we need to speak about? I didn't even reply. "Ms. Hobson. Have you heard from your boyfriend since all of this has happened?" And like clockwork, I handed her my phone so she could read the text message. "Oh! Ok. What time did that message come in?"the counselor asked.

"It just came in. You spoke him up," I replied. I could tell she was adding that into the report.

"Ok. I'm all done. I just need you to read over everything to see if all of the information I typed into the report is correct." I took the two page print out and read over everything thoroughly.

By ten o'clock, I was escorted into a room where I raised my right hand to a Judge, an older white man, who didn't wear a robe. He had on a suit, glasses, and was trying to hang onto the last few strands that existed on his head. "Ms. Hobson. Let me please see your driver's license," he said. He didn't even look at me. I hated that, but it was all good. My energy was dwindling. I had to hold on longer. I was beat, just like I looked. Reaching into my purse, I handed him my ID. "Ok. Raise your right hand. Do you swear to tell the truth and nothing but the truth so help you God?" The judge asked.

"Yes," I replied.

"Ok. You may put your hand down." He barely even looked up to see if I really had my hand up in the first place. Go figure.

"Do you testify that everything written in this report is true?"he asked.

"Yes." I replied.

"Do you feel like your life was in danger?"he asked.

"Uh... yeah," I replied in a sarcastic tone. Finally, the judge looked up at me. Looking at my bloodshot eyeball and shiner, he signed off on a Temporary Restraining Order. I'm sure he had additional questions, but all the dude really needed to do was look at me, and once that was done, I was on my way. The court date was scheduled for two weeks time.

The preliminary process was quick and painless. It took three hours of my time, but this was my life. If it took five hours, I still would have filled out everything and waited. Kelly had it coming. I was relieved when I exited the department because the unit was packed full of women and men who were filling out the same paperwork I had initially completed.

Once I arrived back home, Trina was fixing breakfast and I was hungry. I ate breakfast for the second time, but I didn't care. I just wanted something to stick to my ribs so that I could get some rest. When I finished up my plate, Cash asked again, "Auntie Lynn, what happened to your eye?"

"Cash. I'm not going to go through this with you for the next four weeks. I got beat up. I have a black eye. Don't ask me about my damn eye again," I yelled out to him. I was pissed. I had already told my little godson what happened in a nice way and I was damn sure not about to explain myself every time I came in the house. Trina and Cash just looked at me after I cussed him out as if they didn't even know me. Hell, I didn't even know me. I just pushed my plate away and went up to my room. Taking off my clothes, I texted Diamond to inform her that I had completed everything and that I would touch base with her once I woke up. Then I popped a pill and knocked out. I was too done with the day and it was only noon.

When I awoke, I had too many missed calls to keep count. As I read my text messages and emails, I could still hear Cash downstairs asking his mother a million and one questions about my face. Now, I was more annoyed than embarrassed. It was seven o'clock in the evening, and the day was over for me. I didn't even bother to return any calls. I didn't even bother to tell my interns not to come to work. I just assumed Trina handled everything... and she did. I lay in the bed for two additional days.

"Lynn. Cash and I need to run down to Trenton so Diamond and Twin will pick you up in the AM 'cause you can't stay here alone," Trina yelled up to me. I couldn't believe this. My friends were now handling me like a child, but I couldn't really blame them. I looked crazy.

"When are you coming back?" I asked.

"We'll be back by Monday," she replied.

"Ok," I got up to pack a bag. I wasn't even going to argue with anyone. I knew there would be no winning.

When I arrived at Diamond's, I threw my belongings down in their daughter Jordy's room. Her bed was way too small for me to sleep in so I would just dress in her room and rock out on the couch until Trina's return.

On Friday morning, I attended their son's elementary school graduation in Fort Lee, New Jersey. It had been a few days since I had seen Reem. It was a bit embarrassing to see him with my face still messed up, but I had on dark sunglasses to conceal my bruised eye and busted vessel. At this point any thought of a future with him flew out of the window. I felt as though he had been over exposed in a short amount of time, concerning the logistics of my personal life.

It would be two weeks before I could go outside without wearing sunglasses.

On the initial court date, my mother, father, stepmother Diane, step father Richard, my staff, Trina, Diamond, and anyone else who had love for me, showed up to support and watch Kelly enter a plea of "not guilty." As the Judge began to set the next court date as a result of his plea, I cringed at the thought of knowing he'd be roaming around this earth free.

"Don't worry," said my dad.

"The law will get him," said my step dad. It felt comforting to know that my loved ones were with me. They had all traveled up from DC to support my efforts in following through on the case.

One week prior to the second court date, my mom called my phone. "Hey Ma. What's up? How are you?"

"Oh my goodness, Lynn!" My mom exclaimed.

"What!?" My mom sounded crazy. The type of crazy where she'd be delivering the news of a death in the family.

"Kelly just called me," she said abruptly. I choked on the water I had just sipped on.

Coughing violently, I sat all the way up in the bed. "Are you serious?" I asked.

"Yes. When he called me, he stated that he wanted you to drop the charges and that if you don't then he has some information on you that can possibly ruin your reputation." The nerve of that punk. Did he really just call my mother to threaten me? I was pissed off and on fire. If that dude wants to make threats, then cool, but don't reach out and touch my mother. "Baby. I think you may need to call him. He sounded very adamant about having some serious information on you." I was livid and my blood pressure was through the roof.

"Ma, I apologize in advance for what I'm about to say, but please believe me when I tell you this. If that loser had me on tape sucking his dick, there is no way I'd ever succumb to a threat. Threats are made by bitches."

"Ooooh Lynn. Watch your mouth!" Mommy yelled.

"I'm sorry Mommy. I just needed you to get the severity of my thoughts. I'm never dialing his number for nothing. That low life has had too much of my valuable time and I'm not giving him another millisecond. Is that clear?"

"Alright. Well. I think you should at least report this," she mentioned in a worried manner.

"Ok. I'll do that. I need you to send me an email stating that Kelly called to make a threat." I said.

"Ok. And just be careful Lynn. I reminded him that there was a Temporary Restraining Order in place, but he didn't seem to care." Mommy mentioned.

"Yeah. He's desperate Ma. But don't worry. I'll be fine. Trina and Cash are still here and Diamond, Twin, and Ms. Debbie check on me every few hours."

My reputation as a publicist was solid. I knew I had nothing to worry about in terms of threats. My business was built on relationships and my reputation. Clients came after the other based on my work ethics. There was once a time where I had doubts about my ability to get the job done, but not anymore. I had matured and grown so much in my field of work.

Walking down the street to inform the neighborhood police department about Kelly's breach, I was told by a sergeant that the judge had failed to extend the Temporary Restraining Order until the next court date. I was heated. I felt as though my rights had been violated. Kelly and his attorney called my mother as a safe way of getting a message across. I could tell that they were playing hard ball.

It would be days before the Temporary Restraining Order (TRO) was reinstated; however, this type of carelessness from the Bergen County Court made me rethink representing myself. As I headed home from getting my paper work updated, I ran into Leland Robinson who had already gotten wind of what happened to me. Seeing him in the courthouse's parking lot, I then let him know about the Judge's mistake of failing to extend the TRO.

"You are going to need to get an attorney, Lynn," Leland stated.

"I know, 'cause this is just crazy." I just shook my head and immediately asked, "Can you recommend an attorney for me?"

"Yep. Hold on." Leland reached in his pocket, dialed a number, and got a woman on the line. Explaining everything that he knew about the case, he passed the phone over to me as an introduction, and after that phone call, I had an attorney.

It was now August of 2011. It had been almost two months since my attack and I was still in and out of court, fighting for my life. Yes, I was fighting. So often, women brush off their bruises, sweep their incidents under the rug, and keep it moving, but not me. God didn't build me like that. I had to follow through. I had to at least attempt to make an example out of that cowardice punk. Attorney fees were mounting, but through the grace of God, I was still able to keep up with the pace of living.

Packing my bag for Diamond and Twin's wedding in Turks & Caicos, my attorney called my cell phone.

"Hey Lynn. Kelly's attorney just called and he needs to change the court date. If I don't agree with him to change the date, he will ask for an adjournment from the judge. I don't wanna give him a hard time because Judge Thurber will more than likely give him an adjournment," she stated. I was too pissed. I was ready for this to be over. Now, I was faced with dealing with two wedding ceremonies in the midst of this court hearing.

"Well, what can I say? Just go ahead with what you think is best," I stated. I just wanted to get this over with. This incident was draining me, my pockets, and my time. I was over it. At the end of the day, I can't blame the women who started to report their incidents, but then failed to follow up. This whole ordeal was discouraging. I was tired and empty.

"What's going on now?" Diamond asked me. The two of us were packing our bags for her island wedding to Twin in Turks & Caicos. Diamond asked me to be her Maid of Honor for this wedding since I would be planning the main one in New York.

"My attorney says that Kelly's attorney called to push the date back. He said that he needed more time." I repeated.

"Are you serious?" Diamond could see the look on my

face. This case was really about to drag on additional months. I was too disgusted. I wanted to use this trip to the Caribbean as a celebration of sorts. I wanted to relax and unwind after my win, but things were starting to look too sketchy for my case. At the last court hearing, Kelly's attorney submitted photos of me from my Facebook page just days after the attack. The photos were from Ja's Elementary School Graduation. Ja is Diamond and Twin's Son. My attorney had rebuttled, stating that I was the only person attending an indoor graduation who happened to be wearing sunglasses. In addition to that submission, Kelly's attorney also submitted a marriage license. Get a load of this crap. Kelly managed to find a wife and get married between our last two court dates. His attorney made me out to be an angry ex-girlfriend who just wanted revenge. The points he was trying to make were tight and convincing. I was in so much shock, I had started to wonder if I had been all of those crazy things his attorney made me out to be.

To make matters worse, the Judge started gesturing to my attorney that I didn't have a case unless someone physically witnessed me getting attacked. The bowling alley employee was no where to be found. I searched high and low for him. We even had to push back a court date to buy time to look for him. Though Diamond had seen me on the ground, she did not actually see a blow being delivered to my body.

I was even starting to think my own attorney didn't believe me and that she was just taking on my case for the money. The outcome was looking crazy, to say the least, but if you are a believer like me, please know that there is a God who sits high and looks low. He sees ALL things. He knows ALL things. I prayed and fasted daily leading up to the day of judgment, and just as the Judge was about to deliver her decision, a frail white man stepped into the courtroom, looking tired and timid. It was the bartender. My belly leaped with joy. I nudged my Attorney to inform her that my witness had arrived and she interrupted the Judge to have him acknowledged.

Calling him up to the witness stand, the bartender was sworn in. He gave his account of my bloody beating. Making a final remark to the court, the bartender turned to the Judge and said, "Your Honor. As a bartender at the bowling alley, I've witnessed some crazy fights. I've seen people thrown onto cars in the parking lot and out of the entrance's glass door, but I had never seen a beat down as brutal as this." The Judge's mouth was open in shock.

Rendering her decision following the bartender's testimony, Kelly was then booked and fingerprinted. He is now listed in the Book of Offenders for the state of New Jersey. He now holds a criminal record and he can never become a doctor, lawyer, real estate broker, and/or anything requiring a license.

Thank you Jesus! The entire ordeal lasted four months. I was battered and bruised, but I left that courthouse with my family and my head held high. I fought and won.

The entire summer had passed and I had not seen or spoken to Slow or Bucks. I was so engulfed in the trial and Diamond's wedding, that I had no time to buckle down and focus on my other clients. Though my clients pay was based on my performance, I had not completed anything, and I was hurting financially. The attack had knocked the wind out of me, but I was still standing. While my clients were understanding, the rebuilding process had to begin—again.

The chain of events from what I had endured inspired me to start my own foundation, the Black & Blue Foundation, a foundation that would spark awareness, educate, and guide survivors of domestic violence. My life has been impacted and I am creating an avenue for women such as myself who have been through violent break ups to be able to let their guards down and commune with like minds.

Chapter 24
Sylvia Robinson (Fall 2011)

On the early morning of Thursday, September 29th of 2011, I was awakened by a PING! signal coming from my Blackberry. It was odd considering that I normally turn my phone onto silent mode before going to sleep. I rarely forget to do this because the ring tones to represent the incoming sounds of emails and text messages disrupt my sleep. This particular morning I couldn't believe I had slept through the night without hearing my phone, so it was evident that I must have been extremely tired.

Turning over to retrieve my purple blackberry from the nightstand, I scrolled to my BBM messages. It was from Leland Robinson. The message said, "Hi, Lynn. My mommy died this morning." I sat straight up in my bed as I gasped and read the message again.

I typed back, "Leland. I'm so sorry to hear that your mom passed. You know I'm here for you, right? Do you need anything?"

He texted back, "Call me." I picked up the phone to dial his number. A part of me didn't want to hear his voice. Leland was always so upbeat and silly, and when I heard his tone, it was comforting to know that he was still intact. When he answered, he rolled right into a natural conversation following the text messages.

"Lynn. I need everything right now. I have Greg Walker here with me. He was my mom's Personal Publicist during her prime. I need you to work with him to put a Press Release out about Mommy's passing and then work with him to coordinate the funeral. How soon can you get to my house?" Leland was focused, serious, and direct.

When I hung up the phone with Leland, I immediately yelled downstairs from my duplex to Trina. "Girl, Sylvia Robinson died this morning." I didn't even want to see Trina's reaction and I didn't know how else to put it to her. Though Trina had never met Mama Sylvia, she was definitely one of her biggest fans. Over the years, Trina had established a huge Facebook following with thousands of fans for her one woman relationship inspired show called, "Pillow Talk." Often times, Trina would travel around the country to entertain adults with her poetry, comedic relationship analogies and engaging dialogue with her attendees. Sylvia Robinson's smash hit single, "Pillow Talk" is what inspired Trina to create the show and travel. Sylvia opened the doors for women to be able to express themselves openly and freely through music.

"Are you serious?" she responded. Trina didn't even yell back. She let out the words in a low tone that I could faintly hear. "So you are going over to their house to help out, right?" Cause to Trina, running to help the Robinson's was a no brainer.

"Yeah. I'm on my way now," I replied. Trina was saddened by the news, but her main concern was my good friend, Leland. She was definitely on deck to do whatever needed to be done. When I got downstairs, Trina handed me a banana and some juice. It was early and I had not eaten. I didn't have time to eat.

I jumped into the shower, brushed my teeth, threw on some jeans, a t-shirt, and a pair of Uggs while I waited for my computer to boot up. Surfing the net, I pulled up every bit of information on Sylvia I could possibly muster up. The internet is filled with so much information—and sometimes that information can be wrong so I sifted thoroughly through all of the background information concerning Sylvia's life and career. I then combined the factual net information with what I had already come to know about her in order to create a healthy press release. I wanted the press release to be complete prior to even arriving to Leland's house. I wanted him and his family to not have to over work or over think anything. I placed the word, "DRAFT" at the top of the release, printed it out, and jetted out the door.

My intern Aysha caught up with me in the hallway as I headed to the garage. I just redirected her to follow me. While walking to my car, I went on to inform her of how the day was going to go. Initially, I had planned to start Aysha off on researching all of the components needed for starting a non-profit organization but the day had been re-mixed.

On top of the rush to Leland's side, the weather was muggy and gloomy. A torrential rainstorm came just as Aysha and I got into the car. Driving the two quick minutes to Leland's townhome was almost impossible. The rain was coming down so heavy. I thought my windshield wipers were going to snap, but we kept it moving. The normal two-minute drive damn near took 20 minutes.

There was something about his asking for help that I could not ignore. It was my duty to get up and do something. Leland and his family had been there for me in so many ways, that his call could never be ignored. Plus, if it had not been for Sylvia Robinson pioneering to have Hip-hop recognized, I would not be where I am today.

When news spread like a wild fire about her death, my phone and everyone else's phone in Leland's house would not stop ringing. An icon had died. As the

Founding Mother of Hip-hop, Sylvia's publishing catalogue influenced and fed well-known and established artists such as Jay-Z, Alicia Keys, Kanye West, Kid Rock, Will Smith, Juelz Santana, Master P, and more.

"Lynn, this press release is perfect," Greg Walker mentioned as he went over the final draft of my press release. "Now let's just get it out right away," he snapped. Greg was Sylvia's Personal Publicist for years and for once, I didn't mind taking a back seat to receive instruction. You see, sometimes, you do need to be able to humble yourself and this moment was exactly that for me.

As I loaded up the document to be blasted out to the media, and prepared my finger to press "Send," I knew I was playing a major role in the world of Hip-hop. CNN, Billboard, *The Daily News*, *The New York Times*, *People* magazine, and more completed full featured write-ups on the Mother of Hip-hop. By the day's end, the name Sylvia Robinson had been placed on Twitter as a trending topic. That was huge.

One thing I always seemed to notice, whenever someone passed away that I observed as leaving an impact, it would always rain and rain hard. So that's definitely a question I'ma ask God when I get to heaven. What was the rain all about when people who left a mark on this world died? It's just something that has always made me go "Hmmmmmm."

When a date was set for Sylvia's funeral, I immediately went to work on her obituary and handling the press while Greg picked out the casket, selected the church, and cemetery location. "I want nothing less than the best for Sylvia. She gave me my first shot at being a Publicist so I'm going all out for this funeral honey," he snapped. With a flick of his wrist, I didn't know whether to burst out laughing at his feminine ways or suck it up and do as directed. So I just did a little of both. I nodded and as soon as I got out of his sight, I laughed my ass off. When Aysha and I got to my vehicle we both started laughing uncontrollably. Though Greg was serious, his tongue was too sharp and his hand gestures cracked me up.

Greg and I met on several occasions leading up to the funeral to talk about every last detail from the horse drawn carriage that was to carry her casket, to the run of show for the program. As I constructed the program, Greg, Leland, and his brothers called constantly to make changes to the program. With so many people being affected by her death, it was imperative that several sets of eyes were laid onto the program prior to printing.

Hundreds of friends, family members, fans, and

celebrities poured into Community Baptist Church for Mama Sylvia's home going celebration. The streets of Englewood, New Jersey were blocked off and barricaded as the pearly white horse drawn carriage carried her twenty four thousand dollar casket where her body lay. It was more than obvious that Mama Sylvia was going out in style. Following her carriage was a slew of black Maybachs and shiny Black Escalades to hold the family of 50.

Within the church's sanctuary lay two lifesize photos of Mama Sylvia framed in gold that rested elegantly onto easels. Flower sprays took up the entire width of the pulpit including a huge bright blue Sugar Hill Records themed flower arrangement.

As the first generation of Hip-hop filed in to pay their last respects, so did the second, third and fourth generations. When the likes of Marley Marl and Doug E. Fresh graced the podium to pay homage to the woman who had given them their big breaks, singers Lil' Mo and Angie Stone belted out heartfelt hymns that made even the stiffest person jump up and shout. Hip-hop Artists such as Juelz Santana and Grammy Award-Winning female rapper, Queen Pen were also on hand to say "farewell." I was humbled by the opportunity.

Speakers such as the City of Englewood's Former Mayor and other political notables also took the stage to give their condolences. The Reverend Al Sharpton was one of the speakers who talked about his personal relationship with Mama Sylvia and her deceased husband, Joe. "When I was a young man coming up in New York, I used to take the bus regularly out to the Robinson's for a home cooked meal and financial support," he mentioned. "They saw something in me during my fight for racial justice and I leaned on them during the early stages of my career. They were a rock to me and I will always be eternally grateful to them."he stated.

Doug E. Fresh also made an impression on me as he spoke about a mother's love for her son. As he went on to share his mother's battle with Alzheimer's, he teared up as he gave his condolences to Sylvia's sons Joey, Leland, and Scoochie. He let them know that he understood their pain and though his mother was alive, he dreaded the day of her death. Doug E. Fresh's impromptu speech was moving and motivational.

As the eulogy got under way, I wondered what the Pastor would say. I knew who Sylvia was and I knew what she meant to Hip-hop—a culture that has managed to earn trillions of dollars around the world.

Instead of honing in on her impact, he focused more so on the theme, "Pillow Talk"—a conversation with God. The Reverend Doctor, Lester W. Taylor, Jr. belted out words that had even Juelz sitting on the edge of his seat. "What are you going to do when it's your time to have a conversation with God? What will your pillow talk conversation with the Maker be like? As he threw out questions and analogies, he asked us not to morn for Sylvia, but to celebrate her life by going to God now before it is too late. The Pastors words were poetry in motion. Everyone was listening. He spoke to every single last one of us. Saved or unsaved, he had a message to speak into every last one of our hearts. And as he closed on his remarks, the choir sang the song, "May the Works I've Done (Speak for Me)." The Funeral was perfect. There was nothing broken or nothing missing from the service. I was laying an Icon to rest and it was an honor.

As the crowd started to disperse, I noticed my domestic violence Attorney in the distance. I walked over to her, greeted her with a hug, and thanked her again for helping me win my Domestic Violence case. She was dressed in an all black Gucci Suit and her hair was flawless. She was sharp as a tack.

"Lynn. How are you? You look great." She beamed. Healing from the case was still in progress.

"Thank you. I'm good. One day at a time." I smiled back to her. Today was a milestone for me. The Mother of Hip-hop had passed and I was bidding her a farewell.

Hip-hop as a culture has had a huge impact on the lives of several youth ranging from ages 50 and under. From the music to clothes to movies to culture, I am hip-hop. I am also GOD's child. Get to know HIM for yourself. And I hope you have enjoyed my diary.

EPILOGUE

So many other things have happened since the book was written. From 2012-1015, I most recently finished my bachelor's degree in the Arts at City College in New York City. I am now managing models; doing some Life Coaching; and on the Speaker's circuit. As for the clients in my book, Don Pooh is now managing Mary J. Blige; Sister Souljah has written several books since being my client; Lil' Mo is now on a hit reality show called, *R&B Divas*; DipSet is still in tact and touring; Slo & Bucks went on to sell a t-shirt line for millions of dollars; Trina and Kim are still my BFF's; and I am still doing annual events for my domestic violence foundation. I am closer to God now more than ever. I am not married yet, still single, and my kids are my clients...for now (smile).

Made in the USA
Middletown, DE
02 October 2015